Contemporary Gender Relations and Changes in Legal Cultures

Eds Hanne Petersen, Jose María Lorenzo Villaverde
& Ingrid Lund-Andersen

Contemporary Gender Relations and Changes in Legal Cultures

DJØF Publishing
2013

Eds Hanne Petersen, Jose María Lorenzo Villaverde, Ingrid Lund-Andersen
Contemporary Gender Relations and Changes in Legal Cultures

1. edition

Cover: Bo Helsted
Print & Binding: Ecograf, Højbjerg

Printed in Denmark 2013
ISBN 978-87-574-2768-4

Tak til Det Finneske Legat og Ernst Andersen og Tove Dobels Fond

Sold and distributed in Scandinavia by:
DJØF Publishing
Copenhagen, Denmark
Email: forlag@djoef.dk
www.djoef-forlag.dk

Sold and distributed in North America by:
International Specialized Book Services (ISBS)
Portland, USA
Email: orders@isbs.com
www.isbs.com

Sold in all other countries by:
The Oxford Publicity Partnership Ltd
Towcester, UK
Email: djof@oppuk.co.uk
www.oppuk.co.uk

Distributed in all other countries by:
Marston Book Services
Abingdon, Oxon, UK
Email: trade.orders@marston.co.uk
www.marston.co.uk

List of Contents

Prologue: Measuring Change? Contemporary Gender and Legal Culture

Hanne Petersen

Measuring Change?

In November 2012, two political events of global importance took place.

On Tuesday, November 6, Barack Hussein Obama was re-elected as the first Black president of the United States – a reflection amongst others of a changing demographic composition of the United States of America. It was clear that this president had got his support from men from minority communities and from a majority of women from all parts of American society.[1]

On Thursday, November 8, the Chinese 18th Party Congress started in Beijing in order to appoint the preselected new general secretary of the Chinese Communist Party, Xi Jinping, who is expected to stay in office for the coming decade. His predecessor, Hu Jintao, was described as president of China. Xi Jinping is part of the seven person big all male Politburo Committee, which constitutes the collective leadership of China. Since the establishment

1. I have borrowed part of the title for the introduction from an insightful book on this shift in American politics. See Birthe Christ & Greta Olson (eds): *Obama and the Paradigm Shift. Measuring Change*. Universitätsverlag WINTER, Heidelberg, 2012. Also thanks to my coeditors for comments on this Prologue.

of the People's Republic of China in 1949 only 4 women have ever made it into the Politburo.[2]

On the surface this does not indicate much gender change.

In the 21st century, political, business and professional leadership and economic (property) ownership is dominated by men on a global scale regardless of the prevailing type of regime or culture. This is also the case for religious leadership globally, another normative culture of increasing importance over the last decades.

But over the last one and a half century gendered, social and cultural changes have taken place in a number of important areas, which could seem to have speeded up changes in both gender relations and normative and legal cultures over the last decades.

On a global scale most institutions are organized according to patriarchal gendered and vertical principles, with men, elders and rulers at the top and women, youth and subjects of political-economic management below. However, there are always exceptions. Not all men make it to the top, and not all women are subjected.

The two elections in 2012 however demonstrate that the support to and the power of *white* men on a global scale is waning. They are no longer fully in charge of the construction of 'hegemonic masculinity' – the famous term coined by R. Connell.

This book deals with some of the changes and the continuities in these developments especially over the last decades. In his small and readable book on the *Masculine Domination* from 1998 (in the French version) Bourdieu set out to explain the paradox of the combination of a considerable change having taken place in the field of gender relations during the last part of the 20th century with the considerable conservatism continuing to exist in these same relations. He compared masculinity to aristocracy, to a privilege achieved by birth, to explain some of the persistent resistance to change.[3]

Historically, legal privileges were also related to obligations, even if they conferred considerable power over the subjected and subservient. Today's privileges are primarily economical, and ownership still confers a privileged status in contemporary gender relations be it in the world of business, work or in family life.

2. Jude Howell, Gender and Rural Governance in China. In Kazuki Iwanagi (ed.): *Women's Political Participation and Representation in Asia. Obstacles and Challenges.* Nias Press, 2008, p. 55
3. Pierre Bourdieu, *Den maskuline dominans*, Tiderne Skifter, 1999.

Women's increased participation in paid work over the last century both in industrial and post-industrial and in colonial and post-colonial societies have decreased their economic dependence on husbands and marriage noticeably.

Free abortion is still a political issue especially in Catholic and fundamentalist Christian cultures, but this resistance is in no way as dominant as it was. This is probably a sign of the internal value challenges within these religious communities, where leadership norms and values do not necessarily coincide with those of more reform oriented members.

One of the important changes which have taken place in most of the world during the last 50 years is the expansion of voting rights and the rise of the educational level of both women and working and lower class men. Europe was influenced by the changes after the Russian Revolution in 1917 and the Middle East was influenced by Kemal Atatürk's reforms after he took power in 1923. Chinese women's educational level greatly increased after the establishment of the People's Republic of China in 1949.

The statistician, Philippe Fargues, wrote already in 1997 about the situation in the Middle East, more specifically about Egypt, that *"Just as gender hierarchy is losing little by little, the hierarchy of generations, the foundation which gave a triple advantage to the man – age, education and economic activity – is likewise offset by the diffusion of education."*[4]

We are not experiencing rapid, revolutionary or radical change in the field of neither gender relations nor legal cultures at this time in global history. We are experiencing replacements or certain reversals of hierarchies of gender – and perhaps also of generations.

In her article *The Right to Bare Arms: Reading Michelle Obama's Public Image* M. Michaela Hampf writes about the mixed emotions and stereotypical and anxious perceptions of the American public towards the First Lady. *"White feminists tended to view the First Lady's new public image as 'the nation's stylish first mom' with criticism: An Ivy League-educated former executive has been 'pushed into this stereotypically feminine box.'"*[5] Hampf reminds us that black and white working women have not been playing on the same team. *"The gender norms that have relegated women to the domestic*

4. Philippe Fargues, From Demographic Explosion to Social Rupture. In Nicholas S. Hopkins & Saad Eddin Ibrahim (eds) *Arab Society. Class, Gender, Power and Development*, The American University in Cairo Press, Egypt, 1997 (3rd ed., 4th printing 2003) p. 82.
5. M. Michaela Hampf, The Right to Bare Arms: Reading Michelle Obama's Public Image. In Birthe Christ & Greta Olson (eds): *Obama and the Paradigm Shift. Measuring Change*. Universitätsverlag WINTER, Heidelberg, 2012, p. 65.

sphere were generally white middle-class ones. While they have limited white women's opportunities for education, employment and career, women of color and working class women have faced other challenges."[6] Hampf claims that there is 'something powerful, subversive, and new in Michelle Obama's traditionalism.[7]' This is what I here will call *"subversive traditionalism."*

We are perhaps also experiencing what could be called 'voluntary' contract based and legitimized submission – both class and gender specific.

In 2004 Theo van Gogh's short film "Submission" dealt with violence against women in some Islamic societies and told the stories of four abused Muslim women. Submission was considered unacceptable for modern white women. The film led to public outrage among Muslim fundamentalists and Theo van Gogh was killed by a radical Dutch-Moroccan citizen, who was charged with murder and sentenced to death.

In 2011-2012, the 'erotic' novels, *Fifty Shades of Grey*, by E L James have sold 40 million copies world wide of a book which describes an extremely asymmetric relationship in terms of gender and economy. This relationship is based on a mixture of love and sado-masochism. Submission of the young student of literature, Anastasia Steele, towards the Chief Executive Officer (CEO), Christian Grey, described in the book as '*sexgod*' is planned to be contractually guaranteed. This book has primarily been criticized as low quality literature. One may wonder, whether it is also a legitimization of neoliberal and reactionary change.

These examples may indicate some of the difficulties with measuring cultural change as well as change of traditions both on a local and a global scale.

The present anthology deals with what could perhaps be called conservative change, continuity of both 'conservativism' and 'modernity', symbolic change and perhaps also "subversive traditionalism."

6. Ibid, p. 65-66.
7. Ibid, p. 72.

Gender conservativism and change in traditional legal cultures

Greta Olson, originally American and now professor of literature in Germany, has dealt intensively with the topic of law and literature. In her article in this book she compares two television shows portraying two real life women judges, *Judge Judy* in the US and *Richterin Barbara Salesch* in Germany. Olson claims that these shows need to be considered seriously by students of legal culture in terms of their effect on *living law.*[8] As highly accessible representations of one part of the legal process they may influence the behaviour of litigants in courtrooms and thus courtroom procedure itself. Judge Judy shows reinforce prevailing ideas about normative behaviour and morality and their relation to law. They also model expectations about the appropriate balance between individual responsibility and recourse to the legal process in solving social conflicts. Both shows are enormously popular, and are sometimes derogatorily assessed as 'under-class television."

The shows suggest that a woman taking charge of the court room is normal – which is especially not the case in the US legal culture – and that it is highly beneficial. Olson finds that in the case of *Judge Judy* the shows *"can use their stars to propagate a highly conservative neoliberal ideology. Such an ideology functions to blame overwhelmingly women participants for the problems they have."*

The two shows differ in a number of respects:

"Whereas Judge Judy employs a powerful woman figure to espouse a neoliberal ethos of self-reliance and works to present claimants as at fault for their legal and social conflicts, Richterin Barbara Salesch presents its woman judge as a locus of reason and empathy and as a champion of social justice. Rather than a "no-tolerance" attitude towards deviance, Barbara Salesch's person and judgments bespeak a desire to enable those who have been wrongly accused to speak. Her show demonstrates that the legal process is in harmony with commonly agreed on social norms. Thus the emphasis is on a rehabilitative form of justice rather than a retributive one as in Judge Judy, and this arguably mirrors wider differences in public sentiments concerning penalty in the US and Germany."

The audiences of both of these day television series are primarily women, who are subjected to quite different legal cultures. The American legal culture has been much more punitive than the German since the 1970s and Judge Judy enacts a sensibility that suggests than punishing authority figures are do-

8. Olson refers to Friedman's and Scheiber's use of this term, which is already used by the German (Jewish) sociologist of law, Eugen Ehrlich in his important work *Grundlegung der Soziologie des Rechts*, München 1913.

ing those who are under their power a profound service – "*a woman serves as a palliative mask for punitive neoliberalism.*"

Richterin Barbara Salesch comes from the liberal city state of Hamburg, and her shows quickly became a hit. The female producer of the show has stated that

"Salesch represents the village judge as a woman. The audience has the sense that their value system is being readjusted. At the end of a case, the result can be morally justified. What reassures people is the ritualization, the sense that at the end of the day everything is in order. This is particularly important in the afternoon."[9]

Barbara Salesch is described as a less authoritarian figure than Judge Judy, and espouses what Olson calls a *"a Robin Hood ideal of justice that coheres with Germany's social democratic principles of economic distribution."*

Both shows interact with the larger cultural trends such as the medialization of law, and both meet a desire to see the 'fight for justice' played out in public forum. While Judge Judy has *'an anti-feminist agenda that promotes a victim-blaming ideology'*, Barbara Salesch *'responds to a desire for a public discussion of normative behaviour'* and gender in her show has to be related to representations of class.

Anthropologist, Miriam Koktvedgaard Zeitzen, is Danish and has spent considerable time in the US. During the later years she has also appeared as an expert witness in Canada in cases concerning polygamous marriage by fundamentalist Mormons which is also the topic of her article here, *Claiming the right to polygamy: Fundamentalist Mormon challenges to North American legal cultures.*

Fundamentalist Mormon polygamists are fighting to de-criminalize polygamy. This is part of a growing trend in Western societies, where minority groups are increasingly claiming the right to practice what may for the majority population be a controversial or even illegal cultural or religious tradition. Conflicts over rights often center on a clash between individually based human rights and collectively based cultural or religious rights. In Western legal cultures, 'culture' or religion are not objectified as units with rights, which stand above individuals. Individuals have a right to cultural and religious togetherness, to be part of one or more cultures or religions, but cultures and

9. Olson, this volume, quoting Henryk M. Broder, (2002). "Gerichts-TV. Die Vierte Instanz." *Spiegel Online*. Spiegel Online GmbH, 3 Apr. 2002. Web. 7 Jun. 2011.

religions cannot have rights over individuals or members of those cultures or religions, from a Western legal perspective.

Fundamentalist Mormonism perceives itself as distinct and under threat from secularization and cultural streamlining with surrounding societies. As such, polygamy is about cultural rights, while practicing polygamy is about religious rights. Mormon polygamists are now increasingly visible and vocal in the United States and Canada, and have put polygamy back on the 21st century's legal agenda after a hiatus of half a century.

In Europe, polygamy is considered a practice performed primarily by Muslims and not of relevance to Christian communities and norms. This article demonstrates some of the similarities between fundamentalist parts of the monotheistic religions, where arguments and practices may also be similar. Polygamy alters what in North American – and European – legal culture is the assumed and accepted binary nature of marriage.

In the United States and Canada, Mormons have a long history of refusing to accept anti-polygamy legislation. Up until recent years, ineffective federal and state laws and reluctant law enforcement allowed them to violate anti-polygamy legislation and more or less freely practice polygamy. This unstable equilibrium is now broken, as authorities increasingly prosecute polygamists, and polygamists increasingly challenge anti-polygamy laws which prevent them from freely practicing what they consider their prophet-ordained commandment to be polygamous.

In North America, many people view polygamy as a traditional institution oppressive to women. Polygamous families are generally strongly patriarchal; husbands are heads of the households and expect obedience from their wives and children. Fundamentalist Mormon family life is based on a version of the 19th century's strictly circumscribed gender roles, such as high birth rates and strict enforcement of (sexual) morals outside marriage. Extensive mothering duties mean that few women are able to pursue outside careers. Schooling is often inadequate. Women are usually married young, often in their teens and sometimes while still underage, and sometimes also against their will or without their consent. They may be married as plural wives to men several decades older.

The recent convictions of polygamists in the US signal a change in the legal culture, from a focus on prosecuting polygamist fundamentalist Mormons for being polygamists, to a broader focus which includes specific violations of criminal codes by these polygamists, such as statutory rape, immigration violation or welfare fraud. Parallels are drawn to 1920s America, where authorities were able to convict the notorious Chicago gangster Al Capone of tax evasion, rather than of being a gangster.

At the end of her article, Zeitzen raises some important questions:
"Should minorities have a legally recognized right to live according to their own distinct cultural and religious ways, even if these clash with the laws of the land? Or should there be limits to this tolerance in today's global societies, where all self-proclaimed groups could demand special rights, special rights which might undermine those societies' coherence as societies?"

The fundamentalist Mormon practices remind of the gender and generational hierarchies of more traditional and fundamentalist parts and segments of the Middle East, which are now increasingly being challenged.

In Northern Africa in Morocco, where Danish lawyer and ph.d student, Mira Ramhøj, lived during the first decade of the 21st century with her Moroccan husband and family, polygamy and child marriage has been restricted considerably with the reform of the Moroccan Family Law in force from 2004. Ramhøj has observed the many and diverse actors and strategies involved as well as the tensions amongst different parts of society regarding the reform. The changes of the Middle East during the Arab Spring have also affected Morocco, where Islam light policies have become more influential. Mira Ramhøj discusses this development for the process of future interpretation and implementation of the Family Law. Her article also underlines the importance and presence of non-professional women and religious women, who struggle for a change not only of formal law, but also of misogynist legal cultures and traditions – a struggle which women have been involved in for centuries all over the world. The interconnectedness of different strategies and struggles seems to be the clue to deeper societal and normative change.

Male dominance in conservative normative and legal cultures is the topic of the essay by Turkish assistant professor of law, Eylem Ümit Atilgan *Masculine Domination in Turkish Legal Culture: An Analysis of the High Court Decisions.* She starts with a presentation of anecdotes and examples of experiences of different generations of female Turkish judges, and describes some of the tools and techniques of ostracism, humiliation and physical violence used to intimidate female newcomers to a professional culture. Her focus is upon the way (male) judges in Turkey protect stagnant traditions about male honour in cases concerning blood feud, based upon her fieldwork doing interviews with judges and analysis of court rulings by the Turkish High Court. She is very critical of dominant Turkish ideas about *traditions* as they are used by the courts. They are *"based on the assumption that a tradition is uniform and has an internal consistency, which is different form the position, actions and daily lives of people living 'there.'"*

This is a view of tradition which is not affected by acts of people. *"According to this idea of tradition, which is considered more resistant than all of the modern legal systems, social actors repeat tradition without taking or giving anything to the system like automats? Centuries pass by, states collapse, states are established and traditions are not affected ...*" Everything changes while static ideas of traditions may serve as arguments for upholding ways of life and power balances, which serve specific interests.

Neither culture nor traditions are static, however, and none of them will survive if they do not adapt and change according to the increasing challenges they are faced with. In his brief essay about *The Noble Sàmi Men*, Sámi-Norwegian law professor Ànde Somby reflects on the disappearance and challenges of traditions and cultures. He discusses seven myths about the situation and perception of Sámi men, who are often seen as performing chaotic energy, gender chauvinism, ecological disaster, virility, drunkenness, school drop out and sexual molestation. As a contrast to these myths he reflects on the diversity of Sámi male ideals which require different forms of nurture, care, protection and provision amongst many other situation and relation specific obligations. He claims that some of these traditional male roles can be an important inspiration when attempting to reformulate the new role of being a male in a contemporary Sámi society, which also has to take other challenges into consideration particularly coming from technology and robotisation. Technology may make humans 'not needed', and Sámi men seem to become *"some of the first 'no needed' humans." "These noble savages are perhaps the canaries in our current coalmine."* As such they can show us what we have to expect and as humanity we can observe these phenomena and try to articulate our observations. *"We can be able to articulate which values are at stake, and thereby we can be able to say which principles or values we have to promote."*

In contemporary global capitalism, dominated by neo-liberal ideas and ideals, and strongly influenced by the global financial and economic crisis, more and more humans around the world not least men may experience the fate of 'the noble Sámi men' becoming superfluous, not necessary, not required. This is a considerable challenge and risk for both local and global communities.

States are increasingly being challenged by global market forces, which undermine amongst others their earlier redistributive and protective power towards (especially formerly privileged) citizens. Modern (democratic) states have for some time been forces, which have challenged (some) traditions and traditional communities and cultures – although the dominant heterosexual norms of these cultures have most often been left untouched.

In her article *An egalitarian fiscal culture favours gender equality – the Swedish example,* professor of tax law, Åsa Gunnarsson, from Umeå in

Northern Sweden, discusses the role of fiscal legal cultures in upholding and sometimes also changing traditional gender cultures. Weakened states are experiencing tax evasion, and as a reaction, a global economic order has been on the agenda for some time as a means for fighting harmful tax competition. These fights are however in no way gender innocent or gender just. Tax regulations with redistributive intentions – which are the rule in the Nordic countries – are seen as political interventions in the market economy. The neoliberal tax ideology is based on a special interpretation of what constitutes an optimal taxation for economic growth. The Swedish fiscal culture is the financing part of a welfare economy that has established a universal model of social protection based on a solidarity principle. Despite high levels of social spending, which due to the theory of optimal taxation create dead weight loss, the Swedish economy is growing, as it combines a capitalist society with an egalitarian society with high taxes. Theoretically this is not supposed to happen. However, the egalitarian fiscal culture seems to have been beneficial for a competitive economy.

The Swedish model is based upon a work-fare oriented gender equality model – not on the 'bread winner ideology' which is still dominant in many/most countries in the world. The work-fare model encourages women to participate in the labour market, whilst facilitating married women to combine paid work with family life. This strategy has become a driving force in an active integration of women into the public sphere of social citizenship. Joint taxation of spouses, which is the rule in most countries, is an obstacle for married women to enter the work force, and secures an economic privilege for the male earner in a family. This is a taxation system which supports the male breadwinner family model, linked to a traditional female care regime, which fosters a housewife ideal – as in the case of Germany, the US and Spain. Women are mostly lower paid than men, therefore taxation of the marital unit results in overtaxation of married women. Individual taxation supports the 'dual-earner family model' typical of the Nordic countries. This model makes an increase in working-hours for men more costly in terms of tax than an increase in working-hours for women. One might say that individual taxation might support a new masculinity along the lines of the Sámi men, who have to rethink their societal and family roles.

Experiences from Germany, Japan, Spain and the US show that the joint taxation of spouses contributes to a patriarchal, asymmetrical division between unpaid household work and paid work on the labour market.

The article describes different waves of political-technical changes of the Swedish tax system, some of which have supported gender traditionalism, while others have made it easier for women to contribute to society with their work. Gunnarsson claims that Sweden has managed, partly as an effect of fiscal policies, to achieve a more sustainable level of gender equality than many other countries, although she thinks it is still far from an ideal model of gender just taxation. Her attempt to combine tax models and gender justice are an example of the intricate ways legal cultures and gender interact both in terms of conservation and change.

Symbolic Change and Subversive Traditions. Changing Intimate Relations, Institutions and Legal Cultures

"Thus the family is indeed a fiction, a social artefact, an illusion in the most ordinary sense of the word, but a 'well-founded illusion', because being produced and reproduced with the guarantee of the state, it receives from the state at ever moment the means to exist and persist."[10]

In 1996, Bourdieu wrote that the dominant, legitimate definition of the normal family was based on a constellation of words, "house, home, household, *maison, maisonnée.*"[11] He also described the family as a privilege instituted into a universal norm *"a de facto privilege that implies a symbolic privilege – the privilege of being* comme il faut, *conforming to the norm, and therefore enjoying a symbolic profit of normality."* During the last decades this norm has increasingly been described with the term of *heteronormativity*, indicating that the privileges granted to what is understood as a family, is based upon a certain gendered – and most often also gender hierarchical – pattern. This guarantee of a specific construction of a family is related to both religious influence and technological development. The family model of the monotheist religions have all required and recognized heteronormativity, where families are established based on heterosexual hierarchical relationships.

Many societies have moved from polygamous relationships to monogamous relationships. Modern industrialized societies moved from extended families to nuclear families as the dominant frame for heteronormativity.

Heterosexual monogamous life long marriage has (recently) been seen as an important symbol of Western (Christian) secularity. In 1981, the Danish philosopher and theologian, K.E. Løgstrup, described the nuclear family as an

10. Pierre Bourdieu, On the Family as a Realized Category. In *Theory, Culture & Society* 1996, Vol.13 (3): p. 25.
11. Ibid, p. 19.

unintended 'side effect' of the industrial process brought about by a technological revolution. The unintended consequences and side effect of these technical processes have changed the totality.[12] Legalized abortion, cheap contraception and increased divorces have led to practices, which have sometimes been described as 'serial monogamy.'[13]

With weaker religions, weaker states and fragmented families, the development over the last decades seems to indicate a greater openness in several of these important institutions towards a broadening of the de facto as well as legal privileges granted to marriage to larger groups in society, especially in the area of increasing acceptance of same-sex marriage.

The paradox of symbolic change and subversive traditionalism is demonstrated in the articles in the second part of the book, which mainly come from a Western context – with an Asian exception, giving rise to interesting comparisons.

The majority of these articles deal with issues concerning the changes of the legal culture and legal regulations of intimate relations in a Danish, European and Asian context. These are changes which are of direct importance especially for sexual minorities, and in terms of numbers they do not necessarily relate to very many couples or persons. However, in this as in other regards diminutive numbers may be felt as threatening to majority cultures as Arjun Appadurai underlined in his small book *Fear of Small Numbers.*[14] This book dealt with the period after 1989, which has been marked by "the global endorsement of open markets, the free flow of finance capital and liberal ideas of constitutional rule and the active expansion of human rights."[15] During this period the world has experienced '*a new order of uncertainty in social life.*'[16] Intense globalization has gone together with a proliferation of violence

12. K.E. Løgstrup, 1982, Bivirkningernes verdensforvandlende magt (The world-changing power of side effects) in his *System og symbol. Essays*, Gyldendal, Copenhagen.
13. Wikipedia describes this practice under the entrance "Types of marriage": "In 21st century Western societies, bigamy is illegal and sexual relations outside marriage are generally frowned-upon, though there is a minority view accepting (or even advocating) open marriage. However, divorce and remarriage are relatively easy to undertake in these societies. This has led to a practice called *serial monogamy*, which involves entering into successive marriages over time. Serial monogamy is also sometimes used to refer to cases where the couples cohabitate without getting married."
14. Arjun Appadurai, *Fear of Small Numbers. An Essay on the Geography of Anger.* Duke University Press, Durham and London, 2006.
15. Ibid – back cover text.
16. Ibid, p. 5.

and ethnic cleansing, which has also produced illusions of fixed religious, ethnic and sexual identities. Countries have experienced growing inequality, loss of national sovereignty and diverse developments. Appadurai writes about an 'anxious xenophobia', that he called Pim Fortuyn's Europe.[17] He claims that

"Modern nation-states recognize their common belonging to the vertebrate world, and like the last dinosaurs, see that they are in a desperate struggle for survival as a global formation ... Many states find themselves caught between the need to perform dramas of national sovereignty and simultaneous feasts of openness calculated to invite the blessings of Western capital and the multilaterals."[18]

Appadurai is primarily concerned with explaining the links between globalization and violence, which has been particularly clear in the staged conflicts between national majorities and national minorities – particularly Muslims – during the first decade of the 21st century. He mentions the growing and organized violence against women[19] but does not deal with violence towards sexual minorities, which has also been considerable.

"Minorities are the major site for displacing the anxieties of many states about their own minority or marginality (real or imagined) in a world of a few megastates, of unruly economic flows and compromised sovereignties. Minorities, in a word, are metaphors and reminders of the betrayal of the classical national project."[20]

Is it a paradox that the acceptance of same sex marriage has spread in many parts of the world after the collapse of the Berlin Wall and the Soviet Union? During this same period, we have also experienced a stronger religious movement and religious conflicts and clashes on a global scale. The former communist bloc was both characterized by anti-religious state atheism and homophobia. Religions have become much stronger in this part of the world after 1989, whereas homophobia has not seldom been strengthened. However, in other parts of the world – not least the Nordic countries – it seems as if a very critical attitude towards especially Islam may sometimes have gone hand in hand with increased openness towards same sex relations. The same seems to have been the case in the Netherlands, where Pim Fortuyn, an openly gay Dutch professor of sociology, coming from a Catholic

17. Ibid. p.8. Pim Fortuyn's Europe according to Appadurai is (was in 2006) Austria, Romania, Holland, France.
18. Ibid, p. 21 & 22.
19. Ibid. p. 38.
20. Ibid, p. 43.

family, was running as a candidate for his own populist right wing party, when he was shot in May 2002 about a week before the election. He was very critical of multiculturalism, immigration and Islam, which he called "a backward culture."

Growing religious heteronormative fundamentalism and growing formal acceptance in 'liberal' societies of minorities in general, including sexual minorities produces clashes and confusions about what kind of 'families' should be accepted, as the North American discussion on the Christian fundamentalist polygamist Mormons also illustrates.

During the last decades acceptance of diversity including of same sex relations has grown especially in Northern Europe and in the UK. Same sex activists have increasingly fought for marriage – something that might be described as assimilation and conservativism, but that might also be understood as a subversive approach to the tradition of marriage.

Ingrid Lund-Andersen presents a process which links change and continuity in her article *Restructuring intimate relations: marriage, cohabitation and same-sex relations – a Scandinavian perspective.* The Nordic countries were among the first European countries to grant women suffrage, and they were concomitantly also the first countries, which harmonized family law at the beginning of the 20th century. At the end of the century, however, the regimes for intimate relations developed differently. Denmark was the first to introduce a Partnership Act for registration of same sex relationships, which has been seen as a progressive move. The Act was introduced in 1989 and in 2012 the 'gender neutral' marriage followed – eleven years after it was first introduced in the Netherlands. The other Scandinavian countries, Norway and Sweden, were faster than Denmark in introducing gender neutral marriages already from 2009. According to the article by Theis Munthe-Brun on *Same-Sex Marriage in Denmark and Legal Culture*, the Danish legal system may have been influenced by a normative bias in favour of traditional gender roles and sexual morals. He underlines that people of a nation are not necessarily tolerant or occupied with minority rights, because its legal system momentarily is. Legal recognition does not eradicate existing values and prejudices in the legal system. The Lutheran legal culture of marriage is understood as secular, and its social norms in relation to fidelity, procreation and gender roles are considered unconnected to religion leading to little criticism of the dominant legal culture. This may explain the view by Jens Rydström, quoted by Munthe-Brun, who explains *"how the legal regulation of same-sex partnerships primarily was a project formulated by gay men, and that lesbians were mainly uninterested because of its patriarchal foundations and its lack of custody rights."* Rydström also suggests that there might be a connection between the stronger financial position of gay men and their support for legal regulation.

Symbolic change and expansion of access to the de facto privileges of marriage to same sex couples is not a one way road towards a dismantling of patriarchal domination in gender relationships as Munthe-Brun underlines.

In the division of property between unmarried cohabitants, the legal situation in Denmark as of today is one, where the traditional heterosexual hierarchical economic power relationship is upheld by Supreme Court case law in the 1980s, as is clear from Ingrid Lund-Andersen's article.

Cohabitation has become very common for heterosexual couples in all the Nordic countries, historically as a reaction towards patriarchal marriage, but increasingly as a recognized social norm. However, the combination of a still considerable gender inequality in *paid* work with a very common traditional gender division of *unpaid* work among many cohabiting couples places the Danish cohabiting female partner in a very precarious economic position in case of the break down of the relationship. In the Danish High Court, in a case from 2009, a woman was granted 25.000 DKr as compensation after 28 years of cohabitation during which she had paid for the housekeeping and for the two children of the relationship as well as done housework. The man owned the property, and she was only given a minimal share in this.

José María Lorenzo Villaverde has been doing comparative studies on the development of regulations concerning same-sex marriage in Spain and in Denmark as part of his ph.d. studies at the University of Copenhagen. In his article in this antology *Legal Recognition of Same-Sex Couples in Denmark: From the First Debates to the Enactment of the Registered Partnership Act of 1989,* he describes the development from decriminalization over the criticism of traditional marriage in the wave of left-wing movements in the 60s and 70s to the option of legal effects of marriage through a registration scheme. It is clear from this article, that during this period it was primarily the left wing parties who supported these legal and cultural changes. According to Villaverde, the Danish LGBT movement, at the beginning, suggested a "pick and choose" registration scheme among the legal effects of marriage, both in order not to undermine the heterosexual monopoly over marriage and face less opposition but also because some within the LGBT movement rejected a registration which resembled marriage too much – an institution considered bourgeois and patriarchal. However, the Registered Partnership Act of 1989 mirrored marriage in its horizontal effects.

The development until 1989 is characterized by less visibility and public knowledge about homosexual relations, their numbers and the dominant life styles, than is the case for the following two decades. The early exclusion of

Church marriage is perhaps not surprising in historical hindsight. Rather the rapid changes and increasing acceptance after 1989 might require some explanation. The period before 1989 was a period of less globalization and global interaction, which is also clear from the debates – even if there was political concern before 1989 about Denmark becoming a 'gay haven.'

Kenneth McK.Norrie from Strathclyde University in Scotland in his article *From Decriminalisation to Marriage: Changing Judicial, Political and Religious Attitudes in the United Kingdom to Gay and Lesbian Families* claims that in the UK the general process, of removing criminalization as well as moral disapproval from same-sex sexual conduct, becomes both the start of a process towards equality and non-discrimination as well as the catalyst that makes relationship recognition inevitable. The link between legal change and change in social attitudes are highlighted very clearly in this article, not least due to the data from the British Social Attitudes Survey since 2000. There is a significant age disparity in the acceptance of homosexuality. One might speculate to what extent post-abortion individualized generations generally have different attitudes than the earlier generations, and thus will gradually be less hostile towards greater diversity of life styles. In British common law legal culture the importance of case law has been considerable. Case law demonstrates that homosexual conduct remained immoral in the eyes of the law even after decriminalization, supporting Munthe-Brun's point that formal recognition does not eradicate existing values and prejudices.

Cases concerning lesbian couples early on dealt with issues concerning custody of children in non hegemonic family forms. The fragmentation and dissolution of heterosexual families meant a growing acceptance of same-sex families.

The links between political orientations and recognition of same-sex unions described by Villaverde for Denmark (valid for both the 1989 registration act and the 2012 gender neutral marriage) is also clear in the case of the UK. Throughout the Labour Government's time in power (1997-2010) political hostility to same-sex relationship became confined to the far right. Opposition came mainly from religious bodies, who have long claimed to have a special voice in relation to the institution of marriage. However, the difference between marriage and civil partnership is that 'there is no sex in civil partnership.' A civil partnership cannot be dissolved because of adultery – a canon law crime. Thus it has been easier to isolate civil partnership from the sphere of religion. Quoting Goodall, Norrie writes that religion remains *"the only powerful current ethical framework in Western states, which holds sexual orientation to be a relevant factor by which to make fundamental judgments about the worth of individuals."*

The Church of England generally seems to have difficulties updating itself to the 21st century as demonstrated in the rejection of female and gay priests from becoming bishops in the church. Religious and gender traditionalism in many religions in the world often support (gender) conservativism and the moral superiority of heterosexuality over homosexuality, but this may not make it easier for religious communities to remain relevant to 21st century individuals. The fact that the Dutch and Nordic Protestant Churches have accepted same-sex unions is historically also related to a stronger state influence on the 'state' churches, which has after World War II led to a recognition of female priests in the churches. In line with Bourdieu, Norrie writes that *'marriage has become today a legal institution through which the state identifies who is entitled to certain rights and subjected to certain obligations.'* Although it is not discussed in any of the articles, in the future the obligations may perhaps become more important in times of weakened welfare regimes and less possibilities of (economic) redistribution on behalf of the states. This links back to Gunnarson's article on tax regimes and how they structure marital and intimate relations.

"Traditionally marriage was a relationship characterised by power and dependency with an essential complementarity between the husband's duty of support and the wife's obligation to obey, between male dominance and female subservience", writes Norrie. It is naive at best to see marriage as the solution to society's ills. Marriage has been understood to have an important stabilising influence on society. But it does not follow that it is more effective in providing that stability than good social welfare, parenting support, education and equal opportunities. *"The focus on marriages as a solution is, in other words, dangerously short sighted."*

In this century the market and tax regimes may be the institutions, which will uphold dependencies and obedience, dominance and subservience.

Douglas Sanders has been a visiting professor at Chulalongkorn University, Bangkok in Thailand for a decade from 1998-2008. As a gay rights activist, he describes processes of change in Asia, where same-sex marriage has not yet been recognized. According to him even if marriage may not be a catch all solution it can solve a number of specific problems in one blow – inheritance, hospital visitation, immigration and benefits. Marriage is a simple, easily understood demand, which captures the goal of equality with great clarity.

Further, he writes that minorities are more complicated than majorities, who emerge from long periods of economic, social and cultural integration and assimilation. Majority people have difficulties understanding diverse minorities be they sexual or cultural, and they do not want to pay a lot of attention to minorities, as they are busy with many other things. Same sex marriage has now become an issue also in Catholic Latin America and in selected states in North America – it is spreading from the small liberal northern European countries like Sweden, Denmark and the Netherlands.

It will also happen in Asia, not least because it is not a simple copy of demands from the West, but because it is an old issue, which can be traced in art and literature as well as recently also in scholarly work. In an Asian context a history of same-sex love is also used to distance post-colonial societies from colonial homophobia. Sander's article gives a lot of examples of the activism in Asian countries in favour of same-sex marriage. It is clear that this activism takes place within a different historical and cultural context than the struggles in Northern Europe. Here the steps of legal recognition were ascription, registration and marriage. The changes in marriage law and practices have been of importance (not only) for heterosexual men and women, where they have changed relationship patterns and to some degree also power relations.

The last article in the anthology deals with changes in Greece, which could be said beside the 'noble Sámi men′ to constitute the canary in the coal mine, reacting to the considerable changes, which traditional and modern societies are undergoing during the early 21st century. Shifts of status, loss of status, turbulence and redundancy are characteristics of these dramatic changes taking place at the end of the industrial era and the Gutenberg era.

Greece, which was in the last century amongst the biggest emigration countries in Europe, has become transformed to a country of destination for thousands of foreigners, and has for years now been on the brink of economic and social collapse. In their article on *Gender relations and third country nationals – some thoughts from a Greek perspective*, Eirini Tsifipoulou and Effrosyni Bakirtzi write about some of the legal challenges of the status of third country nationals in Greek territory. Initially immigration concerned work and residence issues, while gender and family relations got little attention. However, proper registration of life events is significant in Greece, as it often allows third country nationals to exercise certain rights such as legal residence rights, family unification rights, social security rights, citizenship rights etc. The legal framework is fragmented and creates bureaucratic barriers to exercise certain rights or to register life events such as marriage, which is recognized as religious and civil marriage by the state. Same-sex marriage has not been recognized so far, but civil registered partnership was introduced in 2008. However, this regulation creates legal uncertainty especially in relation to family reunification issues of third-country nationals or European citizens.

In practice illegal residence is practiced by many migrants to Greece. This also presents an impediment to family reunification. Further it is unclear whether there is a right to acquire autonomous residence permit after the dissolution of a civil partnership. Issues of naming have been contested in many jurisdictions during the process of modernizing gender relations. In the Greek legal system the name/surname is the basic identity element which is connected to fundamental civil and social rights of the individual. Matters regarding the surname of foreigners who are wives of Greek citizens can often cause identity problems before the Greek administration. Differences in the spelling of names/surnames of foreigners that are naturalized Greek are often dealt with by the Greek administration. Such differences between the way a foreigner's name is spelled in Greek and the way his/her foreign name sounds can result in confusion regarding his/her identity.

An increasing number of children are born outside of marriage/civil partnership. This gives rise to several legal problems such as child support obligations, issues of recognition of paternity out of wedlock especially in cases where parents have different nationality, and registration may have been done outside Greece, or where the non-Greek mother does not have a residence permit in Greece. Proper birth registration is important for the right of the child to acquire Greek citizenship.

As the Greek case shows, issues of mobility, migration, (legal) residence and (recognized) identity are of increasing importance in a floating world. It is not only having a name registered which matters; it is also an issue to have an attractive and desirable name, which matters. The Greek legislator deals with this administrative uncertainty by transferring the responsibility to resolve complicated legal issues to the notaries, civil registries and judicial authorities, in case no other solution can be provided by the administration. This creates higher burdens of proof on citizens, considerable loss of time and even legal lacunae.

The changing understanding of marriage and family is clearly linked to globalization, and the changing forms and understandings of a number of important societal institutions – the state, the market, generational relations, gender relations, sexual relations, procreation and maintenance. Patriarchal family forms may no longer be the only sustainable institutions in late modernity, neither in Asia, (North) Africa, nor the so-called Western world. But patriarchal traditions and economic power undoubtedly still structure most relations also in the globalized world.

It is maybe time to realize again that rights on paper – whether established by states or international law – are no guarantee of protection of vulnerable groups and individuals, and that traditions and religions, are not sacrosanct and are in practice negotiated. Peace and justice in the 21st century in all relations – whether intimate or international – is not a given, and it still has to be fought for in many arenas and by very many actors.

PART I

Gender Conservativism and Change in 'Traditional' Legal Cultures

Intersections of Gender and Legal Culture in Two Women Judge Shows: *Judge Judy* and *Richterin Barbara Salesch*

Greta Olson

Introduction

This essay departs from the thesis that the connections between legal culture and gender have not yet been adequately addressed or theorized. Whereas a lively debate has ensued about the meaning and applications of Lawrence M. Friedman's introduction of the concept of legal culture as a prism for scrutinizing a given socio-legal cohort, relatively little attention has been given to the question of how legal cultures are affected by categories of difference, including those of gender, ethnicity, class, disability, and age. By attending to the gender work performed by two 'reality' women judge shows, one US American and one German, this essay aims to further the conversation about how gender interacts with other categories of identity in legal settings.

My first premise is that syndic-court or judge shows need to be considered seriously by students of legal culture in terms of their effects on what Friedman and Harry N. Scheiber have called "*living* law ... what makes the system move and breathe" (1996: 1). This includes the effects judge shows produce not only on perceptions of legal processes but also on how lay people perform in legal settings. Thus I want to counter simplistic perceptions of this genre as yet another outgrowth of reality television, or as a simple diversion – "legal process as entertainment" (Friedman 2000: 539), or, most derogatorily, as "under-class television" (Löhr 2011: n.p.).[1] Particularly in the German context, I have found that judge shows are frequently considered to be laughable representatives of a daytime television programming that caters to those who are not seriously involved in social-political and legal processes and are hence irrelevant.

As the following analysis will demonstrate, popular courtroom shows perform important cultural-political work. In the first place, as highly accessible representations of one part of the legal process, they may influence the behavior of litigants in courtrooms and thus courtroom procedure itself. As Steven Kohm has argued: "As a *cultural* legal text, reality courtroom television hits far more close to home for millions of viewers than the legal doctrine contained in most *official* legal texts" (2006: 694). To the degree that aspects of the adversarial system of court procedure are mimicked in judge shows that take place in Continental European countries featuring inquisitorial procedure, this may lead to an Americanization of lay people's expectations of how their legal systems function. In the second case, judge shows reinforce prevailing ideas about normative behavior and morality and their relation to law. They also model expectations about the appropriate balance between individual responsibility and recourse to the legal process in resolving social conflicts. The enormous popularity of shows such as *Judge Judy* (1996-present) and *Richterin Barbara Salesch* (Judge Barbara Salesch, 1999-2012) speaks for their being vehicles for the values of their recipients ("Gerichtsshows: Realitätsnähe" n.d.: n.p.) as well as their representing the "brand of justice they feel comfortable with" (Krukowski 2009: n.p.). Finally, and no less significantly, these judge shows perform vital, if not always commendable, cultural work in that they reify and occasionally challenge existing hierarchies of exclusion and social difference that are based on categories such as gender, ethnicity, class, and sexual orientation. Social differences are dramatized through the characterizations of legal actors, litigants, and witnesses who are portrayed in them.

In this regard, *Judge Judy* and *Richterin Barbara Salesch* appear most striking in terms of the gender work they perform. Belying the actual underrepresentation of women judges in both US American and German courtrooms, these daily-televised judges suggest that a woman's taking charge of the courtroom is, one, normal and, given their enormous popularity, two, a

1. The original reads: "Wenn der Name Barbara Salesch fällt, ist ein anderes Wort nicht weit: Unterschichtenfernsehen." ("When one hears the name Barbara Salesch, another word is not far off: under-class television.") (Löhr 2011: n.p.). All translations from the German are by the author.

highly beneficial development. Thus Judge Judy and Judge Salesch can be viewed as "empowering" their women viewers (Banks 2008: 56). Accordingly, the over-representation of women judges in fictional television courtrooms can be seen as modeling an imagined gender parity that German and US American society need only catch up to. Yet these shows can also be viewed as highly anti-emancipatory. Because they portray women judges as virtually omnipresent,[2] Judge Judy, Judge Salesch and other popular syndic-court women judges may undermine efforts to increase the representation of women in the courtroom. They may suggest that "the world is more integrated [in this case less sexist] than it truly is" (Steinhorn and Diggs-Brown 1999; qtd. in Banks 2008: 55). (White) women judge shows as well as those that feature Latinas/Latinos or female/male African American judges may somewhat cynically simply cater to the demographic groups who are considered to be most likely to watch them (cf. Ouellette 2009 [2004]; Kohm 2006). Moreover, as I have found to be the case with *Judge Judy*, women judge shows can use their stars to propagate a highly conservative neoliberal ideology. Such an ideology functions to blame overwhelmingly women participants for the problems they have.

In beginning my research, I assumed that *Judge Judy* and *Richterin Barbara Salesch* were likely to perform similar gender work. This was due to *Richterin Barbara Salesch*'s having been conceived of as a German copy-cat product of *Judge Judy* that also featured an actual woman judge, who, at least initially, presided over 'real' civil cases with 'real' litigants. Furthermore, the manner in which *Richterin Barbara Salesch* visually stereotypes particularly working-class women in a manner that reifies prejudices about these women's sexual behavior led me to believe that this judge-centered show also condoned a conservative gender ideology, which was masked by being voiced by a sympathetic woman: Judge Salesch.

Yet an analysis of many episodes of *Richterin Barbara Salesch* in comparison with *Judge Judy* proved my working hypothesis to be incorrect. Whereas *Judge Judy* employs a powerful woman figure to espouse a neoliberal ethos of self-reliance and works to present claimants as at fault for their legal and social conflicts, *Richterin Barbara Salesch* presents its woman judge as a locus of reason and empathy and as a champion of social justice. Rather than a "no-tolerance" attitude towards deviance, Barbara Salesch's person and judgments bespeak a desire to enable those who have been wrongly accused

2. In the United States, women judges overwhelmingly dominate courtroom shows; and where they are not present, African American male judges are in charge (Kohm 2006: 696).

to speak. Her show demonstrates that the legal process is in harmony with commonly agreed on social norms. Thus the emphasis is on a rehabilitative form of justice rather than a retributive one as in *Judge Judy*, and this arguably mirrors wider differences in public sentiments concerning penalty in the US and Germany. Moreover, *Richterin Barbara Salesch*'s frequent reassignment of culpability for a crime from a defendant of lower social-economic status to one who has more material resources reflects upon social democratic ideals. Thus I found that the representations of femininity, morality, justice and law in women judge shows could not be analyzed solely in terms of the intersections of legal culture and gender but have to be seen with greater complexity.

In the essay that follows I will briefly introduce the history of *Judge Judy*, describe its form, and analyze its effect on US American gender politics in conjunction with US American legal culture. I will make the argument that the show masks its highly conservative political ideology and penal philosophy by displacing it onto a woman. The essay shall then go on to describe how *Richterin Barbara Salesch* was intended to be a German *Judge Judy*. Yet its form and effects on gender politics, in particular, and legal culture, in general, differ greatly from *Judge Judy*. This discussion will be further pursued in an analysis of how *Richterin Barbara Salesch*'s gender work overlaps with its interventions into class-related issues. By demonstrating the need for more nuanced analyses of women judge shows in relation to categories of difference, the essay will close with a suggestion that intersectional analysis be utilized in investigations of legal culture.

The Genealogy of *Judge Judy*

Judge shows, also called "courtroom shows" or "syndic-court" evidence what has been called the medialization of law, the trend towards fewer verbally transmitted and more visual and multi-medial representations of law and inclusions of visual means in legal processes (cf. Sherwin, Feigenson, and Spiesel 2006). Furthermore, according to some observers, courtroom shows, like other Hollywood-inspired representations of law, have transnational effects and may lead to an Americanization of perceptions of the legal process (Machura and Ulbrich 2001; Machura 2007: 344). Beginning in the United States, courtroom shows arose in the 1980s as part of the advent of "reality television." They also accompanied decisions such as *Chandler et al. v. Florida* that authorized states to devise their own procedures regarding filming in the courtroom (Porsdam 1999: 92). *The People's Court* (1981-present) was the first courtroom show to feature claimants rather than actors and actual cases. Participants in this alternative small claims court were sought out by the show's production staff and agreed to represent themselves in court without lawyers and to be bound by the arbitration of retired Judge Joseph A. Wapner, who presided over the court-like setting (Porsdam 1999: 93). This quasi-legal proceeding set the model for many courtroom shows that followed it including *Judge Judy*. Here, participants also sign a "binding arbitration agreement" that may call for transfers of money, exchanges of property, or the dismissal of a given case (Sheindlin 2006: n.p.). Philip Kimball describes this form of arbitration as follows:

> In order for a syndic-court judge to have power to adjudicate disputes between parties, each party must agree to arbitrate the dispute. The producers of syndic-court programs have agreements to arbitrate prepared for the parties to sign before the taping of the show. As they are contracts of adhesion, where the parties cannot negotiate the terms of arbitration, the syndic-court judges are able to reserve a wide range of discretion on the substantive, procedural and evidentiary rules that will govern the adjudication of the dispute [...]. (2005: 3-4)

Beginning in 1996, *Judge Judy* was the first court series to feature the judge's name in its title and logo. This formal change reflects the new importance of the judge's personality and person. Former family judge Judith Sheindlin presides over her weekday thirty-minute show. The emphasis of the series is on authenticity, and its audio and visual information all suggest that the courtroom is a genuine one. Opening credits feature an authoritative man's voice stating "You are about to enter the courtroom of Judge Judy. The cases are real. The people are real. The rulings are final. This is Judge Judy." Simultaneously, the camera pans through stately golden columns with a golden statue of blindfolded justice standing in their middle. The camera then cuts to Judy Sheindlin, dressed in her robes and in her courtroom, walking towards the viewer. The statue of justice can now be seen holding cube-shaped screens in her scales that show Judy adjudicating using forceful gestures; another cut follows, and the viewer sees the golden columns again. This time they are presented with an image of a living figure of justice at their center, which is or which resembles Judy Sheindlin. She is shown raising her blindfold on one side as though to see the truth, and a white light shines from the top of the scales of justice she holds in her left hand. Simultaneously, the logo for the show *Judge Judy* swings over this scene; it is printed in the shape of the front of a courthouse, and the shape of the letter D again resembles the form of the front of a columned courthouse. All of these formal elements contribute to the sense that the person of Judge Judy is the locus of clear-sighted justice.

Episodes begin with brief introductions of the plaintiffs and defendants who are filmed walking forward into the courtroom against a backdrop of legal books, while the male announcer describes the substance of the case and Beethoven's Fifth plays quietly in the background. After a commercial break the columns of a stately courthouse are again shown, a restatement of the case is given in voiceover, and the camera cuts to the testimony in front of Judge Judy. Generally, two cases are 'tried' during a half-hour segment, which is interrupted regularly by commercial breaks. Sheindlin places a premium on speed, stating, for instance, that she wants to "make short work of this" (cf. "Forced Haircut" 2002). After initial questioning, she berates one or both of the litigants for their "stupidity," a word she uses frequently, their failure to resolve their conflicts themselves; and, in some cases, their dishonesty for attempting to withhold evidence. There is no one set outcome. Yet in all instances Judy knows best, insults participants, reacts emotively, and retains an iron control over the proceedings. Her authority is underlined by her consistently being filmed from below so that the viewer, like the claimants, has to look up to her.

Judge Sheindlin displays more emotionality and impatience than is allowed for a judge, regularly overstepping her role as arbiter by offering moral judgments about the claimants' intelligence and morality. Thus Judge Judy is frequently compared with Judge Wapner and his *People's Court* in terms of signaling a larger and more general change in prevailing attitudes towards legal culture, which her manner of adjudication reveals. Wapner and his public adjudication have been described as an example of how US Americans see law as a "civil religion" in the United States (Porsdam 1999: 2) with the courtroom (fictional and otherwise) acting as a forum for working out differences in a highly pluralistic society. According to this view, *The People's Court* under Wapner represented a model of law that emphasized democracy, individual rights, and public participation (Kohm 2006). Accordingly, each episode of Wapner's *The People's Court* ended with the following advocation of the legal process as an appropriate public forum for hashing out disagreements: "Remember, if you're involved in a dispute with another party and you can't work it out, don't take the law into your own hands. You take them to *The People's Court*!" (qtd. in Porsdam 1999: 94)

By contrast, Judge Judy's abrasiveness has been viewed as exemplary of newer, more punitive attitudes about deviancy. She reflects retributive attitudes towards defendants that followed after rulings such as *Miranda v. Arizona* (1966), which guaranteed that an arrested person be told her/his right to remain silent and to have legal representation. Arguably, the sense that the Miranda ruling "coddled criminals, at the expense of victims and the public"

(Friedman 2002: 146) only increased after the former star quarterback and celebrity "OJ Simpson" was acquitted from charges of having murdered his ex-wife and her boyfriend in 1995 (*People of the State of California* v. *Orenthal James Simpson*, 1995). A new distrust in the justice process arose and a belief that the justice system had become too solicitous of defendants and could be manipulated by money (Friedman 2002: 96). Moreover, the United States experienced a general departure from rehabilitative notions of punishment to retributive ones since the 1970s. This has been alternatively called the 'culture of fear' or the 'culture of control' and led to the advent of mandatory sentencing and an incarceration binge (cf. Garland 2001, Tonry 2004, Pratt et al. 2005, Simon 2007, Olson 2011). Hence "Sheindlin's take-no-prisoners style has tapped into the public's growing resentment of the legal system. In the post-O.J. world, people crave a jurist who lays down the law with common sense" (Fretts 1998; qtd. in Foust 2004: 279).

Into this picture walked Judith Sheindlin, who became prominent as a tough-minded and straight-talking family judge through a 1993 *LA Times* series of articles, entitled "Law and Disorder," about four Americans who refuse to "give up the fight to help America" (Getlin 1993: n.p.). There, Sheindlin was praised for being a much-needed antidote to an overburdened and ineffective social welfare system: "Tart, tough-talking and hopelessly blunt, Sheindlin runs her court with an impatience that borders on rage. And the ground rules are simple: 'I can't stand stupid, and I can't stand slow'" (1993: n.p.). The article led to her being profiled on the documentary news program *60 Minutes* during the same year, where she was praised for her unconventionality and the speed with which she comes to judgment ("Law and Disorder" 1993). Thereafter, she was asked to star on a courtroom television program.

Sheindlin is the star of the syndicated courtroom. *Judge Judy* rapidly became one of the most popular shows on daytime television and surpassed even the ratings of *Oprah Winfrey* ("Judge Judy" 2011: n.p.). Her popularity reflects the new judge-centrism, in which viewers appeared to wish to have the judge not be an arbitrator but a source of authority: "On average, the frequent viewer believed judges should be more active and opinionated directors of courtroom proceedings" (Condo and Hudso 2011: 4). The public fascination with Sheindlin's Judge Judy has led one researcher to claim that her character is more determinant for public attitudes about law than anything else (Benton 2009: 667-68).

For some, Judge Judy's abrasive, curt, and personally insulting manner appears to have led to larger misperceptions about the US American legal process. According to a study by Kimberlianne Podlas of 241 prospective jurors, frequent viewers of syndic court – that is those who watch court shows more than once a week – make less reliable jurists because of the unrealistic displays of moralism and affect that they regularly witness in courtroom shows: "Eighty-three percent of frequent viewers [...] believed that [...] a judge should 'be aggressive with the litigants or express his/her displeasure with their testimony or behavior'" (2002a: 40). Moreover, frequent viewers fixate on trying to "look for clues" of the judge's opinion (2002a: 40). Thus these same viewers mistakenly understood a judge's silence to mean that she or he "strongly favored with the plaintiff or defendant" (2002a: 40).

In the end, the viewing of daytime courtroom dramas was more important in shaping a prospective juror's perception of judges than their prior experiences of "court service" (Podlas 2002b: 568). Podlas's study thus suggests that the mediated experience of the courtroom makes a greater impact on frequent viewers than time spent in actual proceedings. Acknowledging the skewed view of law that is presented by courtroom shows, the legal practitioners Jordan Condo and Clark Hudson advocate preparing clients for trial by dissuading them of their similarity to Judge Judy-style adjudication. This is part of a larger narrative that reads the medialization of law and its use as a source of televised and digital entertainment quite negatively. Accordingly, televised representations of law pervert the legal process and determine the public's attitude about law. For example, litigants have reported disappointment that "the judge has not humiliated their opponent" (Podlas 2002a: 42), even though they have 'won' the case.[3]

Judge Judy and judge shows that have copied her abrasive manner and authoritarian style do not explain law but issue judgment on participants. According to Nancy Marder of the Kent College of Law, this takes from viewers the opportunity to have legal reasoning explained to them ("Art Imitates Life" 2009: n.p.). Judge Judy's courtroom behavior would seem to directly contradict The Model Code of Judicial Conduct, which requires judges to "act in a manner that promotes public confidence in the integrity and impartiality of the judiciary," and to "be patient, dignified, and courteous to litigants" and to "perform duties without bias or prejudice" (as summarized by Podlas 2002a: 41). Thus one researcher advocates using Judge Judy's antics as a negative standard for how judges should behave: "To rate professionalism and temperament, they [researchers] should consider asking, 'Is the judge

3. See also Friedman on complaints to the *California Commission on Judicial Performance*: Those who believe that judge shows are actually litigating criticize that "Judge Judy goes too far"; or they are disappointed because "when they went to court, the judges didn't act like they do on television" (2000: 552).

more dignified/courteous/patient/controllled/fair-with-unrepresented-people than Judge Judy?'" (Benton 2009: 667-68)

To appreciate how Judge Judy rules over the courtroom one needs to see her in action. It may be useful to compare the footage from the CBS *60 Minutes* profile of her presiding over actual cases while she was still an acting judge. There she is shown spending a great deal of time berating the lawyers who represented the litigants in the family court cases. By contrast in the fictionalized courtroom of *Judge Judy*, abuse is heaped on the litigants who appear without legal representation. Amongst Judge Judy's most frequent behaviors are her expressions of strong negative affect. This includes her regularly yelling at claimants for being stupid, irresponsible, and/or immoral. In a clip that is no longer available on YouTube she screamed at one woman: "Shame on you, shame on you, and triple shame on you!" for having gotten in a fight with her former husband's girlfriend in front of their children. A highpoint in the show, which is evidently eagerly awaited by the live audience, is provided when Judy forcefully dresses down one or both parties in the case. Arguably, this moment suggests that the viewer is similar to Judge Judy in her or his ability to determine the intrinsic fallibility of the litigant. This moment generally occurs after she has heard the claimant and the defendant testify to their versions of what happened.

For instance, in cases from the DVD collection *Judge Judy: Justice Served* (2007), Judy flails into a claimant to tell her not only how flimsy her allegations are but also how emotionally unstable she is. In *Roy v. Tzimeas*, Ms. Roy alleges that her former roommate and landlady, Ms. Tzimeas, assaulted her with Tupperware, causing her emotional trauma for which she wants compensation as well as the costs of moving and paid rent money. This is the key part of Judge Judy's response to the assault charge:

Roy: "[...] I mean I just felt hollow in here. I mean I felt, I did not, uh, I did not feel stable at all. My ..."

JJ: "You're not stable! Anybody that walks into a bedroom, somebody sleeping in their bed, to ask for two pieces of Tupperware and start an argument with them while they're in bed over two pieces of Tupperware isn't too stable to start with." (*Roy v. Tzimeas*: 8:44-9:07)

A statement is made about the problematic essence of Ms. Roy's personality rather than about the validity of her claims for damages. The issue is not legality but the claimant's personality and 'bad behavior,' about which Judge Judy feels authorized to pass judgment.

In the case of *Tucker/Parmann v. Ostley/Brown*, Judge Judy similarly lashes into a seventeen-year-old who claims that she was assaulted by her boyfriend's former girlfriend's friend in the park. This allegedly occurred while her boyfriend and his friends stood by to cheer them on. Judge Judy brings the case to a rapid conclusion with the following exchange:

JJ: "How old are you?"
Parmann: "Seventeen."
JJ: "You should be smarter at seventeen. I don't expect you to be fully cooked but you shouldn't be an idiot. You went there [to the park] looking for trouble, along with him [the former boyfriend]. He especially knew that there was gonna be trouble. And then he and his relatives egged a fight, egged her on to fight with you. Doesn't that say something about him? That he's a moron? And you're a moron for being there! For that you don't get rewarded!" (*Tucker/Parmann v. Ostley/Brown* 11:00-11:44)

Again, an intrinsic value judgment is made about the claimant and not an assessment of the validity of her claims. Despite the perversion of judge demeanor that Judge Judy regularly enacts, her 'no-nonsense manner' is adored by audiences. The reader of this essay may find many lists and assemblages of video clips on the internet of her 'best' (speak most insulting) dramatic moments as well as her most dismissive statements (cf. for instance, Morrissey 2009 or Jefferson 2011). Many of these phrases also feature in Sheindlin's six books.

Judge Judy and Gender Issues

As outlined above, alternative readings have been offered of *Judge Judy*'s influence on gender roles. Positively, she has been viewed as modeling intelligence and strength to the problem-ridden women who participate in her show. According to Nancy Marder, then, her message is as follows: "women: think for yourselves. Men need to act responsibly. Just because a man is unthinking, doesn't mean you have to be unthinking" ("Art Imitates Life" 2009: n.p.). Similarly, she is praised on the blog Jezebel for teaching a "Wife Beater To Have Respect For Women" (Jezebel). Judy Sheindlin fashions herself something of a feminist when she attests in an interview from 2009 that she wants to help people watching daytime television "to be smarter" (Krukowski 2009: n.p.). As she reports on the need for more information in this programing:

I think that programmers of daytime television have done a terrible disservice over the years to the people that watch television in the afternoon. What they have done in daytime TV for too long is to try and dumb it down. And I think that the people who watch daytime TV, the majority of whom are women, have had enough of hair makeovers and behind makeovers and breast makeovers. They want to be smarter. They want information. They want to be able to negotiate the world a little bit better. (Krukowski 2009: n.p.)

By implication, watching *Judge Judy* will help women to be better informed, more intelligent, and better able to negotiate the world.

For many critics, including the author of this essay, Judge Judy's behavior towards women has to be viewed critically. While she embodies a position of power that is relatively unusual for a woman given the overwhelming preponderance of white male judges in US American courts, her effect on marginalized persons, including women, is to shame them and to increase their already present position of subordination within the hierarchy of the pseudo courtroom. Her effect is in no sense emancipatory but rather reifying of social divisions. As Christina Foust has saliently argued, Judge Judy instrumentalizes her status as a woman and a mother to authorize her right to dispense her penalizing form of justice (2004). This interpretation may be verified by Sheindlin's statement in her first book *Don't Pee on My Leg and Tell Me It's Raining* (1996) that her personal status as well as her professional one has led to her impatience with the justice system as it stands: "As a woman, a mother and a judge who has seen our criminal system deteriorate for nearly a quarter of a century, I have had it" (1996: 8-9). Indeed, the image that Sheindlin most frequently seems to inspire in her audiences is that of the tough mother who dispenses so-called tough love. As one can read on AuditionAgency: "[T]he truth is what Sheindlin demands. No bull. No excuses. She's the mom who loves you but wants no 'he made me do it' whining. And she can always tell if you're lying. All she has to do is make eye contact" ("TV Show" n.d.: n.p.).

Verifying this point of view is the statement by Sheindlin's son Adam in the *60 Minutes* portrait from 1993. According to him, when he was a child no appeals were allowed in his mother's court of justice: "It's Judy's law" ("Law and Disorder" 1993). Sheindlin's manner to claimants is that of an omnipotent parent who appears to wish to call out their worst behaviors so that she may reinstate her authority more forcefully. Explaining how Judge Judy embodies a form of "'appropriate' public femininity" based on a morally constructed vision of motherhood, Foust suggests that Sheindlin recurs to middle-class US American women who, during the temperance era, felt justified in leaving the private sphere of the home to speak publically on the basis of their Christian duty to improve the nation. Thus "domestic values" could be combined with the right to "speak in an aggressive style because society respects her moral authority and fears her Christian power" (Foust 2004: 275). The "Tough Mother", as Foust calls her, distinguishes easily between good and evil and sets absolute rules (2004: 25). This allows her to verbally assault parties in the court cases she presides over, to berate them for dressing or speaking or behaving in inappropriate ways, and yet to still be accepted as appropriately 'feminine.' She is also, according to Foust, a figure of a traditional conservative political ideology.

Judge Judy enacts a sensibility that suggests that punishing authority figures are doing those who are under their power a profound service. This is a retributive notion of justice that bespeaks the punitive culture of control that the United States has been involved in since the 1970s: it is characterized by 'expressive justice' or "explicit attempts to express public anger and resentment [that] have become a recurring theme of the rhetoric that accompanies penal legislation and decision making" (Garland 2001: 6). Judge Judy's successful persona as a Tough Mother thus relies on a neoliberal ideology that stresses personal responsibility and self-reliance rather than participatory justice and rehabilitation. As an economic theory, neoliberalism "proposes that human well-being can best be advanced by liberating individual entrepreneurial freedoms and skills within an institutional framework characterized by strong private property rights, free markets and free trade" (Harvey 2005: 2). In terms of social policy, neoliberalism's focus on small government, economic deregulation, and privatization entails the reduction of the state's role in providing support to its weaker citizens and the replacement of the ideal of a common good with that of individual responsibility (adapted from Martinez and Garcia 1999: n.p.).

The Displacement of Retributive Notions of Justice onto a Minority Figure

A retributive notion of justice speaks through Judith Sheindlin's attestations of what needs to be changed in the legal system. The morality she espouses is that of a rigid hierarchy, in which those who have power are also 'right.' This moral code stresses strict consequences, family-based authority, and criticizes those who seek social justice publically. Thus to assemble only a few choice quotes from *Don't Pee on My Leg and Tell Me It's Raining*, she states that "[these legal problems] are a mirror of what has gone wrong in America, a reflection of how far we have strayed from personal responsibility and old-fashioned discipline" (1996: 3). To blame are those who expect schools, government, and the justice system to take responsibility for social issues. Thus Sheindlin blames the justice system itself for having granted prisoners too many rights (1996: 24-26) and advocates a number of punitive measures such as treating juvenile perpetrators like adults, creating harsher prison conditions

(1996: 56), instituting curfews and doing away with parole and probation (1996: 24-61), and radically reducing claims to state support and welfare. Sheindlin's book reads like a platform for neoliberalism: individuals are the sources of their own problems and successes, not the community. Institutionalized and systematic forms of discrimination do not exist or are not relevant, and a government that fosters protection of the so-called weakest only helps to foster delinquents.

In general terms I see *Judge Judy* as a representative of an ideology that renders itself digestible by finding its spokesperson in a woman. Here, I wish to make an argument analogous to one that has been posited about the function of heroic African American protagonists in films such as *The Kingdom* (2007) and series such as *24* (2001-2010) (Bayoumi: 2010; Morey: 2010). In the former, actor Jamie Foxx leads a retributive, action-packed, blood-bath hunt against terrorists in Saudi Arabia; in the latter, an anti-terrorist unit repeatedly saves the United States from ruin by torturing terrorist suspects, often to death. The president of this fictionalized United States is a highly ethical black man. Arguably, these types of popular texts authorize the othering of Muslims, Arabs and Arab-looking individuals by suggesting that racial discrimination has been overcome in the United States. Thus by casting a black man in the position of power, it is suggested that the country has overcome its historical wounds of slavery, Jim Crow, and racism and has moved into a post-racial 'good' society. Hence, the nationalistic, pro-torture, and ultimately highly conservative sentiments of these texts are given the veneer of political correctness and liberalism by having a black man step into the role usually reserved for the white patriarch (cf. Morey 2010).

My sense is that *Judge Judy* performs similar cultural-political work. In that a woman is placed in a prominent position of authority, women's historicall subordination is occluded and a retributive concept of justice can be more palatably dispensed. As Michael Epstein writes about the surplus of courtroom television judges from gender, ethnic, and racial minorities: "Being an other [in racial and/or ethnic terms] allows the judge to pass judgment on a litigant and not be viewed as suspect or abusive of her power" (2001: 134). Thus a woman serves as a palliative mask for punitive neoliberalism. What this means in gender terms is that Judge Judy can be most frequently found beating up her own, that is other women, with whom she finds no common ground: "70 percent of plaintiffs [of judge shows] are female" (2001: 134).

If, as Judge Judy's position suggests, a woman can be an authority figure who metes out judgment in front of millions of viewers daily, then a history of systematic sexism appears to have been visually overcome. This, in turn, allows for the women participants on her show to be scapegoated for what is portrayed as their individual culpability. Thus Judy's rhetoric of responsibility allows her in particular to belittle anyone who perceives herself as a victim. The audience is likewise invited to blame litigants, who are then urged to 'help themselves' rather than seeking community solutions. Her most biting critique is reserved for women who allegedly have the power to prevent harm to themselves and their children and to overcome various forms of material and emotional dependency. As Laurie Ouellette writes: "On Judge Judy all women are presumed to be capable of supporting themselves and their children financially; accepting welfare is constructed not as a reflection of gender or economic inequality but as a character flaw" (2009 [2004]: 233-34).

In terms of the anti-feminist work it performs, then, *Judge Judy* has two important effects. In the first case it suggests to its overwhelmingly women audience that their subordinate economic and political roles are natural and should simply be accepted: "As a consequence of their orientation toward female and marginalized viewers, these programs speak not so much to the American population as whole, but to a segment of the population that has traditionally been denied a powerful role in civic and legal affairs" (Kohm 2006: 696). It thus advises these marginalized groups against taking legal recourse and rather 'solving' their problems by being 'responsible adults.' Read negatively, then, Judge Judy suggests that women have no business bringing issues of domestic abuse or economic want to the courts of law, because these problems are of their own making.

In the second case, Judge Judy's having been the model for day-time courtroom shows' plethora of minority judges[4] belies the reality of the US American law system in which the overwhelming majority of judges are white men. Viewers need not worry about sexism in law school and in court appointments or about the lack of people of color in the courts because the shining examples of Judge Judy and Judge Mathis, an African American man, are there to reassure them. Thus a spectacle of gender and racial/ethnic equality replaces the perceived need for political action. As Taunya Banks summarizes the current situation, "women tend to be concentrated in less prestigious legal jobs" and "comprise 18.67 % of federal judges and twenty percent of state" ones, and the combined percentage of African American women and men judges is between six and eight percent (2008: 39). In

4. "At the beginning of the 2007-2008 viewing season there were still ten [reality court] shows but women judges out-numbered men, and only two judges, Judy Sheindlin and David Young, were white" (Banks 2008: 39). Arguably, Judge Judy is also ethnicized, as she "delves deeply into Brooklyn Jewish schtick and accent from the bench" (Epstein 2001: 134).

recognition of the fact that the vast majority of current US American courtroom show judges are non-white and women, one thus has to analyze them in terms of how their gender politics intersect with racial and ethnic issues.

Judge Judy and Her Copycat? Richterin Barbara Salesch

At first glance, it would appear that the extraordinarily popular *Richterin Barbara Salesch* was simply a copy of Judge Judy. Like Judge Judy, *Richterin Barbara Salesch* originally featured actual civil-law disputes, the only type of case that can be filmed in Germany, where laws concerning cameras in the courtroom are more restrictive than in the United States. As protagonist of the show, Barbara Salesch stated in an interview, the idea for the show came from the States, and hers was the first and only German courtroom show to try "real cases. It was intended to be a German *Judge Judy*" (Löhr 2011: n.p.), featuring a real woman judge with a powerful personality. It was originally a half hour long, including commercial breaks, and was broadcast at 6 PM.

Yet this was by no means the first courtroom show in Germany: *Das Fernsehgericht tagt* reconstructed actual cases with actors and ran from 1961 until 1978. Other court-themed shows followed including one about marriage problems, one that allowed the audience to judge, and one about traffic cases. Many aspects of *Richterin Barbara Salesch* appeared to make it a sure bet in Germany. Barbara Salesch was a judge with a 'large' personality from Hamburg, who might fill Judy's shows. Yet trying actual civil cases did not sell well in Germany. As Salesch herself has stated, no one cared about these boring cases (Salesch 2002: n.p.), and a humorous song was made mocking the trivial content of one of the cases (*Maschen-Draht-Zaun* 1999). Thus in 2000, *Richterin Barbara Salesch* moved to a far more fictionalized form than its US American counterpart and began to 'try' entirely fictitious criminal law cases in an hour-long daytime slot. Murder, rape, and blackmail cases dominate the show in a manner that does not cohere with the actual incidence of these crimes (Wolf 2010: n.p.). *Richterin Barbara Salesch*'s cases have the appearance of authenticity because actual legal practitioners play the roles of the judge(s) and attorneys and amateur actors take on the partly unscripted roles of witnesses and defendants, giving the show the feeling of reality television. *Richterin Barbara Salesch* quickly became a hit, and in 2003 often had well over thirty percent of the entire viewing audience, including the highly coveted market of fourteen to forty-nine-year-old viewers (Schröder 2011: n.p.). The popularity of *Richterin Barbara Salesch* soon led to the advent of other pseudo-reality courtroom shows including *Richter Alexander Hold* (Judge Alexander Hold, 2001-present) and *Das Jugendgericht* (Juvenile Court, 2001-present).

Generally, sexual jealousy, material greed, or a desire for revenge play a role in the perpetrators' criminal motivations. Although the type of cases she tries differs, Barbara Salesch does have similarities to Judge Judy. As Stefan Machura has pointed out, her authority is continuously demonstrated; morality is crystal clear, and arguably social differences are reified through the use of supposedly typical clothing (2006).[5] Young women in lower-wage occupations, for instance, wear low-cut shirts or dresses, large jewelry, and short skirts. Men of the same economic status are often tattooed.

Not only are the cases entirely fictional, but they also mimic aspects of adversarial common-law court procedure in order to amplify their dramatic effects (Machura 2006: 179). Consistently, proceedings are represented as far more emotional and affect-driven than in German courtrooms. As the former protagonist of *Das Jugendgericht*, Judge Ruth Herz, described this process: viewers are led to believe that witnesses and defendants regularly yell at one another in court, and legal actors play to stereotypes. "An element of tension was injected into the characters of 'prosecutor' and 'judge.' [...] [The prosecutor] was meant to be the more aggressive character – his character was meant to be a young person who was 'getting there.' My character was meant to be much more calm and solution oriented" (Herz 2010:10; quoted in Moran et al. 2010: 208).

In the worst case this may lead German viewers to believe that their legal culture is based on an adversarial common law system. Thus litigants may have to be tutored by their legal representatives not to interrupt proceedings, as witnesses and defendants frequently do on *Richterin Barbara Salesch* or to not expect "a brilliant final plea" (Ernst 2010: 745). Thus a similar argument is made as the one about *Judge Judy* – that it and its media successors pervert the legal process by suggesting to audiences that expressive emotionality is the proper communicative mode in the courtroom.

5. An email exchange with the production team of *Richterin Barbara Salesch* asking about participants' clothing revealed that the main characters as well as Frau Salesch, the state and defense attorneys, and the other main protagonists are dressed according to their roles by the production team; the audience members, however, wear their own clothing. The original reads: "die Hauptdarsteller wie Frau Salesch, die Staats- und Rechtsanwälte sowie andere Hauptprotagonisten wurden ihrer Rolle entsprechend vom Produktionsteam ausgestattet, die Komparsen im Gerichtssaal trugen jedoch ihre private Kleidung" (Becker 2012: n.p.).

Effects on German Legal Culture by *Richterin Barbara Salesch* and Other Judge Shows

Just as there is a continuing lively debate about whether courtroom shows have tangible effects on US American legal culture, there is also a disagreement amongst German academics as to whether or not they pervert the audience's impressions of and interactions with law. According to Stefan Ernst, for instance, these shows contribute to clients having unrealistic expectations about their own legal knowledge and the degree to which money can influence the outcome of a trial (2010). One might call this the German OJ Simpson effect. Frequently, *Richterin Barbara Salesch* and the pseudo-reality courtroom shows that followed in the wake of its success like *Richter Alexander Hold* are interpreted, like US American ones, as negative representatives of the demise of law into a form of entertainment (Mackenroth 2002; Mackenroth and Hold 2003; Wolf 2010; Ernst 2010). For those who take a negative view of their misleading effects, German judge shows are said to deform viewers' perceptions of legal process because the cases are dramatized as though they were occurring in an adversarial law courtroom, with the state prosecutor and the defense lawyer attorney yelling at one another; and witnesses expressing anger, fear, and surprise. German shows may also encourage viewers to expect a *deus ex machina* to occur during court cases, which is quite unlike procedure according to the *Amtsermittlungsgrundsatz* (the principle of ex officio investigation) (Machura et al. 2001: 125).

Further skewing the portrayal of courtroom procedure, judge shows follow the 'rules' of series in general by rewarding 'good' characters in keeping them on the show longer (Machura 2006: 178). Moreover, legal actors are divided, like the lay actors, into clearly identifiable types: as described by Ruth Herz, the public prosecutor takes a more adversarial role in German courtroom shows. In the case of *Richterin Barbara Salesch*, public prosecutor Bernd Römer frequently appears to be morally incensed by the wrongs he uncovers inside and outside the courtroom, whereas defense attorneys Ulrike Tasic and Malte Höch react with clever irony, and Judge Salesch keeps her figurative legal progeny under control.

Other commentators counter the view that popular judge shows have a negative impact on viewers' perceptions of legal culture. Arguably the only established German academic who has studied the effect of judge shows with any thoroughness thus far is Stefan Machura. He argues that the courtroom shows' techniques of *Verfremdung* (alienating the audience and reminding them of the shows fictionality as in the epic theater of Brecht) and exaggeration may actually involve a form of teaching (2006: 176). Thus although

Kimberlianne Podlas's work in the United States has shown that frequent viewers of judge shows develop highly unrealistic views about courtroom behavior, Machura's similar study of the correlation between frequent viewing of judge shows and attitudes towards actual courts, which he conducted with students from the University of Bochum, came to quite different conclusions. Frequent viewing did not affect the respondents' attitudes about the correctness of judgments or the trustworthiness of judges in actual courtrooms (2006: 185).

Some critics even argue that courtroom shows have positive social effects. Despite their exaggerated emotionality, they may demonstrate to German viewers that there are, in fact, no juries in German courtrooms; nor do German judges wear white wigs (Engel 2002: n.p.). Moreover, courtroom shows provide a forum for debate about social norms. Thus for Thomas Hausmanninger, courtroom shows have replaced the reality shows of the 1990s, which featured excessive displays of individualism, with a more consensus oriented forum for discussing the interaction between individual agency and community responsibility. In an arguably more conservative era, in which an attention to norms and an emphasis on tolerance are both propagated,

> courtroom shows can contribute principally to the discursive formation of social ethos. As has been seen, they are primarily dedicated to [a discussion of] the social duties to protect and advance others in having a good and successful life. Not only do they contribute to making our law system more transparent, as Hold, Salesch and Herz have repeatedly emphasized (cf. Hold 2002), but, they also do even more than that. Connected to the juridical discourse, they can further a moral discourse amongst the public about these duties (Hausmanninger 2002: 44).[6]

Similarly, the producer of *Richterin Barbara Salesch*, Gisela Marx, has stated about her star: "Salesch represents the village judge as a woman. The audience has the sense that their value system is being readjusted. At the end of a case, the result can be morally justified. What reassures people is the rit-

6. The original reads: "Unter diesen Bedingungen aber können Gerichtsshows grundsätzlich einen hilfreichen Beitrag zur diskursiven Festigung des gesellschaftlichen Rahmenethos leisten. Sie widmen sich ja, wie zu sehen war, vorrangig den sozialen Pflichten zur Wahrung und Förderung fremden guten und gelingenden Lebens. Nicht nur lässt sich mit ihnen demnach, wie Hold, Salesch und Herz wiederholt betont haben, größere Transparenz unseres Rechtssystems für das Publikum erreichen (vlg. etwa Hold 2002). Vielmehr kann, an den juridischen Diskurs geknüpft, so auch ein moralischer Diskurs über die genannten Pflichten beim Publikum angeregt und gefördert werden."

ualization, the sense that at the end of the day everything is in order. This is particularly important in the afternoon" (Broder 2002: n.p.).[7]

Richterin Barbara Salesch and Gender Politics

To understand Salesch's impact on gender issues and its implications for legal culture, I need to briefly describe this syndic-court show's form. Unlike *Judge Judy,* it is an hour long and also, unusually for German television, features commercial breaks, since it is broadcasted on the private network SAT 1. (Public television stations in Germany are supported through indirect taxation and feature few commercials.) The opening credits of roughly twenty seconds are action packed. Images of Judge Salesch are interposed in less than second-long cuts with scenes from violent crimes. The credits begin with a scene of Salesch's black-robed torso looking through the files of a case; a cut is made to what looks like a robbery at gunpoint in a small store; a close-up of Salesch's face at eye level follows in which she looks wisely at the camera and, characteristically, gesticulates with her glasses; another crime scene follows – this time of an arrest, followed by a shot of a police man entering the courtroom. Another cut is to Salesch, shown holding a gun (evidence, perhaps from the first crime scene) while presiding at the bench. Another crime scene follows in which one man threatens another physically; the camera cuts to Salesch appearing to explain a legal point while gesticulating with her hands; a drawn knife is shown, followed by a scene of a man being stabbed and falling to the ground. This is followed by a shot taken from a front angle of Barbara Salesch and the rest of the court arising from the bench. The logo of the show "Richterin Barbara Salesch" appears over the image of the courtroom, which is then faded out. The credits underline what the audience can expect: an exciting violent crime, Salesch's investigation of

7. The original reads: "'Die Salesch ist inzwischen eine Kultfigur – für mich ist sie der Dorfrichter Adam als Frau', erklärt die Produzentin den Erfolg der Serie. 'Die Zuschauer haben das Gefühl, das Wertesystem wird neu justiert. Am Ende eines Falles steht ein Ergebnis, das moralisch zu rechtfertigen ist. Was die Leute sehr beruhigt, ist die Ritualisierung, das Gefühl, es hat alles seine Ordnung. Das ist vor allem am Nachmittag sehr wichtig.'" (Broder 2002). The original quote is more ambivalent than my translation suggests, as it (inadvertently) compares Salesch to the judge protagonist of Heinrich von Kleist's *The Broken Pitcher (Der zerbrochene Krug*, 1806). In this comedy, the judge Adam is revealed to be the perpetrator of the crime whose proceedings he tries.

it in the courtroom, more dramatic action, and a resolution of the action in legal judgment.

The actual show begins with a cut to the courtroom; a male voiceover states the matter of the case in brief dramatic sentences. Richterin Barbara Salesch leads the rest of the judges and/or assessors into the courtroom and announces the case and the type of court that shall try the case. This may either be a *Schöffengericht* (a court of lay assessors), consisting of one judge and two assessors for less grave criminal offences, or a *Schwurgericht*, consisting of three judges and two assessors for capital ones. Judge Salesch questions the defendant by first asking her or him about personal facts such as where s/he lives, whether or not s/he is single and has children, what type of work s/he does, and what her/his monthly income is. She has the charge read by the public prosecutor, and then goes on to question the witnesses. This generally leads to dramatic retellings – some of which are subsequently revealed to be patently false – of the crime, increasingly emotional and accusatory interactions between the witness and the defendant, and/or between the public prosecutor and the defense attorney.

Whereas other legal actors speak harshly to defendants and witnesses, Judge Salesch remains consistently calm, never raises her voice, and interrupts exchanges that grow too vehement. By roughly the middle or the last third of the show, and through the office of Salesch's careful questioning, new insights into the case and surprising plot turns are revealed. The questioning highlights the Continental European judge's role in assessing all of the evidence relevant to a given case. Salesch questions so insightfully that the 'real' perpetrator reveals herself or himself. For instance, in the case of what I will call "The Plastic Surgeon" (episode 2003.12.15), a dancer is accused of having cut off the thumb of the plastic surgeon who performed a disastrously bad breast augmentation operation on her. Rather typical for the show and the voyeurism it encourages, photographs are shown of her post-operative scarred, asymmetrical breasts. One piece of evidence against the defendant consists of the testimony by the surgeon's wife. She testifies that she heard the former patient threaten her husband for having defaced her and ruined her career as an exotic dancer.

Salesch grows increasingly suspicious of discrepancies in the wife's testimony concerning her 'happy marriage' and her anger at her husband for his financial losses, his affairs, and his having insisted that she undergo unnecessary plastic surgeries. The woman who plays the role of Frau Jungmann appears to have unnaturally large breasts, augmented lips, oddly shaped, perhaps surgically adjusted eyelids, and she wears a great deal of garish make-up. The *deux ex machina* occurs in the following exchange:

Salesch: "Frau Jungmann, you seem to be a very independent, confident woman. Isn't that right. And someone like you is so susceptible to being manipulated?"

Jungmann: "You do not know this man. You do not know him. It would start already in the morning at the breakfast table: "Darling, your drooping eyelids are due to be repaired. We will have to take care of that soon," and so on and so forth. He nagged me about it until, in the end, I finally believed it myself. Don't you understand? Fourteen times he operated on me, fourteen times! He even shortened my lower ribs so that I would have a slender waist!"

Salesch: "Frau Jungmann, you know Frau Schleyer [the defendant]. You were there [in the practice] on the sixth and the seventh of June. It could not have been so terribly difficult to find out her private address. And to place the garden shears on her premises so as to link her with the crime would not have been terribly difficult either. Frau Jungmann, don't you think that Frau Schleyer has suffered enough due to your husband's actions? Did you cut off the thumb?

Jungmann: "What? Me? Me?" (44:47-46:03).[8]

In this exchange, Judge Salesch appears to empathize with the witness, and at the same time appeals to her sense of pity for the woman defendant who has been accused of the crime. Thus Salesch is far more moderate than Judge Judy. She reacts to witnesses and defendants with more tact and sympathy, and most viewers would agree that her judgments are reasonable (Machura 2006: 178). Her femininity is consistently described in positive terms, for instance as "motherly, understanding, and always in control, but without any authoritarianism" (Meier 2005: n.p.).[9] Similarly, Susanne Baer, a justice from the Federal Constitutional Court, describes Judge Salesch as follows:

Judge Salesch presents the image of a capable, very nice woman, with henna red hair. ... In Judge Salesch we imagine a person who has her feet on the ground, who is a bit overweight but not obese, and who is understanding, but also firm, a person who seems motherly (Baer 2006; n.p.).[10]

As in the above descriptions, Judge Salesch appears to personify a form of morality and justice that is frequently compared to that of a 'good' mother. However, this gendered form of justice is quite different from that which is disseminated through Judge Judy's Tough Mother persona. Rather than sug-

8. A transcript of the original dialogue is provided in the appendix.
9. The original reads: "Mütterlich, verständnisvoll und stets souverän, doch ohne Autoritätsgehabe – solche Rollenmuster sind durchwegs zu beobachten."
10. The original reads: "Richterin Salesch ist ja diese patente, leicht rot gefärbte, auch ganz nette Frau... Wir stellen uns eben bei Richterin Salesch auch eine eher im Leben stehende, nicht korpulente, aber doch kräftigere Person vor, die verständnisvoll, aber manchmal auch entschieden, also eher mütterlich daher kommt" (Baer 2006).

gesting that marginalized persons should take more responsibility for themselves, Judge Salesch demonstrates that German criminal law, as her court practices it, is fair, kind, and wise. Thus she much more resembles the earlier Judge Wapner – arguably a representative of rehabilitative and participatory notions of justice – rather than Judge Judy with her emphasis on personal responsibility, guilt, and penalization.

Salesch's effect on gender issues also differs from that of Judge Judy's. She shows particular concern for those in her courtroom – women or not – who have experienced social discrimination or emotional pain. Rather than arguing in moralistic and punitive terms, she expresses a desire to uncover evidence and to a degree explain law. Thus at the beginning of the case, she states what kind of court will try the case and cites the regulations for questioning witnesses. At the end of the show, she cites the relevant code (*Paragraphen*) in order to explain the court's decision. Even if court procedure is performed in an unrealistic manner, the legal process itself is rendered accessible. According to Leslie Moran, writing about the effect of Judge Herz's role in *Das Jugendgericht*, courtroom shows have indeed changed the way Germans see law and literally see their judges. "In Germany no trial judge has an official photographic portrait and this gives them a degree of invisibility outside of the court [...]. In part this formal invisibility reflects an image of the judiciary as a selfless bureaucracy devoted to the law in the service of the state" (Moran et al. 2010: 206). With the new visibility of actual, if non-practicing, judges in *Das Jugendgericht*, *Richterin Barbara Salesch*, and *Richter Alexander Hold*, this has changed. Law has literally been given a face and a personality and has been infused with emotions.

Robin Hood Justice and Richterin Barbara Salesch

Richterin Barbara Salesch espouses what I would call a Robin Hood ideal of justice that coheres with Germany's social democratic principles of economic distribution. For instance, in the episode about the plastic surgeon, quoted from above, it is not the struggling dancer defendant who was responsible for the violent crime but rather the surgeon's neglected, materially well-off wife. Similarly, in many other episodes, characters who earn less are shown to have been scapegoated by materially better-off candidates. Ultimately, the wealthier accusers are shown to be guilty (Hausmanninger 2002: 43-44). Arguably, then, judge shows such as *Richterin Barbara Salesch* have to be interpreted not only in terms of their gender impact but also in terms of how they intervene with class-related issues in Germany.

In terms of gender, *Richterin Barbara Salesch*'s function is an ambivalent one. For many she embodies a down-to-earth 'motherly' form of justice that is tolerant and ultimately kind and works to address forms of social inequality, particularly those relating to class membership. Demonstrating her training and legal expertise, she calmly explains court procedure, quotes German criminal code, and ensures that the outcome of judgments are equitable. If anything, and this is entirely speculative, her depiction may contribute to essentialistic notions about women being intrinsically kinder and more compassionate. Judge Salesch's presentation as empathetic and competent as contrasted with public prosecutor Bernd Römer's aggression may cohere with contemporary gender expectations that women are less interested in a binary model of right and wrong than in contingent forms of justice and morality (cf. Gilligan: 1982). Women viewers of *Richterin Barbara Salesch* outnumber men by a factor of more than two to one ("Gerichtsshows: Marktanteile"). Thus it is possible that she and other women judges such as Ruth Herz model an ideal of behavior for their predominantly woman viewers.[11]

Yet the manner in which women defendants and witnesses appear on her show – often in very low-cut shirts or see-through blouses – in combination with their economic positions, reifies notions that women in the last analysis can be reduced to visible markers of erotic capital. Rather in defiance of the series' emphasis on material redistribution, less materially well-off women are more sexualized in terms of their appearance than better-off ones. Moreover, like *Judge Judy*, the presence and prominence of *Richterin Barbara Salesch*, which makes the image of a woman judge a daily reality, belies the dearth of women judges in the German court system, particularly in criminal law ones.

11. With no reflexivity about its own sexism, the report on "Gerichtshows: Marktanteile und Nutzungsmotive" reports that it is not surprising that more women watch afternoon judge shows, since there are more housewives than housemen. The original reads: "Tabelle 1 macht deutlich, dass Gerichtsshows deutlich häufiger von Frauen als von Männern geschaut werden, was jedoch angesichts der Sendezeit am Nachmittag nicht sonderlich verwundert. So gibt es nach wie vor mehr Hausfrauen als Hausmänner."

Consequences of these Judge Shows for Their Respective Legal Cultures

This essay has worked to demonstrate the following points. In the first case, a number of strong similarities between the two women judge shows have been detected: both interact with larger cultural trends such as the medialization of law. Both shows meet a desire to see the 'fight for justice' played out in public forum and to have the authority of a judge with a strong personality bring this struggle to a clear conclusion. Thereby, these shows work to reduce "social complexity" (Hausmanninger 2002: 20): judgments have clear material effects, and personal disputes are resolved by an institution that is given a very human face. Yet *Judge Judy* and *Richterin Barbara Salesch* function quite differently in terms of their overall interventions. To comprehend these differences, their individual legal systems and legal cultures need to be accounted for.[12]

In *Judge Judy*'s case, a desire for punitive justice in the United States and a neoliberal model of morality is dramatized. In this sense, Judy Sheindlin is not incorrect that her many, many viewers get exactly "the brand of justice" they want (Krukowski 2009: n.p.). By contrast, in *Richterin Barbara Salesch*'s enormous popularity, a desire for some consensus about social norms of behavior is expressed as well as an overriding faith in the German justice system. Despite important resemblances, including their featuring women judges and appealing to a day-time audience composed largely of women, *Judge Judy* and *Richterin Barbara Salesch* implement different cultural politics in terms of gender as well as in their overall impact on their respective legal cultures.

Judge Judy responds to a widespread post-Miranda and post-OJ Simpson sensibility that justice is not being served in the US American courtroom. Her response includes a heavy-handed didactic moralism towards pseudo-litigants, who are repeatedly shamed and made to feel that they need to be punished for not being more responsible for their behaviors. A harsh disciplinarian, *Judge Judy* has an anti-feminist agenda that promotes a victim-blaming ideology. Judge Judy's woman-blaming invective is partially obscured by her being placed in a role that is, for the greater part, still reserved for white men. Because Sheindlin voices the blame, it appears that the show cannot be misogynist or support patriarchal values. She functions like male actors in popu-

12. I have argued elsewhere that representations of law have to be contexualized with respect to the preoccupations of the legal cultures out of which they emerge and in which they are received (cf. Olson 2010; 2012).

lar post-9/11 movies and television series who propagate agendas that further prejudice against Muslims by performing them as black men, thus allowing new forms of discrimination to develop by suggesting that old ones have been overcome.

Although it was modeled on *Judge Judy* and is similarly judge-centric, *Richterin Barbara Salesch* responds to a desire for a public discussion of normative behavior. It translates law into lay terms, increases trust in the legal system, and also supports German values such as the need for a social democratic welfare system. Salesch's contribution to gender politics is more ambivalent than Sheindlin's. Whereas the sexualized appearance of the majority of women who participate in her show suggests that they are being objectified, Judge Salesch herself models wisdom, strength, and legal erudition. Aggression and a desire for retributive justice are displaced onto the role of the public prosecutor, Bernd Römer. The analysis of gender in *Richterin Barbara Salesch* demonstrated that it cannot be seen in isolation but has to be related to representations of class. While the status quo of class hierarchy is reified in visual terms, for instance, through the tattooing and body jewelry displayed by less well-off characters and the greater show of skin by women, the question of guilt or innocence for a crime appears to run counter to any class-related expectations. Again and again, characters with a higher socio-economic status are revealed to be the 'true' perpetrators and defendants are exonerated.

This essay has aimed to show that in looking at legal culture considerations of multiple forms of social difference have to be brought into play. Class discourse plays at least as important a role in *Richterin Barbara Salesch* as does gender. Thus although the show is derided by critics for its appeal to a so-called underclass of viewers, it works to critique expectations that those with less education and a lower standard of living are more likely to commit serious crime. Thus representations of gender and class (and ethnicity)[13] need to be seen in relation to *Richterin Barbara Salesch's* overall impact on German legal culture. In the US American context, by contrast, it was the surplus of judges of color and ones with marked ethnic background that demonstrated that the impact of women judge shows goes beyond their representations of gender and femininity.

13. *Richterin Barbara Salesch* and other German courtroom shows have been criticized for reifying prejudices about foreigners and Germans with a Turkish background being more likely to commit crime (Meier 2005: n.p.). If this is the case, then the show functions to ameliorate the negative effects of some social prejudices while strengthening others.

Friedman's original formulation of legal culture provided new tools for considering how individuals interact with institutions and one another on the basis of what might be called the legal imaginary. Yet it failed to address social differences between participants in a given legal culture. Gender is one factor that mitigates a given legal culture. Yet it intersects with other identity categories such as ethnicity and class to create overlapping forms of exclusion or privilege.

As a way of thinking this essay forward, I would thus like to advocate using intersectional analysis to interpret legal cultures. Intersectional theory was initiated by the work of the legal scholar Kimberlé Crenshaw and her insight that black American women are subject to multiple forms of discrimination and violence, which are based on the particular ways they are simultaneously sexed and raced (2004: n.p.). Yet according to US law these women's legal grievances had to be treated as either an instance of sexual or of racial discrimination and not as a combination of both (Crenshaw 1999). By following Crenshaw's lead, one recognizes that social identities are multiply constructed; they are influenced by overlapping but unlike categories such as race, gender, age, ethnicity, material wealth or the lack thereof, and sexual orientation. Taking account of how individuals are gendered, raced, and classed in different ways helps to understand how they engage with and are placed within their respective legal cultures.

In closing, I want to stress the importance of addressing questions of how legal culture relates to and impacts on gender issues. This has been the much-needed emphasis of this volume. Yet I wish to urge researchers to also investigate how other categories of social identity interact with gender within legal cultures. The nexus of factors that create privilege and exclusion has to be considered when describing how medial representations of law such as *Judge Judy* and *Richterin Barbara Salesch* challenge or reify existing social hierarchies and forms of prejudice.

Works Cited

"Art Imitates Life: TV Law Shows & Pop Culture" (2009). *ABA Now*. American Bar Association, 17 May 2011. Web. 12 Sept. 2012.

Baer, Susanne (2006). "Richterin, übernehmen Sie! Justiz im Umbruch?" *SWR.de.* SWR, 2006. Web. 7 Jun. 2011.

Banks, Taunya Lovell (2008). "Here Comes the Judge! Gender Distortion on TV Reality Court Shows." *University of Baltimore Law Forum* 39: 38-56. Print.

Bayoumi, Moustafa (2010). "The Race Is On: Muslims and Arabs in the American Imagination." *Middle East Research and Information Project.* Middle East Research and Information Project, March 2010. Web. 5 Sept. 2012.

Becker, Olaf (2012). "AW: AW: Titel der Barbara Salesch-Folge vom 9.2.2011." Message to Rabea Dahlhausen. 6 Sept. 2012. E-mail.

Benton, Duane (2009). "Comments on the White, Caufield, and Tarr Articles." *Missouri Law Review* 74: 667-74. Print.

Broder, Henryk M. (2002). "Gerichts-TV. Die Vierte Instanz." *Spiegel Online*. Spiegel Online GmbH, 3 Apr. 2002. Web. 7 Jun. 2011.

Condo, Jordan and Hudson, Clark (2011). *Trial Masters – 100 Days Before Trial: Overcoming a Client's Misperceptions of Jury Trial.* Federation of Defense & Corporate Counsel, Tampa, FL. Print.

Crenshaw, Kimberlé W. (2004). "Intersectionality: The Double Bind of Race and Gender." *Perspectives*. American Bar Association (Spring). Web. 12 Sept. 2012.

Crenshaw, Kimberlé W. (1991). "Mapping the Margins: Intersectionality, Identity Politics, and Violence Against Women of Color." *Stanford Law Review* 43.6: 1241-99. Print.

Engel, Peter (2002). "Interview: Manchmal fließen echte Tränen." Saarbrücker Zeitung. 23 Nov. Web. 5 May 2011.

Epstein, Michael M. (2001). "Judging Judy, Mablean, and Mills: How Courtroom Programs Use Law to Parade Private Lives to Mass Audiences." *Television Quarterly.* Summer 2001. Web. 12 Sept. 2012.

Ernst, Stefan (2010). "Medien, Justiz und Rechtswirklichkeit." *Neue Juristische Wochenschrift* 63.11: 744-46. Web. 7 Jun. 2011.

"Forced Haircut." *YouTube.* YouTube, 18 Jan. 2009. Web. 12 Sept. 2012.

Foust, Christina R. (2004). "A Return to Feminine Public Virtue: Judge Judy and the Myth of the Tough Mother." *Women's Studies in Communication* 27.3: 269-93. Print.

Fretts, Bruce (1998). "Here Comes the Judge: In the People vs. Judy, Viewers Find in Favor of Lady Justice." *Entertainment Weekly* 532. Print.

Friedman, Lawrence M. (2002). *Law in America: A Short History.* New York: Modern Library. Print.

Friedman, Lawrence M. (2000). "Lexitainment: Legal Process as Theater." *DePaul Law Review* 50: 539-58. Print.

Friedman, Lawrence M., and Harry N. Scheiber (1996). "Introduction." *Legal Culture and the Legal Profession.* Boulder: Westview Press. 1-6. Print.

Garland, David (2001). *The Culture of Control: Crime and Social Order in Contemporary Society*. Oxford: OUP. Print.

"Gerichtsshows: Realitätsnähe oder -ferne?" *medieninfo bayern.* Staatsinstitut für Schulqualität und Bildungsforschung München, n.d. Web. 12 Sept. 2012.

"Gerichtsshows: Marktanteile und Nutzungsmotive." *medieninfo bayern*. Staatsinstitut für Schulqualität und Bildungsforschung München, n.d. Web. 12 Sept. 2012.

Getlin, Josh (1993). "Law and Disorder: Tart, tough-talking Judge Judith Sheindlin presides over the grim pageant of dysfunction known as Manhattan's family court. 'I can't stand stupid, and I can't stand slow,' she snaps." *Los Angeles Times*. Los Angeles Times, 14 Feb. 1993. Web. 12 Sept. 2012.

Gilligan, Carol (1982). *In a Different Voice*. Harvard: UP. Print.

Harvey, David (2005). *A Brief History of Neoliberalism*. Oxford: UP. Print.

Hausmanninger, Thomas (2002). "Sehnsucht nach Normen? Das neue Ordnungsfernsehen der Gerichtsshows." *TV-diskurs* 20: 40-45. Print.

Jefferson, Whitney (2011). "*Judge Judy* By The Numbers." *Jezebel*. Gawker Media, 5 May 2011. Web. 12 Sept. 2012.

"Judge Judy Makes $865,000 A Day" (2011). *International Business Times*. IBTimes, 27 June 2011. Web. 12 Sept. 2012.

Judge Judy: Justice Served (2007). Dir. Randy Douthit. Prod. Randy Douthit and Timothy Regler. CBS Television. DVD.

Kimball, Philip Z. (2005). "Syndi-Court Justice: Judge Judy and Exploitation of Arbitration." *American Bar Association*, 2005. Web. 18 May 2011.

Kohm, Steven (2006). "The People's Law versus Judge Judy Justice: Two Models of Law in American Reality-Based Courtroom TV." *Law & Society Review* 40.3: 693-725. Print.

Krukowski, Andrew (2009). "Tough but Fair, Judge Judy Rules." *TV Week: In Depth*. 26 Jan. 2009. Web. 12 Sept. 2012.

"Law and Disorder" (1993). *60 Minutes*. CBS Interactive Inc., 22 Oct. 2008. Web. 12 Sept. 2012.

Löhr, Julia (2011). "Barbara Salesch: Die drei Leben der Barbara S." *Frankfurter Allgemeine Zeitung*. Frankfurter Allgemeine Zeitung GmbH, 28 Mar. 2011. Web. 12 Sept. 2012.

Machura, Stefan (2007). "An Analysis Scheme for Law Films." *University of Baltimore Law Revue* 36: 329-345.

Machura, Stefan (2006). "Fernsehgerichtsshows: Spektakel des Rechts." *Paragrana* 15.1: 174-88. Print.

Machura, Stefan, and Stefan Ulbrich (2001). "Law in Film: Globalizing the Hollywood Courtroom Drama." *Journal of Law and Society* 28.1: 117-32. Print.

Mackenroth, Geert, and Alexander Hold (2003). "Brüllen, kratzen und schlagen." *Der Spiegel*, 19. April 2003: 166. Print.

Mackenroth, Geert (2002). "Das ist emotionales Theater." *Der Spiegel*, 14. Oktober 2002: 188. Print

Martinez, Elizabeth and Arnoldo Garcia (1997). "What Is Neoliberalism?" *Corpwatch.org*. Corpwatch, 1997. Web. 12 Sept. 2012.

Meier, Oliver (2005). "Im Zweifel für die Quote. Eine Phänomenologie der TV-Justiz." *medienheft*. Katholischer Mediendienst, 15 June 2005. Web. 12 Sept. 2012.

Moran, Leslie J., Beverley Skeggs and Ruth Herz (2010). "Ruth Herz Judge Playing Judge Ruth Herz: Reflections on the Performance of Judicial Authority." *Law Text Culture* 14.1: 198-219. Print.

Morey, Peter (2010). "Terrorvision: Race, Nation and Muslimness in Fox's 24." *Interventions* 12.2: 251-64.

Morrissey, Tracie E. (2009). "A Decade of *Judge Judy*." *Jezebel.* Gawker Media, 28 Dec. 2009. Web. 12 Sept. 2012.

Olson, Greta (2010). "De-Americanizing Law-and-Literature Narratives: Opening up the Story." *Law & Literature* 22, no. 1: 338-364.

Olson, Greta (2011). "Issues in American Punitivity." *Pólemos* 2: 45-66.

Olson, Greta (2012). Reprint of "De-Americanizing Law and Literature Narratives" (With an Expanded Ending). Ed. Helle Porsdam and Thomas Elholm. *Dialogues on Justice: European Perspectives on Law and Humanities*. Law and Literature Series. Berlin and New York: De Gruyter. 15-43.

Ouellette, Laurie (2009). "'Take Responsibility for Yourself': *Judge Judy* and the Neoliberal Citizen [2004]." *Reality TV: Remaking Television Culture* 2nd ed. Ed. Susan Murray and Laurie Ouellette. New York: New York UP. 223-42. Print.

Podlas, Kimberlianne (2002a). "Should We Blame Judge Judy? The Messages TV Courtrooms Send Viewers." *Judicature* 86.1: 38-43. Print.

Podlas, Kimberlianne (2002b). "Blame Judge Judy: The Effects of Syndicated Television Courtrooms on Jurors." *American Journal of Trial Advocacy* 25: 557- 586. Print.

Porsdam, Helle (1999). *Legally Speaking: Contemporary American Culture and the Law*. Amherst: U of Massachusetts P. Print.

Pratt, John, David Brown, Marc Brown, Simon Hallsworth and Wayne Morrison, eds. (2005). *The New Punitiveness*. Willan: Cullompton. Print.

"Richterin Barbara Salesch (2003.12.15)." *Richterin Barbara Salesch* (1999-2012). filmpool GmbH. 9.2.2011.

Salesch, Barbara (2002). "Richterin Barbara Salesch im Gespräch." *SAT1*. SAT1, 1 Jul. 2002. Web. 12 Sept. 2012.

Schröder, Jens (2011). Nach dem Aus für „Richterin Barbara Salesch" – Gerichtsshows: das sterbende Genre. *Meedia* 13.04.2011. Web. 12.Sept. 2012.

Sheindlin, Judith (2006). Interview by Larry King. *CNN*. Cable News Network, 13 Nov. 2006. Web. 12 Sept. 2012.

Sheindlin, Judith (1996). *Don't Pee on My Leg and Tell Me It's Raining*. New York: Harper Collins Publishers. Print.

Sherwin, Richard K., Neal Feigenson, and Christina Spiesel (2006). "Law in the Digital Age: How Visual Communication Technologies are Transforming the Practice, Theory, and Teaching of Law." *Journal of Science and Technology Law* 12.2: 227-70. Print.

Simon, Jonathan (2007). *Governing through Crime*: *How the War on Crime Transformed American Democracy and Created a Culture of Fear*. Oxford: OUP. Print.

Tonry, Michael (2004). *Thinking about Crime: Sense and Sensibility in American Penal Culture*. Oxford: OUP.

"TV Show Reviews: Judge Judy." *AuditionAgency.com*. n.d. Web. 12. Sept. 2012.

Wolf, Christian (2010). "Alexander Hold oder Landgericht Hannover." *Juristische Arbeitsblätter*. Verlag Franz Vahlen GmbH, Dec. 2010. Web. 12 Sept. 2012.

Appendix

Salesch: "Frau Jungmann, Sie wirken hier auf mich recht selbstständig, selbstbewusste Frau. So. Und sowas lässt sich so gegen den Willen manipulieren?"
Jungmann: "Sie kennen diesen Mann nicht. Sie kennen ihn nicht. Das hat am Morgen, am Frühstückstisch, schon angefangen: *"Schatz, deine Schlupflieder sind wieder mal fällig, die müssen wir demnächst mal machen"*, und so weiter und so fort ging das ständig. Das ging so weit, bis ich's schlussendlich selber geglaubt habe. Ja? Vierzehn Mal hat der mich operiert, vierzehn Mal! Sogar meine unteren Rippen hat er gekürzt, damit ich eine schmale Taille bekomme!"
Salesch: "Frau Jungmann, Sie kennen die Frau Schleyer. Sie waren doch an dem sechsten da, an dem sechsten Juni. Die Adresse von ihr herauszubekommen, kann ja nicht furchtbar schwierig gewesen sein. Und so ´n Tatwerkzeug unterzuschieben, auf die Art und Weise wie es passiert is´, auch nich´ so schwer. Frau Jungmann, meinen Sie nicht, dass die Frau Schleyer hier schon genug gelitten hat durch Ihren Mann? Haben Sie den Daumen abgetrennt?"
Jungmann: "Was, ich? Ich?"

Claiming the Right to Polygamy: Fundamentalist Mormon Challenges to North American Legal Cultures

Miriam Koktvedgaard Zeitzen

Mormon polygamists in the United States and Canada have put polygamy on the political and legal agenda in North America. At issue is polygamy's legitimacy as an institution in societies where monogamy is considered, by the vast majority of the population, to be the only form of marriage permissible, culturally, socially and legally. Contemporary Mormon polygamists, in their fight for their right to practice what they consider to be their heavenly ordained and religiously prescribed marriage and family form in societies where monogamy is the norm, again challenge North American legal cultures. Legal cultures where civil law has traditionally taken precedence over the right to religious freedom, if the exercise of that right involves acts criminalized by civil laws. The chapter will explore this crucial and renewed instrumental link between polygamy and legal cultures in North America, with a focus on polygamy as both a religious right and a cultural right.

For contemporary American and Canadian so-called fundamentalist adherents of Mormonism, a Christian sect established in the early 19th century, polygamy is a religious statement of allegiance to an idealized 19th century Mormonism, where polygamy was part of Church doctrine and practice. Polygamy is a symbol of tradition and continuity with early Mormon heritage. Through polygamy, fundamentalists express allegiance to their version of traditional Mormon culture, sprung from the religious underpinnings of Mormonism, which is perceived as distinct and under constant threat from secularization and cultural streamlining with surrounding societies. As such, polygamy is about cultural rights. Polygamy is also about religious rights. Fundamentalists believe they are following the true teachings of Mormonism, and that through polygamy, they can authentically practice their religion. Polygamous practices can thus be ideologically important as statements of religious identity. It gives practitioners pride in belonging to a moral minority following a higher law.

Mormon polygamists are now increasingly visible and vocal in the United States and Canada, and have put polygamy back on the 21th century's legal agenda after a hiatus of half a century. In the second half of the 20th century, North American polygamists were rarely prosecuted, despite laws criminalizing marriage to, and in some states cohabitation with, multiple spouses. To many Americans, polygamy did not represent a significant harm to the community, there were too many polygamists to prosecute, it was too expensive and there were more important legal and criminal matters to attend to. For some, polygamists represent religious fanatics rather than criminals. At the turn of the 21st century, however, polygamists are once again prosecuted for polygamy related offences. The new wave of prosecutions is fuelled by media stories of very young girls being married off, often against their will, to men up to decades older. Such practices, which apart from polygamy itself are illegal, have generated public controversy.[1] Further fuel is added by stories of young boys, so-called 'Lost Boys', who are expelled from their families and communities so they will not compete with the older men for access to girls as plural wives.[2]

This assumed opposition between polygamy and women's and children's rights has made polygamy both more prominent and more controversial in North America. Polygamous Mormons, typically born, raised and living in Western North America, practice polygamy in officially and fervently monogamous societies, without support or understanding from the overwhelming majority of the populations they form part of. In former polygamous societies, where polygamy is now officially banned, there might be tacit understanding or acceptance of 'illegal' practitioners,[3] but not so among fellow Americans or Canadians. To them, polygamous Mormons violate not only legal but also cultural and religious mores. Increasing social and legal pressures are forcing fundamentalists to turn to the law, to lobby for their right to practice plural marriage. Tacit tolerance of polygamy, prevalent in American

1. See Bennion 2012 for a discussion of polygamy in various media.
2. See Altman & Ginat 1996 and Bramham 2008. The 2010 documentary "*Sons of Perdition*" (Left Turn Films) details the plight of young boys expelled from Warren Jeffs' FLDS community (see note 2). Evidence of expelled boys was heard in the Canadian constitutional reference case (see note 13).
3. Communities in the Cote d'Ivoire (Ivory Coast), for example, have some of the highest levels of polygyny in Africa, though the State legally abolished polygyny in 1964 (Bledsoe & Pison 1994).

legal cultures until recently, as well as potential legal recognition of variant lifestyles such as polygamy, are now under pressure, as authorities and the general public increasingly associate polygamy with the violation of women's and children's bodies and rights.

Polygamy in context

Polygamy is the practice whereby a person is married to more than one spouse at the same time, as opposed to monogamy where a person has only one spouse at a time.[4] In principle, there are three forms of polygamy: polygyny, in which one man is married to several wives, polyandry, where one woman is married to several husbands, and group marriage or polygynandry, in which several husbands are married to several wives, that is, some combination of polygyny and polyandry. Mormons technically practice polygyny, that is, one husband married to several wives. Typically, however, the term polygamy is used when referring to Mormons or other practitioners, in legal texts and public parlance.

In the social sciences, the term polygamy is often used in a de facto sense, applying regardless of whether relations between 'spouses' are legally recognized. In Western societies, where polygamy is not permitted, various forms of de facto polygamy are practiced among minority groups. It can be considered de facto polygamy when, for example, an American Muslim second wife has been married to her husband in a religious ceremony, yet has not had her marriage registered officially in her state of residence. Legally speaking, from the American authorities' perspective, the wife is unmarried. Circumventing civil marriage denies the wife any rights or assistance from authorities in case of divorce, child custody conflicts or other problems. The union is de facto polygamous, however, as she is recognized as married by her religious and cultural peers, and lives socially as her husband's second wife.

Polygamy is hence generally understood to be a union in which several people are married to one common spouse. A Western man who has a wife, but maintains a mistress, is not de facto polygamous, he is legally monogamous but has relations with another woman, whom society or their peers do not usually recognize as his unofficial wife. In order to become polygamous, the Western man would have to marry his mistress, in which case he would

4. When no other source is mentioned, definitions and descriptions of polygamy and polygamous practices throughout this chapter are based on Koktvedgaard Zeitzen 2008.

become a bigamist within most Western law, not a polygamist. A bigamist is someone who has entered into any number of 'secondary' marriages in addition to their one legally recognized marriage. Many countries have specific statutes outlawing bigamy, such that a man with three wives, for example, would be charged with two counts of bigamy, for two 'secondary' marriages after the first legally recognized one. In de facto polygamy, there is typically social recognition of the unofficial second wife within the spouses' cultural or religious community, and her marriage to her husband may be solemnized in a communal religious or cultural ceremony, even if the marriage is not legally recognized by civil authorities. De facto polygamy is hence a useful label to describe a social phenomenon based on the principles of polygamy, but without the transference of legal rights and obligations involved in formal (civil) marriage.

The distinction between formal de jure and informal de facto polygamy is not just a definitional conundrum, of interest to social scientists, however. The legitimacy and legality of the marriages in a polygamous union are of crucial and instrumental importance to polygamists living in states where polygamy (or bigamy) is illegal. In Western monogamous societies, where some minority groups practice polygamy based on their particular religious or cultural traditions, the majority populations generally consider the practice of polygamy a clear violation of their laws. Increasingly, therefore, polygamy has become part of contemporary debates focusing on minorities' rights. Clashing claims to different rights – such as minorities' rights to freely practice their religion or culture versus women's rights to be protected from forced marriage regardless of their religion or culture – has propelled polygamy unto political agendas in Western societies. To many people in monogamous Western societies, practicing polygamy represents a clash between irreconcilable cultural and religious differences. Hence, the majority populations typically reject the righteousness of polygamists' claims of religious and cultural rights. As such, polygamy is not only a legal challenge, but can also be an ideological statement, both for minority groups and majority populations.[5]

5. For a discussion of polygamy as a challenge for Western law and policy, see Bailey & Kaufman 2010. See Okin 1999 for a discussion of polygamy as a challenge to womens rights within multiculturalist concerns to proctect cultural diversity.

Mormon polygamy in North America

The Mormons are a religious body founded in 1830 in New England by the first Mormon Prophet Joseph Smith.[6] Smith had a series of religious visions in which he received a set of gold plates from an angel; based on his translation of the plates he founded Mormonism. Smith and his followers believed that their movement was a restoration of primitive Christianity, and adopted the designation Latter Day Saints, used in the New Testament to refer to members of early Christian communities. They took the name Church of Jesus Christ of Latter Day Saints (LDS), and considered it the New Testament Church, formed again in these latter days.

In the process of re-translating the Bible, Smith claimed to have received a revelation from God regarding plural marriage, and a commandment from God to take more wives. He believed that plural marriage was instituted and practiced by the earliest prophets of the Old Testament and was restored to earth for the Mormon people anew by direct revelation from God to their prophet. Smith secretly introduced the doctrine of plural marriage and instituted its practice among some of his closest associates. Mormons considered the practice to be a requirement for entry into the highest heaven after death, the so-called "third degree" of the Celestial Kingdom. More specifically, a Mormon man must marry at least three wives in order to ascend to heaven. In 1852, the second prophet Brigham Young proclaimed the doctrine of polygamy as a plan to prosper Zion, God's Kingdom on earth. Young had established Zion in 1847 in the Valley of the Great Salt Lake, now Salt Lake City in the state of Utah, in Southwestern United States.[7] Young's proclamation came as a shock to the country, as well as to lay Mormons, most of whom were unaware of the "celestial principle." Many Mormons were bewildered about the principle, yet the reason was clear for those who practiced it – God had told the Mormons to do it.

The general opinion in the rest of the country, among non-Mormons, was that the practice of plural marriage was offensive. In 1862, President Abraham Lincoln signed the Morrill Anti-Bigamy Law, the first of a number of

6. When no other source is mentioned, discriptions of Mormons througtout this chapter are based on: Altman & Ginat 1996; Anderson 1937; Beecher & Anderson 1987; Gordon 1996; Koktvedgaard Zeitzen 2008; Smith & Kunz 1976; Van Wagoner 1989.
7. Contemporary Mormons still live primarily in Utah, where about 2/3 of the 2,800,000 population are members of the Mormon Church, or self identify as Mormons, according to the LDS Church. Source: http://www.utah.gov/ & http://www.mormonnewsroom.org/ (accessed 28.09.12).

laws forbidding the practice in U.S. territories. In 1874, George Reynolds, secretary to Brigham Young, was indicted for bigamy. Church leaders appealed the case to the Supreme Court hoping to set a precedent. In 1879, however, the Supreme Court in Reynolds v. the United States established that although people could freely "believe" in certain religious principles, such as plural marriage, religious belief could not be accepted as justification for an act made criminal by civil law. Reynolds vs. the United States still stands today.

Despite these rulings, Mormons continued to challenge the U.S. government by refusing to obey anti-polygamy laws, arguing that their faith dispensed them from non-Mormon marriage laws and federal legislation. It was a moral and political battle that Mormons could not win, however. In 1890, the LDS Church issued a statement to the press, which became known as the Manifesto. It banned the practice of plural marriage and ordered Mormons to cease polygamous relations. The Manifesto cleared the way for Utah to ascend to statehood in 1896, as Utah could not become a state as long as polygamy was permitted in the territory. Church leaders who continued to seal polygamous marriages quickly undermined the Manifesto, however. The Church was accused of disingenuousness, leading it to issue the Second Manifesto in 1904, declaring that any who participated in additional plural marriages, and those officiating, would be excommunicated from the Church.

In the late 19th century, when anti-polygamy persecutions and prosecutions were at their height, Church leaders established settlements in remote areas of the USA, which they thought were beyond the reach of government harassment, as well as in Mexico and Canada, where laws prohibiting polygamy not enforced. Many more Mormons left the church when it formally began to excommunicate polygamists in the early 20th century. They formed hundreds of small isolated communities where they felt free to follow what they saw as the true principles of Mormonism. These various settlements coalesced into a formal organization in the late 1920s, and this 'fundamentalist' movement developed into the several groups that are active today. The largest group is The Fundamentalist Church of Jesus Christ of Latter Day Saints or FLDS, estimated to have over 10,000 members. Many of FLDS' members live in the twin cities of Colorado City, Arizona and Hildale, Utah (formerly Short Creek).

Fundamentalist Mormons number about 60.000 people. As polygamous Mormons often live in isolated rural communities, where marriages and births may not be officially registered, their precise numbers are difficult to establish. The LDS has attempted to convince the public that the term fundamentalist Mormon is a misrepresentation, because in their view polygamists are not fundamentalists in the sense of upholding the fundamental doctrines of the Mormon Church, which is opposed to polygamy. The official LDS Church has renounced polygamy as a fundamental part of Mormonism, and supports enforcing laws against polygamy. It vigorously disassociates itself from the practice of plural marriage, and continues to excommunicate its polygamous members. Fundamentalists are hence a small excommunicated minority among the world's 14 million mainstream Mormons.[8] Contemporary fundamentalist Mormons, however, consider themselves to be the faithful followers of Joseph Smith and his original theology. Like their 19th century forebears, they consider the practice of plural marriage to be a requirement for entry into the highest heaven. Not all fundamentalists practice plural marriage; many old members as well as new converts are attracted to fundamentalist groups because they feel the mainstream Church is too "liberal." Mormons who continue to practice or condone the principle of plural marriage in clear violations of national and LDS Church laws are thus a minority within a minority.

Civil or celestial marriage

Today, polygamous families face similar legal challenges and pursue similar strategies to circumvent civil laws and practice polygamy as polygamists have done since the early years of Mormonism. To the Mormon prophet Smith, marriages sealed by civil authority were for "time" only, binding a husband and wife together on earth but no longer valid in the hereafter. Marriages sealed by the priesthood, in contrast, were for "time and eternity", extending into the hereafter forever. Such "celestial" marriages were considered sacramental covenants rather than secular contracts, which allowed religious leaders to perform plural marriages within the Church and hence bypass the civil system. Mormon circumvention of secular marriage was legitimized by claims that plural marriages were acts of God.

Contemporary fundamentalist Mormons still adhere strongly to these principles, and maintain that several priesthood holders were secretly commissioned to continue the practice as individuals rather than as Church representatives after the Second Manifesto banned polygamy once and for all. This al-

8. Estimates for the number of fundamentalist Mormons range from as low as 20 000 up to 60 000 people (Bradley 2002). According to the LDS Church, there are 14 million Mormons worldwide; see http://www.mormonnewsroom.org/ (accessed 28.09.12); cf. Bushman 2008.

lows plural marriages to be performed today by special dispensation of priesthood authority independent of the Church organization. Joseph Smith's concept of eternal marriage, in which "families can be together forever", lies at the core of salvation and remains central in Mormon doctrine. The belief that a marriage contracted with proper authority extends into the afterlife hence provides a basis for those Mormons who wish to practice polygamy today. Wives and husbands in contemporary plural families further claim that they practice polygamy to continue meeting "the fullness of the Gospel." By having several wives in a family, all members become "saved." Co-wives may thus 'marry' each other at marriage ceremonies, to underscore the commitment all members of a plural family make to each other, a commitment that has to last into eternity.

Religious sealings without civil registration lead to de facto polygamous Mormon families. This distinguishes them from legally recognized, or de jure, polygamy, which involves formal marriage for all spouses in the union, something near an impossibility for American plural families, as they could be prosecuted for bigamy or polygamy if they registered all of their marriages. For fundamentalist Mormons, therefore, it is probably common to live in de facto polygamous marriages, from a legal perspective. The term acknowledges that the socio-economic and personal arrangements resulting from de facto polygamy are similar to those in recognized polygamy.

The distinction between de jure and de facto polygyny becomes central in a legal context, where the precise marital relationships between the spouses are pivotal in potential prosecution of polygamists. Among Mormons, as mentioned, religious sealings not followed by civil registration are considered legitimate marriages, whereas they may not be considered legitimate by the civil authorities. Thus, legally, the spouses are unmarried, and they cannot be prosecuted based on bigamy laws. They can, however, be considered to live in de facto polygamous unions, and be prosecuted based on cohabitation or having common law marriages – if cohabitation is criminalized or common law marriage is legally applicable in the state. In 1935, the LDS Church was decisive in making the Utah legislature pass a law making unlawful cohabitation a criminal felony rather than as previously a misdemeanour. The law was used in many polygamy prosecutions in the first half of the 20th century.

In the second half of the 20th century, there were few polygamy prosecutions. In 2001 however, the trial of Utah polygamist Tom Green signaled a change in legal culture. Tom Green, who had openly and publically spoken about his polygamous lifestyle in various media, was sentenced to five years in prison for bigamy. To avoid officially engaging in polygamy, Tom Green had married and then divorced each of his five wives, but continued to live with them. The State convicted him of four counts of bigamy, because they considered him married to his five wives by common law.[9] A common law marriage is a conjugal partnership that has not been solemnized in a formal ceremony and is not registered with civil authorities. In Canada and several states in the US, including Utah, common law marriage is legally recognised under civil jurisdiction, if certain requirements are met; typically, the partners must consider themselves and be considered by others to live and cohabit as a married couple; cohabitation for a certain period may be required for the marriage to be valid.[10] Green's case was the first high profile bigamy case in Utah in half a century.

The central importance of legal marriage in relation to polygamy is underscored by some polygamists framing polygamy as a civil right issue. They argue that civil rights include the (man's) right to marry more than one person. Yet Mormon polygamy in North America is practiced based on what practitioners believe to be a mandate or prescription from their religious belief system. Polygamists make a conscious choice to follow religious principles before civil laws; this allows them to define 'family' in a way that maintains their communal culture and family structures. In multi-cultural and multi-religious nations like the United States and Canada, activists argue, polygamy should be recognized as an acceptable lifestyle. Polygamy, however, challenges not only American majority norms, but also legal definitions of what constitutes marriage. Legally speaking, there is a major difference between monogamous marriage between two spouses, and polygamous marriage, which changes the numbers of spouses. American anti-polygamy statutes draw the line at the number of spouses, and limiting the number of spouses does not violate any constitutional rights of American citizens, according to court decisions. Polygamy alters what in North American legal culture is the assumed and accepted binary nature of marriage.[11]

Polygamy as a religious right

In the United States and Canada, Mormons have a long history of refusing to accept anti-polygamy legislation. Up until recent years, ineffective federal and state laws and reluctant law enforcement allowed them to violate anti-polygamy legislation and more or less freely practice polygamy. This unstable

9. See Bennion 2012 for a discussion of Tom Green's case.
10. For an in-depth discussion of common law marriage, see Lind 2008.
11. See for example: http://masscases.com/cases/sic/440/440mass309.html

equilibrium is now broken, as authorities increasingly prosecute polygamists and polygamists increasingly legally challenge anti-polygamy laws preventing them from freely practicing what they consider their prophet-ordained commandment to be polygamous.

In the USA, fundamentalist Mormons have long attempted to argue for their right to practice polygamy by reference to their constitutional rights to freedom of religion. Yet at present, polygamy is not protected by the First Amendment to the US Constitution, which guarantees the free exercise of ones religion. In recent years, however, the hopes of polygamists have been revived by several prosecutions and lawsuits against polygamists in Utah, which have raised a number of constitutional questions. Fundamentalists argue that the First Amendment's Free Establishment and Exercise Clauses relating to religious freedom allow them to practice their religious beliefs freely, including heavenly ordained plural marriage. It is their right to express themselves religiously and form associations by practicing the principle of plural marriage, that is, a polygamous lifestyle as an expression of their religion. This argument is usually refuted by arguing that the right to religious freedom does not put a person over federal law, which clearly prohibits marriage to more than one spouse.

In Canada in 1890, like in the USA, the government passed anti-polygamy laws which still stand today. Yet Canadian polygamous Mormons, like their US brethren, continue to argue for polygamy by referring to their constitutional rights to freedom of religion. They argue that the Canadian Charter of Rights and Freedoms allows them to freely exercise their religious beliefs and establish themselves as religious groups practicing plural marriage. From the Canadian authorities' perspective, the right to religious freedom does not exempt a person from following civil law, which prohibits marriage to several spouses. The Charter of Rights and Freedoms has generally been interpreted to mean that people can freely "believe" in certain religious principles, such as plural marriage, but that religious belief cannot be accepted as justification for exercising such religious principles, if they constitute acts considered criminal by the civil laws.

There have been very few prosecutions of polygamists in Canada, however. When authorities have arrested and charged alleged polygamists, the charges have been struck down because of uncertainty over whether the law criminalizing polygamy could hold in court, if set against the right to religious freedom. This has meant that, for decades, there have been no substantial criminal convictions involving polygamy. Canadian authorities therefore initiated a constitutional reference case to firmly settle the question of whether the law criminalizing polygamy is unconstitutional.

At the center of the legal battle is Bountiful, a small isolated fundamentalist Mormon community of about 1000 people in the Western Canadian province British Columbia. In 2009, Winston Blackmore and James Oler, leaders of rival factions in Bountiful, were charged with practicing polygamy. The charges were dropped on procedural grounds, but precipitated the constitutional reference case. Blackmore has, in court on tax evasion charges, acknowledged that he has 22 wives and 67 children; some suggest that he has had up to 30 wives and over 100 children.[12] Bountiful's Mormons, with reference to Canada's Charter of Rights and Freedoms relating to religious freedom, argue that polygamy is essential for them in order to live in accordance with their religion. As fundamentalists, they argue that polygamy is a religious prescription in Mormonism, going back to their founding prophet Joseph Smith. For fundamentalists, there is an unbroken link between the Mormon past and present, for the beliefs on which they base and legitimize their polygamous practices are the same. Today's polygamists see themselves as descendants and defenders of earlier polygamists; their belief in the practice as both church doctrine and Mormon tradition, and the condemnation and prosecution they suffer because of it, act as self-perpetuating forces.

The government of British Columbia (BC), partly in response to their difficulties in securing convictions when prosecuting even self-professed polygamists like Blackmore for polygamy-offences, therefore took the unusual step of calling a constitutional reference case, to settle decisively whether the Canadian criminal code's section 293, which criminalizes polygamy, is unconstitutional. The case was set to clarify whether section 293, if upheld, violates other constitutionally guaranteed basic rights, such as freedom of religion, contained in the Charter of Rights and Freedoms. The case's principal parties were the Attorney General of British Columbia, who argued that the law could be upheld, and an amicus curiae (impartial advisor), a private lawyer appointed by the government to respond and argue that the law is unconstitutional and should be struck down. For the Canadian and BC governments, the purpose of the court case was clear, namely to establish whether there was legally safe ground for prosecuting people practicing polygamy based on their religious beliefs.

The provincial government ran the case in the BC Supreme Court, which as a trial court allows witnesses to be called. A string of experts and representatives from different organizations gave evidence about all aspects of all

12. For a description of Bountiful, see Campbell 2010 2008, and various Canadian media, for example: http://www.vancouversun.com/
and http://www.cbc.ca/ (accessed 28.09.12); see also Bramham 2008.

kinds of polygamy. People personally touched by polygamy also gave evidence. Women who live in polygamous marriages talked about the delights of this family form, in anonymous statements. Women who escaped from violent or forced marriages in Bountiful and other communities gave evidence. Evidence was heard of marriage exchanges of very young girls between American and Canadian fundamentalist communities. For the provincial government, these personal and perhaps personally traumatized witnesses were used to establish whether polygamy necessarily causes harm to women and children. The amicus curiae, on the other hand, argued that degrading treatment of women and children among fundamentalist Mormons is due to a few individuals who handle an otherwise well-functioning lifestyle badly. These few individuals should be prosecuted for their crimes, such as sexual exploitation when forcing though marriage of underage girls. They should not be prosecuted for being polygamously married, because polygamy is a lifestyle which adults should have the right and freedom to choose.

For the provincial government, however, degradation of and harm to women and children is a systematic and structural part of polygamy. That, they argue, is exposed in witness accounts and documented by most studies of polygamy cross-culturally. A pivotal argument for upholding section 293 was hence that potential (and not necessarily actual) harm to women and children is an inherent aspect of polygamy. If it could be established that polygamy as a marriage and family form leads to an increased risk or threat of harm to women and children, and hence is inherently harmful for women and children's rights and well-being, then it would supercede any religious rights, and the law could be upheld. As such, polygamy as an institution was on trial. In the spring of 2011, witness depositions and court proceedings in the case ended. In the fall of 2011, the verdict came in – article 293 was upheld.

Presiding B.C. Supreme Court Justice Robert Bauman, when deciding whether criminalizing polygamy is unconstitutional, had to weigh people's constitutionally guaranteed rights to religious freedom and to freedom of expression and association against the potential harm polygamy can cause women and children. Chief Justice Bauman ruled that the ban on polygamy infringes on some sections of the Charter of Rights and Freedoms, and partly impairs the constitutional right of religious freedom, but that the criminalization of polygamy was justified by the harm polygamy causes to women, children and society. The ruling has not been appealed by British Columbia, although having the case referred to, and upheld in, the B.C. Court of Appeal would give the law banning polygamy more legal weight. If the law is to be upheld across Canada, the case would have to go to the Supreme Court of Canada. For now, the B.C. government believes the lower court ruling is powerful enough to carry criminal charges against polygamists, and it has cleared the way for a special prosecutor to charge the Bountiful leaders with engaging in polygamy.[13]

Polygamy as a cultural right

Fundamentalist Mormons who practice polygamy believe it to be legitimate according to their own sacred beliefs, absolving them of their duty to respect civil laws banning polygamy. While civil law in North America does not recognize polygamous marriage, laws directly banning living a polygamous lifestyle are only found in some US states. The laws criminalizing polygamous lifestyles originated as anti-polygamy legislation designed to allow Utah to ascend to Statehood within the USA. The prevalent legal culture in the second half of the 20th century, however, meant that the laws were rarely enforced, allowing fundamentalist Mormons to live as de facto polygamists. Recent convictions have signaled a change in this legal culture, and laws are now enforced. The focus may be on enforcing a broader set of laws than in the 19th and 20th centuries, however, and not just those directly relating to polygamy.

Fundamentalist Mormons are forced to respond to this re-enforced criminalization of their lifestyles. They continue to argue, as they have from the early days of Mormonism, for their constitutional right to freedom of religion. Today, however, emphasis may be placed on the practice of plural marriage as part of their distinct lifestyles, lifestyles based on the exercise of their religious beliefs and doctrines. These lifestyles may be said to form part of a distinct Mormon fundamentalist culture.[14] Once a group of people has a distinct culture, they may claim cultural rights. Cultural rights may include a group's right to preserve its culture, to use its own language, to protect its economic foundations, to raise its children in traditional ways – to practice lifestyles which may be termed its intangible cultural heritage.[15]

13. The B.C. Supreme Court ruling can be seen at: http://www.courts.gov.bc.ca/jdb-txt/SC/11/15/2011BCSC1588.htm; see also reports in http://www.cbc.ca/ (accessed 28.09.12)
14. See Bushman 2008.
15. According to UNESCO, intangible cultural heritage includes traditions or living expressions inherited from ancestors and passed on to descendants, such as oral traditions, performing arts, social practices, rituals, festive events, knowledge and practices concerning nature and the universe; see http://www.unesco.org/culture/ich/ (accessed 28.09.12).

The concept of cultural rights has grown out of the use of a rights discourse in still more contexts. It gained momentum particularly through anthropological research into non-Western and 'exotic' cultures, research which often displayed an implicit mission to encourage respect for these other cultures, and argue for peoples' right to cultural diversity. It helped establish cultural difference as fundamental for differences between peoples. The focus on cultural difference contributed to many more peoples being aware of having a distinct culture, a culture that can be objectified, take on material form, be destroyed, sold or lost. Ever more peoples are now demanding protection of their cultural rights and cultural heritage. The idea of cultural rights contains a form of ethnocentrism, in a tendency to highlight ones own cultural values compared to those of people who orient themselves through other cultures. It can help create social solidarity, a feeling of shared values and coherence among people who share cultural worlds. People everywhere consider, in varying degrees, their own ways to be the most correct, suitable and morally right. Herein lies the basis for differentiating oneself culturally from surrounding peoples.[16]

Mormons have always considered themselves religiously distinct from neighbouring peoples, and their lifestyles have reflected this perceived distinction. Mormons have endured persecution for their faith ever since the religion was founded in 1830; they have been derided for their religious beliefs, their secrecy, their hierarchical organization, their unquestioning obedience to self-proclaimed prophets. For many converts, acceptance of Mormonism meant to be cast out by family and community. Common violation of conventional behavioural and religious norms unified the Mormons, however, who early on became convinced of the peculiarity of their ways. Mormons today continue to feel distinct from non-Mormons. They cultivate their exclusivity by a tendency to orient themselves more towards the norms of 19th century American family life, as they understand it, than towards contemporary norms. Years of derision have strengthened Mormon belief in their religious righteousness. Today's polygamists hence frame their struggle as a continuation of their 19th century forebears opposition to a federal government bent on preventing the Lord's chosen people from practicing their God-ordained right.

Unlike other forms of contemporary polygamy, which have generally developed as part of cultural processes stretching over generations, Mormon po-

16. See Hastrup 2004, Sahlins 1999 and Wikan 2002 for different perspectives on cultural rights.

lygamy was proclaimed by a named individual at a given time in history. It was presented as a revealed doctrine, but imposed upon a group which had no cultural or religious premises for accepting and understanding it. Mormon polygamy, unlike most polygamy in other cultures, was developed within a relative short period and without any coherent set of guiding principles or firm traditions for its practice. This is one of the greatest challenges facing contemporary plural families. The challenge is especially great for converts who join the fundamentalist movement as adults or when their parents join. They typically come from mainstream Mormon monogamous families and have little or no personal experience of living a polygamous lifestyle. They have to experiment to solve all those everyday issues facing them both as individuals and as a family. Familial adjustment problems are often compounded by personal adjustment problems faced by converts raised as mainstream Mormons, who are now rejected by their parent Church and perhaps by their natal families as well. Converts must, in other words, attempt to live a lifestyle which is not only completely unfamiliar, but also contradicts everything they were brought up to believe about family life. Converts, like all other fundamentalists, must create their own plural family style.

The result is that many plural Mormon families struggle to find idiosyncratic solutions to such problems as how to organize a very large family made up of several mothers with an often very large amount of children. There are no set patterns of plural living arrangements, which are administered by individual families to fit their particular circumstances. Joseph Smith practiced the principle, but was more interested in discussing its theological implications than its practical arrangements. Living arrangements of polygamists hence reflect the variable, 'experimental' nature of much of their cultural practices. In the 19th century, a diversity of arrangements emerged as Mormons struggled to come to terms with this new and radical marital principle. Among fundamentalists today, there are still no fixed living arrangements, with co-wives living either alone, in pairs or in family groups. For fundamentalists to define their culture as distinct, and their lifestyles as particular, they must thus define their culture and intangible cultural heritage based on heavenly ordained plural marriage, whatever the tangible form it takes in everyday life.

Contemporary Mormon polygamy is hence the same sort of cultural reinvention as it was for 19th century Mormons. Polygamy, like all societal institutions, takes shape from the way people practice it. Mormon polygamy can thus be defined and practiced to fit the needs and purposes of modern fundamentalist polygamists. What is new about today's polygamous practices, is that fundamentalist Mormons, in arguing for their right to exercise their religious beliefs through polygamy, that is, their right to practice polygamous lifestyles, may in effect be arguing for their cultural rights as members of a distinct culture. As other minority groups, they might insist on the inalienability of their cultural rights. Thus, for the fundamentalist Mormons of Bountiful, the principle of plural marriage may, as intangible cultural heritage, be a strategic resource in their ongoing dealings with local and national governments hostile to the principle. In Canada, if a community like Bountiful can argue that it has a distinct culture – as have for example First Nations (Canada's native aboriginal populations) – then it can be granted special legal, social and economic rights.[17]

Were fundamentalist Mormons to claim cultural rights as a culturally distinct people, and be able to secure legal entitlement to live the principle of plural marriage, as part of what could be consider their religiously based cultural heritage, they would face similar obstacles as those obstructing their claim of religious rights to polygamy. Such claims would also be subject to one of the paradoxes of cultural rights, namely how to distinguish between an individual Mormon's rights and freedoms and those rights Mormons have as members of cultural (or religious) groups. An individual Mormon could only claim a cultural right to practice polygamy as part of a distinct fundamentalist Mormon culture. This would, in turn, require that culture to be so recognized by the surrounding society, making itessential for fundamentalist Mormons to legally establish, as a collective, that they have a distinct religious-based culture or a lifestyle which includes polygamy.[18]

Women's and children's rights

In Canada, the rights of fundamentalist Mormons to practice the tenets of their religion and culture are now set against the rights of women and children to be protected from harm. The focus on women's and children's rights in the Canadian case is pertinent, for polygamy, or more specifically polygyny, inherently involves gender asymmetry: the fact that one man can be married to several women but one woman can only be married to one man.

17. See for example Cassell 2009.
18. It is important to note that chief justice Bauman, in his canadian reference judgement, stated his opinion that a conjugal union required a sanctifying event or ceremony to mark its start, and so ensured that polyamourists would not be caught by the provision. Polyamourists have multiple partners, and some live lives resembling polygamous unions; they are not married to each other, however. See f.ex.: http://polyadvocacy.ca

Building on this basic gender inequity of polygyny, many researchers suggest that polygyny entails oppression of women on various levels. In the 19th century, women were seen as dehumanized by polygamy. Yet contrary to popular stereotypes, many early Mormon women endorsed plural marriage. Plural wives saw themselves as part of a sisterhood whose underlying principle was a conviction that plural marriage was a 'holy principle.' Mormon co-wives are still known as "sister-wives." Today, women in polygamous groups are similarly often portrayed as subjugated and helpless victims of a male dominated culture. Yet some studies of women in contemporary polygamous communities show that polygamy can allow women to achieve economic security and personal autonomy through their female networks. For some women, polygamy may be seen as a solution to such difficulties as spinsterhood, single-motherhood, poverty and loneliness. For women already 'living the principle', often in isolated polygamous settlements, new wives can be friends and co-workers who will help run the household and cope with an often hostile outside world.[19] Women who are comfortable with polygamous marriages and enter them voluntarily may therefore object to the argument that polygamy necessarily causes them harm.

One can find studies to both support and reject the notion that polygamy is harmful to women, yet most studies cross-culturally seem to suggest that polygyny reduces female autonomy and can cause considerable more stress than monogamy.[20] In North America, many people indeed still view polygamy as a traditional institution oppressive to women. Polygamous families are generally strongly patriarchal, and fundamentalist Mormon family life is based on a version of the 19th century's strictly circumscribed gender roles, seen through high birth rates and strict enforcement of (sexual) morals outside marriage. Plural wives' extensive mothering duties mean that few are able to pursue outside careers. Schooling is often inadequate. Women may be married young, often in their teens and sometimes while still underage. They may be sealed as plural wives to men several decades older, sometimes against their will or without their consent.

Today, as in the 19th century, some women, including very young girls, appear to enter polygamous marriage involuntarily and under pressure. For them polygamy may represent clear harm. In the 19th century, if plural marriage caused individual women suffering, they would rarely have made it

19. See for example Bennion 2008 & 2012.
20. For different perspectives on gender dynamics and potential harm to women in polygamy, see Bailey & Kaufman 2010, Donovan & Andersen 2003 and Koktvedgaard Zeitzen 2008.

public, as loyalty to their Church and fellow Saints would have been primary. Acknowledging non-Mormon feelings towards polygamy, early Mormons might have tended to present a "storybook polygamy" rather than exposing the difficulties involved in trying to live such a complex and challenging lifestyle. Contemporary polygamists similarly attempt to portray the positive aspects of their polygamous lifestyles in public and legal fora. The difference is that today, unhappy plural wives do go public, and some of those women found their way to the constitutional reference case as witnesses.

The Canadian case illustrates that today's legal culture concerning polygamy is not primarily fuelled by moral outrage, as it was in the 19th century. Legal action is not solely focused on the practice of plural marriage as a crime in and of itself, rather it may focus on specific issues such as forcible marriage of very young girls. Underage girls being forced into polygamy is one of the issues of most concern to the American and Canadian public. Critics claim that polygamy fosters and condones child abuse, statutory rape and sexual exploitation. There are also claims that underage girls are trafficked across state and international lines for purposes of polygamy. In the U.S., this is a federal offence under the Mann act, which prohibits transportation of women across state boundaries for 'immoral purposes.' Evidence of exchange of very young girls between fundamentalist communities for purposes of plural marriage was heard in the constitutional reference case in Canada. The B.C. government has now initiated investigations into young Canadian girls being trafficked across the border to US polygamist communities. Forced marriage of underage girls can provide further legal basis for prosecuting polygamists.[21]

The general public's view that polygamy entails violations of women and children's bodies and rights is reinforced by media stories of 14 year old girls being bartered between fundamentalist communities, and forced into marriage as plural wives of men several decades their seniors. From a fundamentalist Mormon perspective, they are merely following the traditional 19th century Mormon marriage pattern, in which church leaders decided on marriage partners, and girls often married at age 14. Some fundamentalist groups defer sexual relations when a girl is so young, but many do not. They can point to their first Prophet Smith, whose youngest plural wife, Helen Mar Kimball, was 14 when she married him. Most people in the US and Canada today find it unacceptable for a girl of 14 to marry or have sexual relations, however. It

21. In her 2008 book '*The Secret Lives of Saints*', journalist Daphne Bramham describes this 'trafficking' of B.C. women to the USA to supply brides to related fundamentalist communities. See also note 13.

is also illegal. In Canada, the legal age of consent is 16. A 14 year old can consent to sexual activity with a partner as long as the partner is less than five years older and there is no relationship of trust, authority or dependency or any other exploitation of the young person. In the various US states, the age of consent ranges from 16 to 18, with some states providing for age-gap exemptions, as in Canada.[22]

There have been a number of prosecutions of fundamentalist Mormons accused of practicing or aiding in the practice of polygamy relating to underage girls. In Utah in 2001, as mentioned, Tom Green was sentenced to five years in prison for bigamy. On a more serious charge, he was sentenced to five years to life in prison for statutory rape of a minor. The child-rape conviction stemmed from Green having had sexual relations with his first wife Linda Kunz when she was only 13 years old, and he was 37. Tom Green's five sister-wives are literally two sets of sisters, and all married him when they were 14 or 15 years old. The large Green family with over 30 children lived in a collection of trailers, making up an isolated Utah desert community. Green, like many contemporary Mormon polygamists, has continued the 'tradition' of establishing new polygamist communities across the Western United States and Canada, when they outgrow or become disaffected with their settlements of origin. A marriage pattern involving the arranged marriage of very young girls can take place because of, and be reinforced by, the social, economic and geographical isolation polygamous families often live in, ostracized from the mainstream Mormon Church and American society at large, and perhaps from rival polygamous communities.

In 2008, authorities raided the ranch Yearning for Zion, in El Dorado, Texas, whose residents are members of the FLDS. They removed over 400 children, alleging that very young girls were becoming mothers as a result of incestuous relations and forced marriages. Incestuous relations among polygamists can rarely be proven if suspected, as people have been disciplined not to reveal their parentage in order to avoid potential prosecution. The removed children were DNA tested to establish their parentage. The raid caused controversy, and most children were reunited with their mothers and returned to their compound within a few months. In 1953, the Short Creek polygamous community was similary raided and children removed, and that raid was like wise criticized for its insensitive approach. Its main effects was to strengthen

22. For Canada: http://www.justice.gc.ca/;
USA: http://www.age-of-consent.info/ (accessed 28.09.12).

fundamentalist belief in their cause as well as to extinguish non-Mormon desire to prosecute them, a reluctance lasting until the turn of the 21st century.[23]

The controversial raids illustrate the challenges faced by authorities seeking to safeguard the rights of children and women in polygamy. Records uncovered at the Yearning for Zion ranch, however, as well as testimony from some of the young wives and mothers who were willing to speak with the authorities, revealed several men married to underage girls. Evidence recovered from the raid formed part of the basis for convicting FLDS leader Warren Jeffs. Jeffs, the second son of his late father's fourth wife, was arrested in 2006 after being on the run for two years, and was at the time of his arrest on the FBI Ten Most Wanted list. In 2011, Jeffs was charged with sexually assaulting two of his under-age brides, and sentenced to life in prison, among other serious charges. The girls were 12 and 15 years old when they married him, and his 15 year old 'spiritual wife' gave birth to his child.[24]

The right to polygamy

Fundamentalist Mormon polygamists fighting to de-criminalize polygamy, while authorities are working to uphold and, increasingly, enforce the criminalization of polygamy, are part of a growing trend in Western societies, where minority groups are increasingly claiming the right to practice what may for the majority population be a controversial or even illegal cultural or religious tradition. Conflicts over rights often center on a clash between individually based human rights and collectively based cultural or religious rights. In Western legal cultures, 'culture' or religion are not objectified as units with rights, which stands above individuals. Individuals have a right to cultural and religious togetherness, to be part of one or more cultures or religions, but cultures and religions cannot have rights over individuals or members of those cultures or religions, from a Western legal perspective.[25] Hence, a Mormon woman's individual human right to choose a marriage partner outweighs her community's collective cultural or religious right to assign her a partner in order to maintain certain preferred polygamous patterns, even if

23. For more in-depth information and analysis of the raids, see Bailey & Kaufman 2010, Bennion 2012 and Jacobson & Burton 2011.
24. Jeffs' trial was widely reported in US media; see for example CNN.com (accessed 28.09.12).
25. See note 16. See also Okin 1999 for a discussion of the potential consequences for individual women of protection of (minority) groups cultural rights.

these patterns are seen as crucial for fundamentalist Mormons' cultural and religious identity. In American legal culture, claims of cultural and religious distinctiveness can thus not support the claim that Mormon tradition allows for arranged marriages of very young girls – a girl's human right to choose her own spouse and laws regulating underage marriage and sexual relations, will come before Mormon cultural or religious rights.

In the Canadian reference case on polygamy, it was argued that polygamy should not be criminalized, yet not be legalized. This would mean that people who are part of polygamous marriages would not be 'fully' married according to the law, and not have the same rights and obligations as regularly monogamously married couples, yet it would not be a criminal act for several people to live together in conjugal like relations. Complete legalization was never the focal point of the case; the argument was rather whether some people, as part of their religious lifestyle, should be allowed to practice this strongly held belief in polygamy. Allowing polygamy as part of a religious lifestyle or culture would form a constitutional exemption, and not give all people the possibility of being polygamous. The 'not criminalize, not legalize' argument did not succeed, because the BC government successfully established that polygamy inherently involves potential harm to women, children and society, whatever the level or scope of legalization. The general public was skeptical of the argument as well, for it was seen as the first step towards complete legalization.

Legalization of polygamy, as some activists agitate for, would have far reaching consequences not only for Mormon polygamists, but for other minority groups practicing polygamy as well. Legalization would affect immigrants who are refused entry to the USA or Canada, or are forced to live 'underground', if they are part of 'illegal' polygamous marriages. Such scenarios have generated fears among some Canadians that Canada would develop into a polygamy 'magnet' for all the world's would-be polygamy immigrants, as no other Western country allows for unrestricted legal polygamy.[26] Such politically divisive immigration issues will keep polygamy on the political and legal agenda in North America. Among fundamentalists Mormons, immigration issues are no less prominent – American girls bartered as polygamous brides with Canadian girls may be violating immigration laws when residing with their husband, to whom they may not be registered as legally married, and hence face deportation.

26. See for example: http://www.vancouversun.com/
and http://www.cbc.ca/ (accessed 28.09.12).

The recent convictions of polygamists like Green and Jeffs in the USA indeed signal a change in the legal culture, from a focus on prosecuting polygamists for being polygamists, to a broader focus which includes specific violations of criminal codes by polygamists, such as statutory rape, immigration violation or welfare fraud. One of the charges which lead to Tom Green's arrest and conviction was that he cheated the state of $54,000 in child support after his 'wives' had sought public assistance; he was convicted of failure to pay child support. In Canada, Blackmore is facing tax evasion charges. It has led to suggestions that Canadian authorities may be seeking to prosecute polygamists through other charges than polygamy itself, because of the past difficulties in securing convictions in cases involving polygamy. Parallels are drawn to 1920s America, where authorities were able to convict the notorious Chicago gangster Al Capone of tax evasion, rather than of being a gangster. Canadian authorities vigorously deny such suggestions, and insist that Blackmore is charged with tax evasion because he is a taxpayer, not because he is a polygamist.[27] North American legal culture is thus adapting to the challenge of polygamy, as authorities are slowly revising their reluctant approach towards polygamists.

While the focus of the Canadian reference case was polygamy, it leads to broader reflections about the tolerance of difference and alternative lifestyles within societies. Should minorities have a legally recognized right to live according to their own distinct cultural and religious ways, or should there be limits to this tolerance in today's global societies, where all self-proclaimed groups might otherwise demand special rights. The Canadian court case gave a clear answer to where the limits to this tolerance should be drawn. Yet some Canadians may still be pondering whether Bountiful's Mormons represent a culture to be protected, or a cult to be controlled.

References

Altman, I. & J. Ginat (1996), Polygamous Families in Contemporary Society, Cambridge: Cambridge University Press.

Anderson, N. (1937), 'The Mormon Family', American Sociological Review, 2 (5): 601-8.

Bailey, M. & A.J. Kaufman (2010), Polygamy in the Monogamous World. Multicultural challenges for Western Law and Policy, Santa Barbara, CA: Praeger.

27. See http://www.cbc.ca/news/canada/british-columbia/story/2012/05/03/bc-polygamous-leader-taxes.html (accessed 28.09.12).

Beecher, M. & L. Anderson (eds.) (1987), Sisters in Spirit. Mormon Women in Historical and Cultural Perspective, Chicago: University of Illinois Press.

Bennion, J. (2008), Evaluating the Effects of Polygamy on Women and Children in Four North American Mormon Fundamentalist Groups: An Anthropological Study. Edwin Mellen Press Ltd

Bennion, J. (2012), Polygamy in Primetime. Media, Gender, and Politics in Mormon Fundamentalism, Waltham, MA: Brandeis University Press.

Bledsoe, C. & G. Pison (eds.) (1994), Nuptiality in Sub-Saharan Africa, Oxford: Clarendon Press.

Bradley, M.S. (2002), 'Polygamy-Practicing Mormons' in Melton, J.G. & M. Baumann (eds.), Religions of the World: A Comprehensive Encyclopedia 3:1023-1024.

Bramham, D. (2008), 'The Secret Lives of Saints. Child Brides and Lost Boys in Canada's Polygamous Mormon Sect', Random House Canada.

Bushman, R.L. (2008), Mormonism: A Very Short Introduction, New York: Oxford University Press.

Campbell, E. Angela (2010). Bountiful's plural marriages, *International Journal of Law in Context* 6 (4): 343-361.

Cassell, E. (2009), 'Anthropologists in the Canadian Courts', in Freeman, M. & D. Napier (eds.) Law and Anthropology. Current Legal Issues 2008 (12): 187-217.

Donovan, J.M. & H.E. Anderson III (2003), Anthropology and Law, New York: Berghahn Books.

Gordon, S. (1996), 'The Liberty of Self-Degradation: Polygamy, Woman Suffrage, and Consent in Nineteenth-Century America', The Journal of American History, 83 (3): 815-847.

Hastrup, K. (2004): Kultur. Det Fleksible Fællesskab. Århus: Univers

Jacobson, C. & L. Burton (eds.) (2011), Modern Polygamy in the United States: Historical, Cultural, and Legal Issues. OUP.

Koktvedgaard Zeitzen, M. (2008): Polygamy. A Cross-Cultural Analysis. Oxford: Berg Publishers.

Lind, G. (2008), Common Law Marriage: A Legal Institution for Cohabitation. Oxford University Press.

Okin, S.M. (1999), Is multiculturalism bad for women? Princeton: Princeton University Press.

Sahlins, M. (1999): 'Two or Three Things that I Know about Culture', The Journal of the Royal Anthropological Institute 5 (3): s. 399-421.

Smith, J.E. & P.R. Kunz (1976), 'Polygyny and Fertility in Nineteenth Century America', Population Studies, 30 (3): 465-480.

van Wagoner, R. (1989), Mormon Polygamy. A History (2.ed.), Salt Lake City: Signature Books.

Wikan, U. (2002) Generous Betrayal. Politics of Culture in the New Europe. Chicago: University of Chicago Press.

Masculine Domination in Turkish Legal Culture: An Analysis of the High Court Decisions

Eylem Ümit Atılgan[1]

Quis custodiet ipsos custodes?
Who will guard the guards themselves?

At the very beginning of my academic career the chair members used to regularly visit an emeritus woman professor of our chair, Hamide Topçuoğlu, who had retired long ago.[2] The senior professor of the chair was a very loyal visitor of this admirable lady, who very rarely leaves the home, but enjoys the visits of her former students and young academics. She was one of the first woman students (1935), and the first woman scholar of Ankara University Law Faculty (1943). She was a pioneer of the Modern Turkish Republic: a well educated scholar, fluent in several languages and the diva of Philosophy and Sociology of Law. We, the new members of the chair, carried on this tradition and enjoyed the conversations and listening to memories of this charismatic lady.

The reason for remembering her in this article is a story that I heard from her. She always had on her mind amazing and inspirational real stories about the last century of Turkish society regarding legal and academic culture, gender etc. Most of them were own experiences and they were introducing an influential panorama of society and cultural change. One of these experiential stories motivated me to question masculinity in the legal culture especially the legal culture of professionals. I would like to begin with discussing masculinity and legal culture with the story which aroused my scientific curiosity:

1. Assistant Professor in Ankara University Law Faculty, Turkey.
2. Prof. Dr. Hamide Topçuoğlu, 1918-2009.

The background of the story relies upon the most incredible era of Professor Topçuoğlu's biography. In the summer of 1939, she had succeeded in Civil Judge exams and deserved to be appointed as a civil judge. But she had to wait for three years for vacancy. Because in the 1940s there was a quota against women: % 95 of the seats was reserved for male judges. After three years of waiting she resigns and gives up her dreams of being a judge. A conversation among a senior male judge and a junior female judge, when she was a trainee, was a very popular anecdote told by her:

> "A newly appointed female judge makes a visit to the chief judge of the court in a small city. When she knocks at the door and enters the room, the Chief doesn't look at her face and ignores her. She tries to attract his attention several times but she can't succeed. After a while he starts talking without looking her in the face:
>
> 'A wife and husband sit in their living room. The husband says, looking at the window, "Wow! A camel is flying over our house"
>
> The wife says calmly 'Well. God willing, it won't fall on our roof."
>
> After finishing the story the chief stares her in the eye and continues to talk:
>
> "Hey you! What is needed here is a kind of woman who doesn't ask questions like "How is it possible for a camel to fly? Or where is it? I want to see it? Now go to your office and learn working with no question!"

Whenever I remember this story, I feel the terrorizing power of a senior judge on a young inexperienced judge. But before all, I am terrified by the absolute dominance of the masculinity. Even today, more than half a ntury later and in spite of my age and career, I always feel like a little school girl, whenever I step into a court or the office of a judge. I conducted field research at the courts and made in depth interviews with judges on different topics several times. During the long hours of in depth interviews the role that was given to me as a young woman was to be "unconditionally obedient." I always had that feeling: The walls of the court, the furniture of the court rooms, the judicial language, they were so masculine that you have to leave your femininity outside of the court if you expect to be respected or taken in to account by the others.

I had to wait for another admirable woman who came into my world to be able to name and define this intuition. A few years ago in Beijing (six years after we first met in Granada) I had a nice conversation with Professor Hanne Petersen[3] during a very restricted time in spite of a heavy agenda at an international conference on philosophy of law. She was so kind to listen to my recent field study on the "Equity Perception of Turkish Judges." With her mar-

3. I will always remain grateful for Professor Hanne Petersen's inspirational friendship.

velous apprehension she revealed an exciting dimension which was concealed by other issues in my study. She introduced me to the book of Bourdieu "*Masculine Domination*", which is shadowed by his other works nowadays. Although I refer to the huge literature of masculinity studies, the keyword that defines the phenomenon, I experience at the court room is "masculine domination."

Here I need to discuss the question "Why Bourdieu?" According to Bourdieu, the paradigmatic form of a mode of domination operates essentially with symbolic violence. Bourdieu highlights in *Masculine Domination,* how symbolic violence manifests its power essentially in *face-to-face* interactions. "Symbolic violence is exercised only through an act of knowledge and practical recognition which takes place below the level of the consciousness and will and which gives all its manifestations – injunctions, suggestions, seduction, threats, reproaches, orders or calls to order – their 'hypnotic power.'"[4] I had a crush on this definition because it makes sense, when I try to explain the meaning of an interesting situation which I heard from woman judges. In depth interviews, woman judges told me that they used to subclass men in the trials who address them "Mr. Judge." In Turkish, there are two different forms for addressing male and female judges. These men were refusing to say "your honour" in the female form. I think this represents symbolic violence.

I also think Bourdieu's vocabulary offers appropriate tools to understand a lot of complicated social facts and events such as a traumatic event which happened in Turkey a few years ago:

In 2007 a woman judge was attacked right after the trial where she declined the acquittal of a defendant accused of theft. The defendant's brother smashed her skull, leaving her with a broken nose and concussion in the courtroom. He shouted, "She should stay at home and look after her children instead of interfering in peoples life." When I watched him shouting on the TV screen, I remembered the answers of Bourdieu about how masculinity dominates asymmetric social positions. The cultural field is constructed through the fundamental principle of division between the active male and the passive female and this principle creates, organizes, expresses and directs the positions: The obedient position of women and the determinant-dominant position of men differentiate from each other.

4. Pierre Bourdieu, *Masculine Domination*, translated by Richard Nice, Stanford University Press; 1st edition, 2002, p. 42.

With all these intuitions and experiences, I have conducted a research on analysis of the codes of masculine domination in the Turkish legal culture in light of the Supreme Courts' decisions.

In this article I would like to discuss one of the judicial decisions which I analyzed in detail for the research. This decision of the Supreme Court is about the blood feud. Although numbers are dwindling in years, it is evident that blood feud still exists in Turkey. A large number of sociological field research focusing on blood feud specifies the connection between male honour and blood feud. It can be said that blood feud is a part of the honour code of masculinity. But the judicial discourse prefers a definition of blood feud related to the discourse on tradition. I think this is not an innocent preference but that it has a vital function in the social reproduction of masculine domination.

My last answer to "Why Bourdieu?" is right here. Masculine domination is organized around three central themes: the naturalization of masculine domination; the misrecognition of this domination; and the mechanisms of social reproduction of this domination.[5] From my point of view, to unveil the codes of masculine domination in the culture of legal professionals is a very important step to analyze the mechanisms of social reproduction of the gender domination.

In this research I concentrate on all forms of hegemonic masculinities.[6] As it is stressed by Jeff Hearn, it is not necessary for the cultural sustainers of hegemonic masculinities to be the closest ones to the hegemonic masculine image.[7] Based on the terminology of Connell, one could say that the position and the function of legal professionals in Turkey correspond with "complicit masculinity."[8]

5. Veronique Mottier, *Masculine Domination: Gender and Power in Bourdieu's Writings*, Feminist Theory, vol. 3 (3), 2002, p. 345-359.
6. Field research on Turkish hegemonic masculinity helped me to find out the pieces of masculinity in Turkish culture. By comparing these field research findings I reached a list of the codes of masculine domination. Subsequently I scanned these codes in Supreme Court Decisions. "Honour" was one of these codes.
7. Jeff Hearn, *From Hegemonic Masculinity to the Hegemony of Men*, Feminist Theory, April, Vol 5 (1), 2004, p. 57.
8. The forms of hegemonic masculinities are as it is widely accepted: 1) Hegemonic masculinity: legitimating patriarchy 2) Complicit masculinity: bringing benefit without effort 3) Subordinated masculinity: by gender related relation, sex, gay 4) Marginalized masculinity: by class, ethnicity etc. R.W. Connell, *Masculinities*, St. Leonards: Allen and Unwin, 1995, p. 79, Jeff Hearn, *Deconstructing the hegemony of*

Giving some highlights of the methodology would help to see a map of my research before dealing with the judgments. In my project I use critical discourse analysis in order to unveil the value judgments, attitudes and behaviours of legal professionals in judicial decisions and in-depth interviews with judges, and in focusing on the best examples of Supreme Court decisions, which take account of masculine domination codes. In the study I intend to illuminate the role of legal elites with regard to the reconstruction of masculine domination in Turkish legal culture. In accordance with this purpose I prefer "interdisciplinary"[9] perspectives to dislocate the superficial and false opinions about popular legal culture and professionals' legal culture comparison.

My study particularly aims to give insights into the role of legal elites in reconstruction of the masculine domination in the Turkish legal culture by conducting an internal –external legal culture study. Superficially and incorrectly it is believed that there is a conflict between (secular, elite) legal professionals' and (conservative, uneducated) lower class peoples' legal culture and consciousness in Turkey. However I assume that an internal and external legal culture study based on qualitative method could dislocate this common opinion.

The methodology I prefer for this study is to administer interview forms that used qualitative and quantitative survey designs concurrently, on judges and prosecutors, and to record the interviews via an audio recorder. In line with this purpose, I prepared interview forms including open-ended and closed ended questions. In this context, the project is not only a "co-relational research" which aims to reach a hypothesis with reference to the relations observed between the social facts, actions, behaviours, but also a "descriptive research" intended to take a picture of the social reality. I have made 50 interviews and I have analysed 98 hours of records of interviews.

This analysis goes much further than the interpretation of norms. It is obvious that considering law as a cultural phenomenon requires a multi-dimensional perspective of law. Unlike the conceptualizations of law as a formal and logical system of legal rules or a set of ideals or values which can be discovered by human reasoning, the multi-dimensional perspective of law refers

men and masculinities–presentation of the research theme, GEXcel Work in Progress Report, vol. V, 2008, p. 16.

9. I refer the term "interdisciplinarity" as integrating and organizing traditional forms of knowledge, skill and experience in a new and original fashion. Joe Moran, *Interdisciplinarity,* London & New York: Routledge, 2002.

to three dimensions of law: social fact, norms, and value hold a strategic importance for the cultural component of the legal system.

The cultural component is composed by value and attitudes which bind the system together and which determine the place of a legal system in the culture of the society as a whole. And legal culture is still the term we apply to those values and attitudes in a society which determine what structures were used and why; which rules work and which do not and why.[10]

According to the commonly used legal culture definition, it is one way of describing relatively stable patterns of legally oriented social behaviour and attitudes. Like culture itself, legal culture is about whom we are, not just what we do.[11]

Now let's look at the judicial decisions and listen to the voices of judges on blood feud and honour. At the beginning of 2010, with its revolutionary decision, the High Court increased the distance between morals and law. In one of these decisions, the specification of the family council in crimes known as honour killing was made available and this opened the way to include this crime into this scope. In another decision, the High Court removed the permanent provision that is used in order to define a crime as blood feud; the provision was: *"the murder should occur after the suspect is released from pain and anger caused by the loss of a relative."* After having been thrilled with this ruling, we learnt in a few months that the High Court made a decision on May 2010. Here it opened the way to exemplify blood feuds as crimes committed after unjust provocation, and thus masculine domination codes entered into courtrooms.

It is stated that when you tell something like a story, all problems may be endurable, therefore let me tell everything like a story so that we can endure. In fact the judicial decision tells us the story:

The incident takes place in a Penal Institution; E kills K's brother on 26.07.2001 and therefore he is in prison. *Five years later*, after he was transferred to another Penal Institution, he learns that K., whose brother he killed is in the same prison. He hands in a petition to the Administration of Prison and requests to be transferred to another prison. On the day of the event, the sub-manager of the prison calls K. and asks him about the problem. K. sees E.'s petition on the table and learns the wing where E. is staying. When he goes back to his wing, he and other prisoners prepare a needle by using a refrigerator's shelves. On the very

10. Lawrence M. Friedman, *Legal Culture and Social Development*, in Law and the Behavioral Sciences, Lawrence M Friedman& Stewart Macaulay, The Bobbs- Merrill, NY, 1969, p.1003.
11. David Nelken, *Using the Concept of Legal Culture,* Australian Journal of Legal Philosophy, vol.29, 2004, p. 1.

same day, one of the prisoners who stay in the same wing, acts as if he is sick and makes the guardians open the door. When the door is opened, other prisoners get out of the wing; two of them wait at the corridor and prevent guardians from interfering with the incident. K goes to E.'s wing with the others and starts spitting at E. The judge of the first instance court hears the wounded victim, witnesses and offenders by looking into their eyes and says that this is a blood feud. But the Supreme Court which only analyzes trial reports and documents overturns the judgment: K. did not kill the man who killed his brother as a blood feud; he killed him after unjust provocation. The Supreme Court states the justification: "The persons of interest decided to kill the victim beforehand; they were determined and insistent in their decision. Although there was a long amount of time until the action, which was also enough for planning, there was not enough evidence to prove that they committed the crime in cold blood, (...) murderer's murder does not constitute blood feud inducement and the action is accepted to be the suspect K.'s crime of attempting to kill the murderer of his brother under unjust provocation."

If this is not considered to be a blood feud, we should question the approach of the Supreme Court about what is in fact a blood feud. According to the Supreme Court, there must be a time period between the first death and the second so that the offender can let go of any anger, pain or hatred and act under the effect of customs. The definition of the Supreme Court is not enough to clean the concept of blood feud. Most of the judgments are given on the basis of "being under unjust provocation" rather than blood feud. Because the Supreme Court's clauses that are defined as the elements of homicide with the intention of blood feud are rarely found together in events. This list of elements is prepared without taking sociologic and anthropologic information into consideration and made of a paradigm that has long lost validity. Without benefiting from the data of sociological research on blood feud; by ignoring discussions that continue in different areas of social sciences about traditions, discourse, gender, ethics and social moral, the Supreme Court is criticized in the studies. Adjudication focuses on whether the criminal went through grief and indignation instead of taking into consideration that honour and revenge concepts are shaped by masculine domination codes. How many hours are needed to forget about the grief and indignation? When the starting point is put here, it is really hard to reach a consistent reason. So, the Supreme Court has difficulties and sometimes the words "I took my brother's revenge" is written in trial records and blood feud inducement is not mentioned.

There are two important mistakes in the legal reasoning process that determines this decision. The first mistake is demonstrated in the discourse of tradition and it results in rebuilding the tradition. The second is the mistake of basing the legal judgment on value judgment instead of value itself, leading to an incorrect assessment in the legal reasoning. In both mistakes, there are perception and mentality forms that are shaped by masculine domination, and reproduce these mentalities repeatedly.

Let's start pointing out these mistakes with "reproducing traditions with discourses about traditions." In the study of the role of tradition discourses in the process of naturalization of gender hierarchy, Dicle Koğacıoğlu points out that tradition discourses are based on the assumption that a tradition is uniform and has an internal consistency, which is different form the position, actions and daily lives of people living 'there.'[12]

This discourse leads us to get used to a concept of "customs" which is almost materially separated from social relations. This idea of tradition, which is produced within the professional actors' discourses, and the information that is spread by media organs shapes people's lives. But it is somehow not affected by the acts of people. According to this idea of tradition, which is considered more resistant than all of the modern legal systems, social actors repeat tradition without taking or giving anything to the system like automats? Centuries pass by, states collapse, states are established and traditions are not affected. People migrate, they are forced to migrate, and they fall apart, different ethnic and religious groups, army and paramilitary powers conflict with each other. Production and trading styles, produced and changed goods, groups that produce and trade the products change, but these traditions do not![13]

This discourse of tradition is popular in the court room in Turkey. Sometimes judges justify the discourse of tradition as such:

> "Although the victim is unofficially married to the brother of A.T, A.T tries to kill her since she had a forbidden relation. It is a well known truth that people living in the region then feel compelled to response harshly to this forbidden relationship because they know, they would be excluded from the society in case they do not response against this relationship. So, all these facts result in violence against women. When the probability of harsh reactions by the family members who believe that the family's virtue and honour has been attacked, is taken into consideration, it is necessary to accept the existence of A.T's will to use violence against his aunt because of her behaviors that are inappropriate with social rules and disapproved by the society."

12. Dicle Koğacıoğlu, *Gelenek Söylemleri ve İktidarın Doğallaşması*: Namus Cinayetleri Örneği. (Discourses of Tradition and the Naturalization of Power: Honour Killings), http://research.sabanciuniv.edu/5862/1/feministyaklasimlardicle.doc, p. 7. Also see Dicle Koğacıoğlu, *The Tradition Effect: Framing Honour Crimes in Turkey*, Differences: A Journal of Feminist Cultural Studies, Vol.15, No.2, 2004, pp. 118-151.
13. Koğacıoğlu, *Discourses of Tradition and the Naturalization of Power...*, pp. 4-5.

In this discourse, tradition which is related to social relations and hegemonic structures, is removed from the transformation of these structures and defined as something "that stands almost materially separate." For instance in order to define a homicide as an honour killing, there must be a "family council decision" and this decision should be proven legally! This is the best example of a perception of "material thing." Another example which is as clear as this is the jurisprudence which mentions that taking revenge to protect and clean the family honour is not enough for define it as blood feud. According to the jurisprudence, we can only accept situations, which correspond to formal sections written in the book of traditions, as blood feud or honour killing. In the judgment given below, judges say that it is possible to define an event as blood feud if it awakes orientalist and hegemonic feelings:

"With the stimulation of rusty and old fashioned custom, the person who has an incentive to blood feud takes it as his duty to kill an innocent person, who had no provocative acts, and whose only fault is to be a relative of the person who killed his relative. He has the thought of blood for blood; and in case he kills the killer will lose its validity."

When blood feud is legally analyzed, it should not be forgotten that it is a concept based on masculine domination codes. The actors of the judiciary must be fed by the data of field studies and anthropological approaches which determines these acts in relation to social morals such as retaliation and honour. This is where I see the second mistake. This concept of honour should not be confused with the "concept of human dignity", the core of human rights. In prison interviews these answers are given to the question of "value vendetta?":

"These are customs in our region, you must take revenge."

"I wouldn't look into anybody's eyes if I didn't shoot."

"If you don't take revenge, you'd be humiliated and they would question your manhood."

"If I wouldn't kill for blood, neither my father nor my brother could show up at the coffee house"[14] When we look at these answers, we see that the concept of honour is related

14. Mahmut Tezcan, *Kan Davalari: Sosyal Antropolojik Yaklasim* (Blood Feud: Social-Anthropological Explanations), Ankara Universitesi Egitim Fakultesi Yayinlari, 1981, p.45; Mahmut Tezcan, *Türkiye'de Kan Davası ve Önlenmesi Çareleri*, (Blood Feud in Turkey and Preventive Measures, Journal of Justice) Adalet Dergisi, vol. 65, no. 8, Ankara, 1974, p. 668; Yücel Türkben, *Kan Gütme Olayları ve Mülki İdare Amirleri*, (Blood Feud and Local Authorities, Journal of Turkish Administra-

to collective honour and closely connected to gender and to distribution of pecuniary and spiritual resources.[15]

"Honour" is the basic point of manhood in terms of social norms. When a judge tries to fill in the parts in the legal reasoning without basing the process on information, he tries to make a judgment based on "Knowledge of life" and "Knowledge of human character" which moves him away from the correct evaluation norms. According to Kuçuradi, evaluation, as a cognitive activity, is different from attributing value or ascribing value.[16] But a judgment based on value judgment is nothing but attribution of value. In order to make a correct judgment, judges should start from the knowledge of the value of human being and the judgment should not destroy human value. Social moral is the body of judgments that change from society to society and sometimes it changes within one society in the same period. Placing value judgment instead of values themselves means giving the role of tradition to law.

Although the Turkish feminists and women's movement endeavour to free Codes from masculine domination forms, the judicial exercise goes on sticking to the value judgement instead of "the value" because the patterns of perception and mindset are the results of masculine power. Moral laws are away from "us", close to "them", not "here", but "there" for elite legal professionals. It is the moral law which belongs to" them" who are ignorant, barbaric, eastern, goods of tribes. Saba Mahmood mentions that the idea of "their moral law" has been the founding element of traditions' rhetoric and defines the traditions' rhetoric as the tendency to relate the repeating practices of the actors and actors' identities.[17]

However, the tradition of masculine domination is now being reconstructed right here, in the courtroom, Your Honour! I would have liked to utter this sentence during the in-depth interviews I conducted with judges at the field research, when they often opened up the subject of being "unable" to go to

tion),Türk İdare Dergisi, vol. 48, no: 357, İçişleri Bakanlığı Tetkik Kurulu Yayın Müdürlüğü, Ankara, 1977, p. 128.

15. Sefa Şimşek, *Törelerin Aynasında Doğu ile Batı,* (The Code of Honour in the East and in the West), Bursa, 1998, pp. 22,36, p. 59; Artun Ünsal, *Anadolu'da Kan Davası*, (Blood Feud in Anatolia),(Original in French: La Vendetta, 1995) translated by Emre&Niyazi Öktem, İstanbul, 2005, pp. 47-58.
16. Ioanna Kuçuradi, Ethic, Ankara, 2006, pp. 15-29; Kuçuradi, *İnsan ve Değerleri* (Human and Values), Türkiye Felsefe Kurumu, Ankara 1988, pp. 12-14.
17. Mahmood, Saba, *Politics of Piety: the Islamic Revival and the feminist Subject*, Princeton, Princeton University Press, 2005, p. 53.

coffeehouses.[18] This "inability" to go to coffeehouses is so important that a point is always made about it during the conversations. Sentimentality is so intense that it is as if those who are unable to go to coffeehouses are the real victims of the custom not the dead one:

I shall quote a male judge of a first degree court approaching retirement in his profession instead of saying a lot about the relation between coffeehouses and male honour:

Interviewer 53 *"(...) the person had been imprisoned for a short time and was released. Every day, he started to pass by the street where the family whose sons had been murdered by him lived. Without any shame, he went to that coffeehouse where the father used to show up and started sitting in front of him. The father was highly offended. In fact, such a case would particularly hurt fathers and brothers; it would hurt the family of course, but men would be hurt in a different way. That is a very difficult situation. And the father killed him. See! Historical facts are so important in this case, so important! Homicide is of course such a grave matter; in the Penal Code, I use that vast discretionary power. All cases should be examined in depth and discussed; evidence should be collected carefully; if a party is injured, then a decision that would relieve them must be made. If the balance was disturbed, it should be stabilized! We should protect those individuals who respect the social order and others."*

The actors of the modern legal system in Turkey have an opinion in common. For most of the legal actors, the adaption of the Western Codes such as the Civil, Penal and Commercial Code, by the Turkish legal system has been of vital importance. They consider themselves part of the Western law circle thanks to those receptions. However, even though the codes are word-for-word translations of the western originals, the outcome of implementation by judicial decisions is quite different from the western circle of which they feel proud to be a member.

18. In Turkish masculine culture, coffee houses have a significant role in creating a sense of sameness among men. There, they play card games chat, gossip and share their secrets. Each district has a coffee house and they are "men only." Recently there are an increasing number of ethnological researches in Turkey which are based upon the argument that masculinity is socially constructed in and intertwined with relations of power. Most of these researches are focused on masculine practices like coffee house masculinities: Serdar Öztürk, Coffe house and Power in Republic Era of Turkey 1930-1945, Istanbul, 2006, Çağdaş Demren, *Coffee house masculinity: A Case of a Gecekondu District in Ankara*, Ph.D. Dissertation, Ankara, 2007. Also coffee house is an interesting subject of near eastern cultural studies, such as the well known book of Ralph Hattox, Coffee and Coffehouses, The origins of Social Beverage in the Medieval Near East, Washington Press, 2000.

These actors of legal culture apply the mitigation of unjust provocation to the penalty of accused males of honour killings although the honour killing is defined as an aggravation in the new Penal Code. If you kill your sister, who is raped by your uncle in Turkey, you can find a supporter among secular elite judges, claiming that you are under the influence of unjust provocation. Although adultery is not a crime in the criminal code the guardians –the watchdogs of the regime (the judges of the appeal court call themselves guardians of the secular regime) through a wide interpretation of compensation law condemns, that the woman who commits adultery should give compensation to the wife of the man who participates inadultery. And by this "a contrario" interpretation, a masculine domination mindset again finds the way of punishing only the woman, but not the man who commits adultery. They love to point to the "traditional Turkish family structure", and "traditional values" as scapegoats. However, we know that this is the harshest practice of masculine domination on woman's body. And I assume that by doing that they sustain masculine domination as complicity.

It is evident that they do not act differently from the Kadis, from whom they drifted apart by the legal revolution a century ago. Although the Sharia rules and the Sultan's decrees were viewed as the formal sources of law that was applied by Kadis, we know that Kadis were often used to give decisions that connived at the efficiency of customs contrary to the Sharia by legal history studies.[19] In other words, they were hiding and running the customs, which were incompatible with laws by the Trojan horses. A custom contrary to the law cannot continue to exist in the legal sphere; the Kadi would have to keep away from it. However, the Kadi was "giving rulings which recognize the customs with the aim of not having any dispute with local order and customs."[20] It was one century ago in Turkey. Now actors in the modern Turkish legal system tolerate not all traditions but traditional structures that were constituted by masculine ways of thinking, seeing, making and relying on sexist value judgements.

The Codes do not have the final word in the confrontation of the "law" and the law of masculinity. It is a prevailing opinion among the judges, that a man who committed such a homicide (killing to protect family virtue or male

19. Leslie Pierce, Morality Tales: *Law and Gender in the Ottoman Court of Aintab*, University of California Press, 2003, pp. 149-167; Halime Doğru, *In the Light of Kadi Registration Life in Rumelia*, İstanbul, 2008, Halil İnalcık, "*Suleiman the Lawgiver and Ottoman Law, Archivum Ottomanicum*, 1, 1969, p. 111-114.
20. İlber Ortaylı, Custom and Sharia in The Ottoman Family Law of, Turkish Family in the Process of Cultural Change, II, Ankara 1992, p. 458.

honour) acted under the influence of unjust provocation and that he was obliged to act in that way. As far as I am concerned this proves how powerful the law of masculinity is within perceptions and mindsets of judges. In fact when a lawyer correctly makes the legal reasoning and evaluation, he should not give the answer "with blood" to the question "how do you clean blood." The decision that spoils the game of masculine domination relies on the value of human being and this is LAW.

Family Law and Gender in Morocco Strategies for Change

Mira M. Ramhøj

The Family law in Morocco aims at providing equality between the sexes even though it contains articles that can still provide for a non egalitarian and discriminatory decision making, such as the article that opens the possibility of marriage of minors and which in reality will always involve a minor girl.

Where lawmakers have left a gap open for interpretation the decision making seems to be incoherent with a normative approach that should have been left abolished with the Family Law of 2004.

The focus in this article is to describe how the Family Law has been affected from areas and actors both inside and outside the legal sphere: by female participants and activists; by researchers in Islamic law; by women active in women's rights organizations; by legal practitioners whether judges or practicing lawyers The aim is to indicate to what extent these actors (may) play a role in the process of changing normative, primarily patriarchal, understandings and interpretations of the Family law and decision making regarding issues of the Family Law.

How is gender affecting the legal culture in the Moroccan Family Law?

Law is a social construction by which the social order between the sexes is maintained in any given society at any given time. The family law in Morocco is a tool to secure a social order in society. How to secure marriage as the social norm, as a dominating factor for social structure, but at the same time let it evolve and provide for equal rights between men and women? Culture and religion are sources of (traditional) gender construction.[1] Creating gender equality is considered a necessity for the making of democratic progress.[2]

1. Raday, Frances, Culture, religion and gender, 2003 p. 665.
2. Mernissi, Fatima, The Veil and The Male Elite, 1991.

Lawmaking as a strategy for change

With the adaption of the Moroccan Family Law of 2004 major legal changes were made for Moroccan society. The Family Law changed from being a law based on a patriarchal model to being based on an egalitarian model.[3] One of the important changes was that the union of marriage is now a union under the direction of both the man and the woman, whereas in the former law it was a union under the direction of the man only. With the new law divorce became more accessible for women and the age of marriage was raised from 15 to18, though exceptions can still be made. Polygamy is still legal but due to the wording, it is in practice made almost impossible. All these changes made the Family Law one of the most progressive Family laws based on Islamic sources. The preamble of the law also clearly states, that equality between the sexes is of importance in order to progress into and develop a modern society.[4]

The Family Law has been in force for almost a decade. Despite the language of the articles and the overall egalitarian ideology and despite various initiatives by the government, there are still great problems with the implementation of the law. Family courts have been established. There were no specific courts dealing with family matters before the 2004 law change. Judges have been re-educated in interpreting the new articles of the law. Information desks, at some of the family courts, have been set up to enable people to get information on how to go about the juridical system and to receive information about their rights and to follow up on their own cases. Many of these measures have been on paper for a long time. But they are still not used in practice as could have been expected after so many years. Much of the work of informing women about their actual rights according to the Family law is initiated and carried out by various women's rights NGO's. Providing actual and accurate knowledge about what rights the Family law grants women is still a subject of importance.

Gender equality, anti-discrimination and a strengthening of the legal system are key areas of Morocco's recently adopted Constitution. The new Constitution was an outcome of the relatively calm protests that have taken place in Morocco demanding political change and change of the power balance. If the right actions are taken the Constitution can be a strong tool used for the

3. Badran, Margot, Feminism in Islam, 2009.
4. Preambule, du Guide Pratique du Code de la Famille, 2005.

continuous demand for a change of the legal framework and for improving women's rights.

Morocco has also recently fully ratified the CEDAW Convention with the inclusion of article 16 (equality in marriage and divorce) and Art 9(2) (transfer of nationality to children born of a father who is non Moroccan), that before were left out on the basis of being incompatible with Shari'a. The formal legal framework for change has largely improved, but the question is how this will be implemented?

Changing the Family Law in Morocco has been a step forward in granting women the possibility for equal rights, but still much has to been done so women can fully benefit from the rights they are given. The *adouls*, who are facilitating the marriage contracting, and the judges who are given a large margin for interpretive discretion, are both groups with conservative norms and traditions. The *adouls* are the traditional judges working side by side with the modern legal system. Changing the norms and traditions in relation to both these groups and society at large is a considerable challenge. Article 400 of the Family Law makes it possible for a judge to make a judgement that is in coherence with malikite doctrine and the values in Islam for all circumstances that are not foreseen ("prevu") in the law.

A change of societal norms is also a necessity in order that people will not want to transform exceptions into rules. Exceptions should be left as exception. Minor marriages (marriages with women under 18) are an example of how some practices can still be conducted, because the judge can make an exception to the legal marriage age of 18.

It is very tempting to use the term "surface law"[5] in referring to some of the main articles of the Family Law, to the overall egalitarian principles stated in the preamble and also to the ratifications to international conventions.

Strategies for changing the religious legal culture

The Family Law is based on the Islamic malikite doctrine. It is the only law in Morocco based directly on religious sources, which is codified in a structure of positive law. It is emphasized in the preamble that the use of a jurisprudential effort, *ijtihad,* and openness towards "l'esprit du époque" is at-

5. See William Twining, Surface Law. In Hanne Petersen, Anne Lise Kjær, Helle Krunke & Mikael Rask Madsen (eds), *Paradoxes of European Legal Integration,* 2008, pp. 157-183.

tempted.[6] But what does that actually mean when defining and interpreting the exact rules in the Family Law?

The reference to Islamic law, both in the Constitution and in the Family Law is not giving any exact clarification of how the articles in the Family Law should be formulated and less indication on how specific interpretation should be carried out. It was the use of *ijtihad* that made the changes possible in the making of the 2004 Family Law, changes that were almost impossible to reach when sticking to the religious framework. Nonetheless these changes were accomplished.

According to article 41 of the Constitution the Counsel of the Ulemas, "Conseil des Oulemas" an official counsel under the authority of the Ministry of Religious Affairs consisting of religious scholars, is the only authority that can pronounce *fatwas*, religious decrees. Fatwas, pronounced by the Counsel of Ulemas, are neither legally nor religiously binding, but they have an impact on how the authorities legislate and it would be hard for any government not to take into account the religious considerations of the Counsel of the Ulemas.

Making the changes to the Family Law of 2004 the Counsel of the Ulemas provided the analytical parts. Their Guidance Committee consisted of three women one of them Rajaa El Mekkaoui, a professor of law. She was also also the first female to give a religious lecture before the King, when the changes to the Family Law were made in 2004.

Some years ago a centre for studies in feminine Islam, *"Centre d'etudes Feminines en Islam"* was established, in Rabat, by the Counsel of the Ulema, being the first of its kind in the Arabic world. The objective of this centre is to carry out scientific research and draw up scientific material on the issue of feminine Islam. This centre is under the direction of Asma Lamrabet, who is according to her own words not a traditionalist. She has been chosen for this task in order to make changes and progress in women's rights issues[7]

One of the difficulties for the work being done by this centre is that the awareness of its existence and the research it carries out is still little known to the greater public. Various women's rights groups contact the centre on specific topics, but there is no connection between the legal world and the centre. The Centre is under the Ulema and it does not hold any legal power. Howev-

6. Guide practique du Code de la Famille, Preambule, "... d'effort jurisprudentiel (ijtihad et ouverture sur l'esprit de l'epoque et les exigences du developpement et du progres)", 2005.
7. Interview carried out in Rabat on the 10th of September 2012 with Asma Lamrabet. "pour faire avance des choose."

er, it may still have an impact which can be seen and felt if their criticism of for instance minor marriages will catch on and be followed by a lowering of the numbers of minor marriage.

Another way in which women have entered the sphere of religious knowledge and authority is at a more practical level by working as *mutjahids,* in some mosques in Morocco. *Mutjahids* will be able to give basic religious instructions in mosques, but cannot lead the prayer. The profession of female *mutjahids* has been established in the hope that women will receive more gender neutral advise on issues related to family and women.

The main contribution of the Islamic feminists to the general discourse is to try to prove that the heritage of religious norms is not in conflict with norms on equality. One of the major differences to the Western feminist movement is that the Islamic feminist movement is using religion and religious arguments as an important source for their discourse. Their goal is not to give a theoretical evaluation of the significance of the sources, but rather to describe how Muslim women are using religion as a tool for arguing against women's oppressions. Religion has an important place in Morrocan society and plays a big role for Morrocans as such.[8] The battle for *just* interpretations (providing equal rights between the sexes) is a battle of great importance.

The use of *ijithad* in order to show women's equality in the Quran has been demonstrated by other female academics such as Leila Ahmed and Fatima Mernissi. Mernissi is describing the Muslim society as suffering from a *mal du present*. This means that the Muslim society is stuck to its past not being capable of entering into to the future. By constantly referring to a glorious past and looking for answers in the past not in the future, Morocco is therefore not making the changes needed to progress and develop. Mernissi claims that gender equality is necessary for the making of democratic progress.

Gender in the courts

Before the 2004 Family Law came into practice family law matters were primarily solved outside the modern legal system. The *adouls* had the authority to establish and dissolve marriage. The adouls are schooled in the religious texts and they are still taking part in making the marriage contract, but it is no longer the adouls who have neither the authority to validate the mar-

8. A recent international survey carried out by PEW Research Center showed that 89 % of all Moroccans places religion as something important in their lives.

riage and dissolve it nor the authority for other matters in the Family Law. Many adouls have been quite conservative in their approach to the Family Law thus creating problems for women to benefit fully from their rights. It is possible to insert an article in a marriage contract, where the women states that she will not accept the man to engage in another marriage. But if the adoul is not informing the woman of her right to include such a condition, a clause concerning polygamy might not be made.

At present it is the judges who take the final decision in validating and dissolving a marriage and in all other matters concerning the Family Law. Much criticism has been raised against the interpretive measures made by the judges in the Family Courts. Women have complained that when seeking divorce they would be met by a patronising judge discouraging them from divorce.

Women judges make up approximately 20 % of all judges in Morocco, which seems to be a growing figure, but women do not hold many positions at higher levels in the tribunals.

Recently women judges have organized themselves in an association. This has been made possible after the Constitution was changed, making it legal for judges to organize themselves in groups as long as the principles of impartiality and independence can be guarantied.

The female judges have organized themselves among other things to raise awareness of the fact that the legal system is very much a male dominated system. Their objective is to be better represented in the courts and especially at higher courts. Focus is on defending the interest and rights for the female judges, to reinforce the ties of solidarity between judges in different regions and also to organize cultural and social activities between the female judges.

Social media is being used by the association for female judges to establish networks and voice their dissatisfaction with a legal system, where women are not equally represented.

The fight for authority

Women's rights movements have throughout the history of Morocco been active in making public awareness of gender inequalities and advocating for women's rights.[9] Family law as a state controlled and religiously based codification of women's rights has been a main focus of attention. In 1992 femi-

9. Fatima Sadiqi, Facing Challenges and pioneering Feminist and Gender Studies, p. 449, African and Asian Studies 7, 2008.

nist groups mobilized in a mass rally against the *Moudawana*, the former Family Law, and collected one million signatures against the inequalities codified in the law.

In 2000 mass demonstrations took place, on one side by the secular feminist movements adhering to the international human rights law and on the other side by the Islamists opposing a change of the Family Law. The secular women's rights groups worked in close relation with the King and embraced the religious sources as a mean for achieving change. Nouzia Skalli, a well known feminist became the minister of family affairs.

One case that has recently mobilized the women's rights groups is the case of a young girl being married to her rapist. The young girl, Amina Filali, was raped by a man much older than herself. To protect the honour of the family her parents agreed for the rapist to marry their daughter. The penal code in Morocco states that a "kidnapper" can stay free of charges if he marries his victim. This article is not clear and it is contested, how it should be interpreted by the courts. But before a minor can be married according to the Family Law the judges must carry out an investigation of the minor's psychological as well as physical health in order to grant the marriage.

This case clearly demonstrates the problem with the margin of discretion left to the judges. The judge in this case valued the honour of the family as a higher priority than the safety and psychological impact a marriage would have on Amina Filali, who later committed suicide.

Demonstrations were carried out in many towns in Morocco; social media were used to mobilize and create awareness as well as raise the debate of minor marriages in general and on the articles in the penal code. The case was an opportunity for the women's groups to raise the overall question of minor marriages. More disturbingly the Amina Filali case has showed that it was not the only case of a minor being married to her rapist.

Changing the age of marriage from 15 to 18 was one of the significant changes made to the Family law of 2004. However, minor marriage was not made illegal altogether but can be granted by a judge in the Family courts after an overall investigation of the minor's situation.

During the recent years there has been a continuous raise in the number of minor marriages from approximately 30,000 a year in 2008 to 35,000 in 2010. Thus a problem that seemed to be solved with the codification in the law still remains a very large problem.

Problems regarding gender inequality are often stated to be related to practice rather than to principles. The legal framework is of significant importance, but the battle for peoples' mind and their normative values is of great significance too in order to change the practices.

After the 'Arab Spring' the new February 20th Movement positions itself against the state, whereas the "old" feminists were in a position, where the state was considered the "ally of the feminists" and not the opponent as is in the case of the February 20th movement.[10] In the process leading to the Family Law women's rights groups and a few notable women were working in close collaboration with the official institutions and at the highest level with the King, in order to make the changes. The February 20th movement is in opposition to the official institutions and to the present balance of power in Morocco and works for change from the "outside." So where the earlier feminists saw the connections with the official institutions as a necessary tool for making significant change the February 20th movement has a very different position.

Gender and Law in a changing context

Moroccan society has undergone significant sociocultural and socioeconomic changes in the past three decades. Changes that to some extent have gone much further than the codes in the Family Law has provided for. Women are becoming more educated, even though illiteracy rates are still high especially in rural areas, and women do not necessarily have marriage as such as a goal, but will also make their education and career their priority.

The average age of marriage has raised to 26-27 years in urban areas being only 17 years thirty years ago and the average Moroccan woman will not give birth to more than 2.2 children. Pre-marital sex is not unheard of, even if this can still have fatal consequences for a woman especially in rural areas. A medical document proving virginity still needs to be provided before marriage can be concluded. In 30 % of households the woman is the one being responsible for the economy.

Despite all these very real and sometimes obvious changes, traditions and patriarchal ideologies still have a great impact on what is accepted and expected of a woman in today's Morocco.

10. Salime, Zakia, A New Feminism? Gender Dynamics in Morocco's February 20th Movement, Journal of International Women's Studies, Vol. 13#5, October 2012.

Paradoxes and Dilemmas

The fight for women's rights is an area, which somehow portrays modern Morocco.

It presents the paradox of a traditional viewpoint coexisting with a desire for modernization, where marriage should be based on equality if one asked the liberals and based on a patriarchal structure if one asked the conservatives.[11]

On one side the liberal secular women's groups want to have a Family Law that is not based on religious sources. On the other side the feminine Islamists want to grant equality to women, but to keep the religious sources. The February 20th Movement is a Moroccan uprising for political and structural change in society. It is a secular movement but nonetheless it has included the Islamist organization, Justice and Spirituality, in its fight for change. The Justice and Spirituality organization is notorious for it opposition to the monarchy in Morocco.

The only female in the present government is the minister of Family, Bassima el Hakkaoui, coming from the conservative Islamist party. Her dilemma will be to be in coherence with her political conservative allies and at the same time pave the way for the process of change that the public demands.

Conclusion

The Family Law of 2004 set out to grant more equal rights to women and start a process of change.

Changes have been made and changing the law has been an important beginning. But as long as the Family Law still contains articles that can be interpreted in favour of patriarchal and conservative norms, and as long as the judges are left with a large margin of discretionary power, the overall intention of equality seems to fade.

Awareness campaigns both by official sources and probably more importantly by various groups raising the question of women's rights and equality will be of great importance for changing the norms and traditions in a society that still suppresses women.

11. Fatima Sadiqi, Facing Challenges and Pioneering Feminist and Gender Studies, p. 449, African and Asian Studies 7 (2008).

Still many actions needs to be taken and much attention needs to be given for women to achieve equal rights in Moroccan society. Changing the laws is a necessary and important step, but by no means a measure that can stand for itself if substantive changes have to be made.

It will be interesting to see which groups will play a role in the near future for securing women's rights in Morocco.

Literature

Badran, Margot, *Feminism in Islam,* Oneworld Publications 2009

Dupret, Baudouin, *La charia aujourd'hui, Edition La Decouverte,* Paris 2012

Lamrabet, Asma, *Femmes et Hommes dans le Coran:Quelle Egalite?,* Dar Albouraq, 2012

Mehdi, Rubya, Hanne Petersen, Erik Reenberg Sand og Gordon E. Woodman, *Law and Religion in Multicultural Societies*, Djøf Publishing Copenhagen 2008

Mernissi, Fatima, *The Veil and the Male Elite,* Perseus Books Publishing, L.L.C 1991

Raday, Frances, *Culture, Religion, and Gender*, Oxford University Press and New York University School of Law 2003, I.CON, Vol. 1, number 4, 2003, pp 663-715

Sadiqi, Fatima, *Facing Challenges and Pioneering Feminist and Gender Studies,* African and Asian Studies7, 2008

Salime, Zakia, *A New Feminism? Gender Dynamics in Morocco's 20th February Movement,* Journal of International Women's Studies Vol 13 #5 October 2012

Twining, William, Surface Law. In Hanne Petersen, Anne Lise Kjær, Helle Krunke & Mikael Rask Madsen (eds), *Paradoxes of European Legal Integration,* Ashgate 2008, pp 157-183

Guide Practique du Code de la Famille, Ministere de la Justice, A.D.I.J.J., 2eme edition Mars 2005

The Noble Sámi Men

Ande Somby

Do the noble Sámi men exist? This text aims to explore whether we can insist on that.

At least the Sami exist. We are focusing on the little population on top of Europe that has carried important aspects of the mystery of Europe through the times. The Sami people have since time immemorial been populating the areas that today are known as northern Norway, northern Sweden, northern Finland and north western part of Russia. Traditionally the Samis have been living of fisheries, arctic farming, reindeer herding and hunting and gathering.

The arctic is a tough place to live in. It can be cold. The circumstances can change pretty rapidly. From one moment to the other the weather can change pretty drastically. Also the seasons can vary dramatically. There are times when the gracing lands for the reindeers can be covered by ice. There are also times when either the forests or the fjords can "go black." It means that they can be empty for game or fish.

The answer is migration. Fish do that. Animals do that. Migrating birds definitively do that. Traditionally the practice of migration has been deeply embedded in the Sami culture as well. All the different Sami livelihoods have practised migration in one form or the other. Migration in space has been practiced according to the fact that animals and plants have their parties in different locations at different times. In addition to migration in space it has also been practical to migrate in professions. When times have been bad for fishing, people would have to migrate over to hunting and arctic farming.

In the European tradition the Sami have had an important role. They have been different. It means something to be the different one. People compare their lives and societies to your life and society. In that respect the Sami society has been observed, described, characterized and commented extensively in European literature.

Practically it meant that people had to multiprofessionals. In their lives they also had to have the competence of improvisation. That is somewhat contrary to the popular image of the Sami. The Sami has through history been iconised as the reindeer herding people on the tundra. As any other icon, this one too can be problematic. There are lots of other reindeer herding people in this world. And traditionally the Sami only had a minority in reindeer herding. Many Samis do not recognize themselves or their ancestors as reindeer herders.

In addition nowadays the structure of the Sami society resembles any other modern society. There are teachers, doctors, bus drivers and every other walk of life among the Sami as well. Still the Sami culture still has something in particular. Many Samis are negative towards being depicted as reindeer herders.

In this text we are going to meet the boys. The boys work with their reindeers through the year. They live an outdoor life, and they produce reindeer meat on the tundra. In many respects the boys live a dreamlike life. Their practises are pretty ecological compared with other meat producers. Their life is very much more "free" than the life of farmers or other professionals. And they traditionally carry many positive myths ranging from the image of being "noble" savages who are do respect their women, are not hash against children and who are connected to their tradition through a deep respect for their ancestors.[1] Somehow these men then appear as a bit godlike. They carry characteristics that we all would want to carry.

However it is not easy to live a human life like an angel. If you fall then you are condemned. Here we shall visit some episodes of angles falling, and then comment on them.

Myth 1: The chaotic energy

It is oftentimes told stories bout Sámi men that when you have agreed to meet at a certain time they will tend to show up much later. They will be at total ease with that and if you start addressing that, they will say that "if you are in such a hurry – why didnt we meet up yesterday.

Myth 2: The gender chauvinist

Sámi men are from time to time accused as other men for that they dont let women get access to power positions. One example has been the claim both

1. Actually these among other characteristics were used against the Samis in a text that The Apostle of the Samis – Thomas von Westens wrote 17th of July 1716 when authorising and instructing the two missionaries Kjell Stub and Jens Blok. (http://somban.com/bahkinNOR1.htm)

regarding under representation of woman both in the Norwegian Sámi Parliament.[2]

Myth 3: The ecological disaster machine
Sámi men are accused for that the reindeer gracing lands are overgrased and that they mistreat their animals.[3] But not only that they are also accused for overfishing and that they use *atvs* on the tundra causing wounds on the tundra.

Myth 4: The virile
Back in 1997 there was a story about some research about how long men from different races would keep up their sexual virility. The conclusion was that Sámi men and men from the Australian aborigines were the two groups of men who lasted the longest. The explanation was that they had higher levels of the so called LH hormone.

Myth 5: The drinker
Sámi men are often characterised in popular belief as heavy drinkers. That they drink a lot and get very drunk. The more extreme versions of this myth is that they also get involved in fighting. Sometimes it is fist fighting other times knives can be used.

Myth 6: The school drop out
There are claims that the Sámi boys often tend to drop out from the educational institutions. The claim is that they exit either to a life in the tundra, or that they live their lives depending on their moms.

Myth 7: The sexual Molester
There has been two types of claims against the sámi men. The one is that they tend to buy sex. One story was from the time when the borders between Norway and Russia opened up. Then many Russian women came across, and they had sexual encounters and sexual relationships based on that the men paid them. The other was a bit related. It was exposed that in Kautokeino the grown up men bought sex from under aged girls by giving them prepaid calling cards.[4]

2. http://kjonn.maktutredningen.no/aktuelt/760
3. http://www.nrk.no/nyheter/distrikt/troms_og_finnmark/1.8199725
4. http://www.aftenposten.no/nyheter/iriks/article1242769.ece

Sámi Male ideals

Traditionally you could have many roles within a traditional Sámi clan – as you have many roles as a man in any other given context. In a traditional Sámi context we have a huge nomenclature for how we can be related to each other, and I will pick out some of the ways a Sami man can be related to a given Sámi woman. We intend to link them to your expected tasks in that given role and try to extract the traditional male virtues out of that.

Being somebody's father meant that you have an all-expected presence, and the Sámi fathers do not differ dramatically from fathers in our neighbouring culture. You have to provide to, nurture, care for, protect and sometimes direct your daughters.

Being somebody's brother means that you act as an allied in all of the situations, a life can offer. You are supposed to be the buddy, who assist you sister when she is in need for assistance. Sometime that would imply that you lift the load if it becomes to heavy for her, and other times you have to give her protection if that is what is needed.

Being somebody's Grandfather means that you are supposed to be the bank of knowledge and wisdom. When your grand daughter is small you oftentimes represent the rules of exception. Even if the child is supposed to get sweets only on Saturday, grandfather can give exemption from that rule, and thereby the child gets to know the existence of exceptions and how they work. When the grand daughter gets older the grand father gets the role of being an advisor and one who gives comfort if life becomes difficult. Then the grandfather is a bank of experience, wisdom and advices.

Being somebody's uncle implies to be a back up person. We differentiate between an uncle who is mother's brother, an uncle who is a younger brother of your father and an uncle who is an older brother of your father. There are nuances between the roles of different uncles, but for our purpose it is not necessary to go into details on that. If the father, brother or the grandfather is not present, an uncle's obligation is to step into any of these roles. In addition the uncle would have the obligation to tell the stories to the child, which have been kept secret from the child. That applies to both small children, when small secrets get revealed. When the child becomes bigger it can be time to reveal bigger secrets.

Being somebody's "vilbealli" – male cousin is a role where you have approximately the same role as a brother and an uncle, and sometimes when these two characters are absent you have to step into these roles and fill them. If they are present, then your role is to be a modifying character. You can represent more of the fun side of life to your cousin, for example by being the humorous character in her life or being the one who reveals contemporary secrets. You exchange gossip with your cousin. The concept of cousins is that there is a numerical system that you can be first cousin when you are children of siblings. When you are a child of somebody who are first cousins then you are second cousin, when you are a child of second cousins then you are third cousins and so forth. The characteristic aspect in Sami culture is that the significance of being cousins follows you through to fifth or sixth cousins.

The traditional male roles that can be found within the family nomenclature of relationship can be an important inspiration when we attempt to reformulate the role of being a male in a contemporary society. There can be important reminders of how one both could take care, give care be taken care of.

The other important source of inspiration is the contemporary ideologies on equality between human beings including equality between men and women. These principles are bought to expensive prices in the form of former human suffering, and in moments of frustration it could be easy to slip into both misogynist considerations and also to expose our Nordic brothers for hate blaming the Sámi men of being too uneasy existences. The goal to avoid misogyny and sexism has to be mentioned explicitly. So we also have to state the goal to be guided by other core values in the humanity we know from the tradition of human rights discourse.

When formulating the new male roles in addition to define the direction on the basis of the guidance of some core values, we also need to have an understanding of the nature of the contemporary situation. Apparently it is a matter of how to configure the relationship that men should have to women, but somehow it seems to be a part of a bigger question. How human beings shall find their place when technology and in particular robotisation takes more and more of the space and the work of human beings.

I would claim that an increased robotisation is taking place and that "the knives that technology provides us with become sharper and sharper." In my eyes that is a very good thing. We don't have to do dangerous work – such as looking up explosives on the ground neither do we have to do boring work. The problem is however how we are able to adapt ourselves to new circumstances. Our ability to adapt has perhaps never been more important than now. These waves of the technological takeovers have hit many of our men first. They have sort of become "not needed" anymore, and thereby the meaning of existence is questioned. I would claim that there are more waves to come. When the robots "learn" how to drive buses and cars, human bus- and taxi drivers will not be that much in demand as they are today. When the robots "learn" how to nurse then the same thing perhaps happen to nurses.

I think these developments will present big challenges to humanity.. The utopian scenarios are there. If we can use all the time that we will get from the robots doing our work, we perhaps will get more time to use on generosity, beauty, truth, tolerance and wisdom. In such a scenario the best moments in humanity are yet to come. But the dystopian scenarios are also there. If all this spare time has taken so much of the drama of our lives away, then we start to get bored, abusive, manipulative, addicted and indifferent. As we know that both utopia and dystopia is within human potentiality our obligation is to try to nurture the utopian potentialities within us and try to reduce and fight against the dystopian ones.

If we look at the noble Sámi men in such a context, they are very important for our current humanity. Since they seem to become some of the first "no needed" humans, they can show us what we have to expect, and as a humanity we can observe these phenomena and try to articulate our observations. We can be able to articulate which values are at stake, and thereby we can be able to say which principles or values we have to promote.

These noble savages are perhaps the canaries in our current coalmine.

An Egalitarian Fiscal Culture Favours Gender Equality – the Swedish Example

Åsa Gunnarsson

Introduction

I will reflect upon the Swedish individual income tax reform from 1971 that was the first step away from joint taxation of spouses. It incentivised married women's increased labour market participation on a large scale, which is an effect well recognised as a best practises for economic gender equality. In comparison with joint income tax models the Nordic individual income tax systems also seem to contribute to dynamic effects on the economy. However, this aspect is quite neglected in the international arenas for tax policy discussions. One of the reasons could be that the international debate has been occupied with the vision of a neutral and non-distributive income tax model in opposition with tax policies that promote a social justice driven interventionist, egalitarian fiscal culture. My purpose with this text is to upgrade the importance of gender equality concerns in tax policy making. This is interesting from both a social justice and an economic growth perspective.

Contradictory fiscal legal cultures – a problem for gender just taxation

The power to raise and spend public revenues remains fundamentally associated with the nation state at a time when states increasingly set their fiscal directions in response to pressures associated with global economic integration, capital mobility and market deregulation. Nation states have also agreed to collaborate on matters of fiscal governance and policies in the Organisation for Economic Co-operation and Development, the World Bank Group and the International Monetary Fund. Apart from having a strong global influence on world trade, these organizations also have a worldwide influence on multinational commitments to engage in stimulus budgeting and on cooperating in preventing tax evasion. A global economic order has been on the agenda for a while as a means for fighting harmful tax competition. Tax law reforms are regarded as valuable instruments for achieving this aim (Mumford 2010, 36-37). The recent series of economic crises starting with the global economic crisis in 2008 has also led to new multinational commitments. The interventions of international organizations in the economic and fiscal governance of national states is exposed, for example, in the way Greece has been forced to submit to massive budgets cuts and fiscal restrains.

Many OECD countries have reformed their income tax over the last three decades. Even though a common understanding of the ideal income tax system has never been expressed openly, there are common strands in the various tax reforms. Based on a neoliberal tax ideology, a special interpretation of what constitutes an optimal taxation for economic growth has guided the international trend in redesigning national budgets and fiscal systems. A line between fiscal purposes and social justice has been drawn, meaning that tax regulations with redistributive intentions are seen as political interventions in the market economy. Economic intervention creates excess burdens or welfare losses, which can be restricting for economic growth. As redistribution of wealth and income are based on political ideals concerning economic equality, such interventions are seen as creating inefficiency in the economy (Hayek 1956; Korpi, Palme 1993; Prop. 1989/90:110, 620-632; Birch Sørensen 2010). This legal culture of tax system design developed inside the OECD community has resulted in a normative standard whereby distributional neutrality is a part of the concept of fiscal taxation, which aims to preserve the status quo.

In contrast to the concept of fiscal taxation, Swedish welfare economy represents a more egalitarian culture with a high tax burden, and a comprehensive and generous social welfare system. The egalitarian fiscal culture is based on a combination of the ability to pay principle and the social policy. The theoretical frame of the ability to pay concept originally emerged from the philosophical idea of the state as a social organism in which there exists a mutual dependency between state and individual. Later, the theory of ability to pay has been taken as a basis for the welfare state view on the distribution of the tax burden. Regardless of the approach chosen, the measurement of the individual taxpaying capacity should be equal to the amount or degree of private satisfaction of needs that the taxpaying citizen can achieve. This position of satisfaction of needs can, in turn, be measured in two different ways. One is to measure the satisfaction of needs from the source of income, the other to measure the satisfaction of needs on the basis of the use of income. The interventionist function of the welfare state is most strongly reflected in the social policy tax theory. The principle of social policy is based on the objective to use taxation for equalisation through redistribution of economic resources. The redistribution objective of taxation has been motivated in different ways. One of them is to draw upon the same hypothesis as the marginal utility theory, namely that the subjective utility decreases for every utility unit acquired. This argument has been used to establish an objective reason for the justification of progressive taxation. Another argument is that the ability to pay tax increases in a higher proportion than the increase in income. It is easier to increase ones income, the wealthier one is. I would say that the social policy principle is most of all based in the ethics of social justice. If social justice is implemented as a solidarity principle, which has been the case for Sweden, it provides the ethical argument in favour of a progressive income tax system (Gunnarsson 1995, 115-134).

The Swedish fiscal culture is the financing part of a welfare economy that has established a universal model of social protection based on a solidarity principle. The comprehensive scope of the Swedish welfare state, with respect to the range of publicly provided benefits and services, the population coverage, and the high level of benefits, can be divided into two parts. One part has the features of a 'social service state', which is a definition used to emphasize the general welfare services and benefits strategy, and the centrality of public services. Compared with other models or typologies for welfare states, this has been regarded as an inclusive policy. The other part of the Swedish welfare regime can be defined as 'the social insurance state' protecting against income loss, under which benefits based on earnings-related schemes should be categorized (Sainsbury 1996, 31-32; Vahlne Westerhäll 1996; Vahlne Westerhäll, 2002, 640-641; Anttonen 1998).

The combination of a heavy tax burden and a generous social welfare system gives a redistributive effect (OECD, Forum, 2011), which is one pre-requisite for an egalitarian society. Despite high levels of social spending, which due to the theory of optimal taxation create dead weight losses, the Swedish economy is growing. The egalitarian fiscal culture seems to have brought some good for a competitive economy. However, that aspect seems to be neglected in contemporary tax policy analyses. Sweden has been the focus of a great deal of academic interest for a number of years for the simple reason that according to traditional economic analyses it should not be able to survive. The economy is not supposed to grow as it combines capitalism and high taxes. Nevertheless, Sweden is a highly productive and technologically advanced economy, home to some of the world's most successful capitalist enterprises and enjoys one of the highest standards of living in the world. Quite simply, Sweden merges a capitalist society with an egalitarian society, which in the fiscal tax system discourses are incompatible things. The Swedish model is often compared to a bumblebee, in the same way's as the law of aerodynamics tells us that it is not possible for something constructed as a bumblebee to be able to fly, the established laws of economy tells us that an economy such as the Swedish cannot grow (Kielos 2009). Sven Steinmo has listed those features of the Swedish welfare economy that can be an obstacle for economic growth:

- high levels of income equality
- universalist social welfare and tax policies
- high levels of union organization and economic concentration
- long history of labour/capital peace and cooperation
- highest taxes in the world
- highest level of social spending in the world and
- high levels of gender equality (Steinmo 2010).

One can see that the list is inspired by the message learned from the theory of optimal taxation that taxes should be designed to avoid dead weight losses. The wedge between pre-tax and after tax income distorts economic incentives, which reduces the total size of the pie available for redistribution. This theorem promotes principles of uniformity, neutrality and horizontal equality in taxation. The linear income tax is the ideal model that best fulfils these principles. However the theory of optimal taxation constitutes two theorems. The second theorem shows that there exists a cross-effect between men's low income elasticity and women's high income elasticity. All tax reforms that promote lower taxes for the primary earners have a negative impact on the secondary earners labour market participation (McCafferey 1997, 178-180; Apps 2009). So it is equally possible in relation to the dead weight loss axiom, to build a normative case on the axiom that gender equality is an important pre-requisite for economic growth in welfare economies as it promotes an increase in labour market participation. The individual income tax reform from 1971 was also, in the preparatory work, argued in similar terms. However, the argumentation was not based in neoliberal or optimal tax theory. My analysis is that individual taxation is rooted in a welfare state legal culture, which in Sweden is expressed in what can be labelled as a work-fare gender equality model. So, the legal cultural frame for individual income tax is about welfare state policies.

Work-fare Oriented Gender Equality – The Swedish Model

The representation of the Swedish state as a form of state feminism, or at least as a women-friendly welfare state, has its roots in how it has actively advanced women's interests. The idea of 'workfare' is at the core of the Swedish welfare state model that is based on an egalitarian ideology of social citizenship, and so also central to the policy of promoting gender equality. In contrast to a 'bread-winner' ideology, under the notion of 'workfare' men and women alike have been regarded as self-supporting individuals within a labour market in line with the ideal of a dual income-earner family ideology (Gunnarsson et. al. 2004; Wennberg 2008; Pylkkänen 2009).

A prominent characteristic of the Swedish model is truly the fact that gender equality policy is closely intertwined with the Swedish welfare state ideology. In the formation of the welfare state gender equality has been a major concern in many welfare reforms, and has been particularly important in those reforms oriented at the labour market. Employment strategies have acknowledged the significance of work in achieving economic independence and in earning the right to social security (Hernes 1987, Sainsbury 1996, Bradley 1996, Bergquist et. al. 1999; Gunnarsson, Svensson 2012). The overall objective of Sweden's gender equality policy is to ensure that women and men have the same power to shape society and their own lives. The policy should be read from the perspective that it points in the direction of shared power and shared responsibilities, based on Yvonne Hirdman's gender system theory. This theory represents a structural understanding of inequality. Hirdman claims that the principles of separation of the sexes and the male norm feeds gender inequalities on three interacting levels, which are the structural, the individual and the symbolic (Gunnarsson, Svensson 2012; Hirdman in SOU 1990:44).

By promoting a socially egalitarian citizenship based on notions of solidarity and redistributive social justice the Swedish social democratic welfare state has had a comparatively high degree of universalism regarding social benefits (Kautto et al 1999; 2001 and SOU 2000: 83; Gunnarsson et. al. 2004). General services and benefits available for eligible residents are the most inclusive part of Swedish social citizenship, in contrast to earnings-related social insurance benefits (Sainsbury, 1996, 1999; Gunnarsson 2007). Flat-rate benefits for households with children, such as the child allowance, health and childcare services and means-tested benefits, such as the housing allowance, have had a significant redistributive effect in favour of women (Skatteverket 2007: 2, Prop. 2009/10: 1).

At an early stage of the welfare state project a combination strategy was developed to enable women to fulfil the responsibilities of care whilst pursuing their wish to be self-supporting. Radical reforms in the 1960s and 1970s addressed gender equality based on the narrow egalitarian idea of promoting married women's labour market participation (Gunnarsson and Stattin 2001; Gunnarsson et al 2004; Pylkkänen 2009; 123-149). The combination strategy aimed to further encourage women to participate in the labour market, whilst facilitating married women to combine paid work with family life. It thereby became a driving force in the active integration of women into the public sphere of social citizenship (Gunnarsson, Svensson 2009, 50; Gunnarsson, Svensson 2012). In my view, the abolition of joint taxation, together with progressive social reforms such as the introduction of publicly financed day care for children and sex neutral parental leave, constitutes the women-friendly welfare state.

Individual Income Tax and the Abolition of Family Taxation in Sweden

The Swedish income tax system has moved away from joint income taxation of spouses and the delivery of income support to families as tax expenditures to individual income taxation and family income support in cash and in-kind payments over the public budget. Family tax expenditures have been constructed as both jointly and individually assessed family-related tax allowances, deductions and tax credits. Today Sweden together with the other Nordic countries apply a dual-earner family income tax model (Pakarinen 2011). This is the result mainly of two tax reforms, one in 1971 and that of 1991. They represent the major principal fundaments in the process in which the abolition of elements of jointness in the tax system step-by-step have been replaced by individual based tax regulations.

In the context of the differential treatment of taxpayers in different working and family situations, the question of the appropriate unit of taxation has been the most discussed issue in Sweden throughout the years. The joint taxation of the marital unit was not seriously questioned in Sweden until a commission report was presented in 1969 (Fi 1969: 4). When the change to an individual tax unit, following the proposals in the report, was carried through in 1971, it was only partial. The termination of the joint taxation of spouses took a long time, and the last remnants of the partial joint taxation of income were abolished as late as 1991 in connection with the thorough restructuring of the tax system. Joint taxation of net wealth did exist until 2007, when it was finally decided that wealth taxation should not be carried out.

The arguments against joint taxation have been many over the years. One of the main arguments put forward by the commission that proposed the partial joint taxation, introduced in 1971 was that the assessment of ability to pay should not be made dependent on sex or civil status. Such a dependency could have an impact on the expected increase in demand for labor supply in the future as joint taxation was seen as an obstacle for married women to get into the work force. Thus it would obstruct the aim of equality between men and women. Another argument made by the commission as well as by scholars was that joint taxation is not in line with the ability-to-pay principle, which follows from the fact that income tax should be related to the individual tax subject. The correlation between labor market participation of the secondary earner and the income of the primary earner in a household, was also openly recognized (Fi 1969:4, 60-, and Gunnarsson, 1995, 178-79). After the introduction of the individual as the appropriate tax unit, the effective marginal tax rate became higher for married men at the same time as the marginal tax rate was generally lower for women. An increase in working-hours for men was therefore more costly for the households in terms of tax, than an increase in working-hours for women.

In contrast to the 1971 tax reform, the 1991 tax reform was not at all occupied with family and joint taxation issues. Its major objective following the neo-liberal international tax trend at that time, was to achieve tax neutrality by adjusting taxation to the first theorem of optimal tax theory. As I explained earlier, this concept of fiscal taxation did, in particular in the Swedish context, lead to a shift from social concerns in tax legislation. They were regarded as non-fiscal tax measures as they in theory create excess burdens and therefore act as a hinder for an efficient allocation of resources in the market economy. The reform clearly stated that family taxation and social justice objectives were to be regarded as non-fiscal. Welfare state schemes were delegated to the transfer system of the public budget and were not to be carried out as tax expenditures (Prop. 1989/90: 110).

The Swedish design of fiscal taxation was expressed in the introduction of a dual income tax, in which the global state income tax was split into one tax on earned income and one on income from capital. So, instead of a global income tax on the aggregated income from all sources at the individual level, taxed at a single tax rate, each of the two income taxes was set at a proportional rate, 20 percent on earned income and 30 percent on capital income. A threshold for the state income tax on earned income was also introduced, at such a high level that almost 90 percent of the taxpayers was expected to be exempted from paying state income tax on earned income. As a result of the reform, the only elements of progressive taxation left in the system were the use of an increased basic deduction for low-income groups and the threshold effect when a taxpayer's income was taxable for state income tax on earned income. This meant that most of the taxpayers were only obligated to pay the proportional local municipality tax on earned income. Depending on community residence, the taxes varied between 27 to 30 percent with an average on 31 percent, in the beginning of the 1990s. The large reductions of the marginal income tax rates, from the high 70-percent rate applied before the reform to around 50 percent at the top, inevitably led to huge revenue losses. The idea behind was that the distribution policy should be left undisturbed by the reform. No income group should benefit or loose more in relation to other groups as an effect of the reform. However, the exemption of almost 90 procent of tax payers from income taxation on earned income and the massive marginal income tax cuts for high-income earners were not neutral tax measures. A package of base broadening of income tax on both capital and earned income was supposed to give an acceptable effect on the income distribution, and to cover a part of the revenue losses. An extensive tax-switch from direct to indirect taxation, by a raise of the rate and a broader tax base for value-added tax, secured most of the remaining part of the revenue required. The tax-switch from income tax to VAT needed some kind of supplementary income distribution concept in order to fulfil the distribution-neutrality objective. This was done by the introduction of a progressive basic deduction from the municipal income tax base for low-income earners and an increase in housing and child allowances. Still, the reform was expected to be slightly more beneficial for high-income earners (Prop 1989/90: 110, 620-632, SOU 1995: 104, 61-62, 83-84).

The structure of the reform gave the opposite effect in relation to the individual income tax reform in 1971. The cuts of effective marginal tax rates had a moderating impact on women's labor supply as the marginal net of tax salaries increased for men. This behavior strengthened as secondary earners women also are more sensitive to income transfers, such as the increase of transfer payments to households with children. Altogether, the reform led to a reallocation of household production within the households. Men increased their hours of paid work much more than women did (Aronsson and Palme, 1994).

The ability-to pay-principle has in the Swedish tax policy setting been given a very strong position in defending the individual as the appropriate tax unit. Obviously, it is in line with the second theorem of optimal taxation and it has also in practice promoted women's labor market participation. In contrast, the 1991 tax reform was a backlash in relation to the individual tax unit interpretation of the ability-to-pay principle. Here, the first theorem of optimal tax theory was given priority. The dominant view was that economic growth demands neutrality in taxation. Tax cuts were defined as one of the most important means to achieve neutrality. Particularly in relation to the need to protect the income tax base, high-income earners and the capital they control are regarded as very mobile over the boarders, and to promote an increase in labor market supply. The reform did also give up the global income tax, which is another well-established interpretation of the ability-to-pay principle. The global, individually based income tax was earlier in tax policy discussions regarded as the true measure of the ability to pay taxes. The dual income tax system has, by its division of income tax objects, pushed aside the former principal orientation based on the individual's total ability to pay.

The International Context of Gender Equality in Relation to Tax/Benefit Units and Tax Credits for Domestic Services

Even though the 1991 tax reform went the opposite way in relation to what could be regarded as beneficial for gender equality, one can still claim that the fiscal culture, in an international context, continues to be a vital part in the sustainability of gender equality in Sweden. I draw this conclusion from studies of three areas of fiscal policies. The first area concerns the old issue regarding tax ability, the tax unit and women's market participation. The other two are fiscal policy areas that represent fairly new trends, earned income/work tax credits and public subsidies of domestic services.

Broadly, comparative studies show two main normative positions regarding tax and social policies concerning spouses, families and children. One is the male breadwinner family model linked to a traditional female, care regime, which fosters a housewife ideal – as in the case of Germany, the U.S and Spain. Consequently, the legal system rests on a normative base where the family or the marriage is the unit of assessment for social entitlements and taxation, in which the carer has only supplementary and no individual rights. (Sainsbury 1996, 44-45; Sainsbury 1999, 77-80; 314; Lahey 2011, Wersig 2011). The other is the dual-earner family model for which the Nordic countries are renowned. Social entitlements and income taxation are based on the individual's work performance, citizenship or residence, not marital status. Individual obligations via income tax, and individual social rights based on earnings-related social security schemes are measures that, as one of several objectives, aim to increase economic autonomy for married women. (Gunnarsson 2003; Sainsbury 1999, 77-80). Today joint filing of aggregated marital income is normally voluntary in those countries that base their income tax on a joint fiscal model. However, the freedom of the choice is imaginary as it often means that the family will loose a substantial amount of disposable income after tax. As long as income tax is progressive, the technique of splitting the aggregated income of both spouses and each spouse filing for half the income will reduce the total tax burden as the spouse with the highest income will be taxed at a lower rate of marginal income tax. This tax relief is magnified for one-earner families. As the income structures in heterosexual families follows gendered lines, income taxation of the marital unit results in the overtaxing of married women. This is truly a disincentive for housewives to enter the workforce, which for example is the case for women in western Germany and in Spain. It also traps many of those married women who work in the position of being secondary earner in the family. Contrary to the claimed neutrality between one-earner and dual-earner families, joint income and wealth taxation favour the marital tax unit. Experiences from Germany, Japan, Spain and the US show that the joint taxation of spouses contributes to a patriarchal, asymmetrical division between unpaid household work and paid work on the labour market. In contemporary tax systems income splitting between conjugal partners almost always has negative consequences for gender equality. Normally tax regulations allowing income splitting, is merely used as a fictive, technique with the purpose to reduce tax for the primary earner. A substantive transfer of income is not conditional. The tax liability of the receiving spouse will not correspond to a legal claim on the assets or income for which she will be taxed (Lahey, 2011; de Villota, 2011; de Villota & Ferrari, 2004; Wersig, 2011; Gottfried & O'Reilly, 2002).

A trend in tax policy among OECD countries since the 1990s has been the use of various types of tax credits as a part of an active labour market policy to incentivize particularly low-earning families' but also middle-income families' labour supply. The term tax credit describes mainly two different concepts. One is a recognition of partial payment already made towards taxes due. The other is the concept where a state benefit is paid to workers through the tax system, which has the effect of increasing (rather than reducing) net income. A tax credit is generally more valuable than a tax deduction or tax allowance of the same magnitude because a tax credit reduces tax directly, while a deduction or allowance only reduces taxable income and so the reduction in tax is only a fraction (the marginal tax rate) of the deduction or allowance. Many of these working family tax credits are assessed on the basis of spouses' or partners' conjugal income. The idea is that the family will get a tax credit if they increase their hours of paid work on the labour market (Brewer et al. 2008).

New Zealand introduced working family tax credits as early as in 1986 through the Family Support Tax Credit (FSTC) and Guaranteed Minimum Family Income (GMFI), which targeted poor families. In 1996, the FSTC was replaced by the Independent Family Tax Credit (IFTC). Both types of working family tax credits tax have used the aggregated parental income to determine the size of the tax reduction. By introducing income-targeted support for families, based on the household income, a new form of joint taxation has been enforced. (Gunnarsson 1999). Similarly, the U.K. introduced a Working Family Tax Credit (WFTC) at the beginning of the 1990s, aimed at stimulating increased labour market participation for families with small children, focusing particularly on single parents. The WFTC was later replaced by a Working Tax Credit (WTC), embracing all low-earning families, and an additional subsidy for families with children in the form of a Child Tax Credit (CTC). Both WTC and CTC are assessed on the basis of family income, number of children and working hours per week (Brewer et al 2008). Australia also introduced a version of family tax credit in the 1990s, assessed on the basis of joint, family income. It is delivered as a Family Tax Benefit A (FTB-A) and a Family Tax There are many other examples of how reforms of earned income tax credits and tax-delivered benefits, particularly for child subsidies, have introduced a joint tax-benefit unit. This means that individual taxation has become eroded in many OECD countries. Several of these reforms have also raised the tax rates for the secondary earner. In summary, tax credits that are based on joint, family income have the same lock-in effect on women's labour market supply as joint taxation and income splitting of spouses or co-habitant heterosexual partners (Lahey 2005; Philipps 2011; Apps 2006; Apps 2010; Stewart 1999). The Swedish working tax credit reform does not follow this trend. When it came into force in 2007, each individual taxpayer became the unit of assessment for the earned income tax credit (Prop. 2006/07: 1, Vol. 1, 137).

Recently a new type of tax expenditure has been introduced in several EU countries. As part of job growth policies, stimulation of the domestic services sector has led to reforms that in different ways subsidise paid domestic work. The Nordic countries – Sweden, Denmark and Finland – have used tax credits. Germany has applied a mini-job model, which is a specific category of employment for the household sector with low wages and low social contribution costs. Belgium, France and Austria have introduced a voucher model, which at least France combines with a tax credit provision. The voucher is pre-paid service check that the user of domestic services can purchase and use as a salary for the domestic worker. It aims to simplify the process of hiring and paying salaries as well as social contributions for employees in private homes. If the vouchers model is combined with a tax credit, the employers of domestic workers also can claim an income tax reduction of parts of the costs for the voucher (Kvist 2011). In all, it seems that domestic services vouchers and mini-jobs are more commonly used policy options in breadwinner model countries that practise joint income taxation of spouses, and that tax credits is the common tax policy for the Nordic individual income tax systems (Gunnarsson, Kvist 2011).

Individual Taxes and Benefits – Best Practises for Gender Equality

Despite the backlashes in the 1990s one can see that Swedish policies for economic gender equality are still present. When the Swedish type of work tax credit was introduced, it was not constructed as an earning family tax credit type. It was not based on the household income, but the individual income. And it also seems that the Swedish public subsidies for domestic work are more in line with sustainable gender equality than the public expenditures for domestic work that are in practise in the central European and Mediterranean countries. The stimulation of domestic services through mini-jobs and vouchers reforms are designed to replace the unpaid work of the housewife or the servant tradition carried out by maids. The way in which the different tax credits for domestic services are constructed in the Nordic countries, are much more in line with a work-fare oriented gender equality tradition. The awareness of how the divide of paid and unpaid work between the public and the private spheres of economy contribute to gender gaps in relation to income and wealth seems to be present in the Swedish political debate. In this respect I claim that Sweden has managed, partly as an effect of fiscal policies, to achieve a more sustainable level of gender equality than many other countries. However, the Swedish tax system is far from what I think is an ideal model for gender just taxation. Based on Swedish best practise on what constitutes a women-friendly income tax system I think a good income tax system would be global not dual. A progressive rate on the aggregated income from all sources should be applied with the individual as the tax and benefit unit not the household. If this income tax could be combined with an universal child benefit and an individual, parental leave insurance, I think the welfare economies in the OECD community would have a good chance to meet the future welfare challenges of which the organization and financing of care work and reproduction are a massively gendered social risk.

Reference list

Anttonen, Anneli (1998), Den sociala servicesstaten som feministiskt kampbegrepp. In Eliasson-Lappalainen, Rosmari, Szebehely, Marta (Eds.), *Vad förgår och vad består? En antologi om äldreomsorg, kvinnosyn och socialpolitik.* Eslöv: Arkiv Förlag

Apps, Patricia (2009), "Tax Reform, Targeting, and the Burden on Women." Paper prepared for National Foundation for Australian Women for submission to the Review of Australia's Future Tax System

Aronssson, Thomas and Palme, Mårten (1994), 'A Decade of Tax and Benefit Reforms in Sweden – Effects on Labour Supply, Welfare and Inequality' *3 Tax Reform Evalutaion Report* 1994 (Stockholm: Ekonomiska rådet)

Bergquist, C., Borchorst, A., Christensen, A-D., Ramstedt-Silén, V., Raaum, N. C. and Styrkardóttir, A. (eds.) (1999), *Equal Democracies? Gender and politics in the Nordic countries.* Oslo: Scandinavian University Press

Birch Sørensen, Peter (2010), 'Swedish Tax Policy: Recent Trends and Future Challenges.' *Report to the Expert Group on Public Economics 2010: 4.* Stockholm: Fritzes

Bradley, David (1996), *Family Law and Political Culture.* London: Sweet & Maxwell Fi 1969: 4,

Gottfried, H. & O'Reilly, J. (2002), 'Reregulating Breadwinner Models in Socially Conservative Welfare Systems: Comparing Germany and Japan.' *Social Politics*, Oxford University Press.

Gunnarsson, Åsa (1995), *Skatterättvisa.* Uppsala: Iustus Förlag

Gunnarsson, Åsa (1999), 'Equity Trends in Taxation – with Examples from Swedish and New Zealand Tax Reforms' in *Liber Amicorum Leif Mutén.* Amsterdam: Kluwer

Gunnarsson, Åsa, Stattin, Chris, (2001), 'Jämställdhetsnormen i skatte- och socialrätten.' In Monica Burman and Åsa Gunnarson (eds), *Familjeföreställningar. Om familjens betydelse inom juridik, ekonomi och forskning.* Uppsala: Iustus Förlag AB

Gunnarsson, Åsa (2003), *Fördelningen av familjens skatter och sociala förmåner.* Iustus Förlag AB: Uppsala

Gunnarsson, Åsa, Burman, Monica, Wennberg, Lena (2004), Economic dependence and self-support in family, tax and social law. In Svensson, Eva-Maria, Pylkkänen Anu and Niemi-Kiesiläinen, Johanna (eds.) (2004), *Nordic Equality at a Crossroads. Feminist Legal Studies Coping with Difference*

Gunnarsson, Åsa (2007), Gender Equality and the Diversity of Rights and Obligations. In Gunnarsson, Åsa, Svensson, Eva-Maria and Davies, Margaret (eds.) *Exploting the Limits of Law. Swedish Feminims and the Challenge to Pessimism.* Aldershot: Ashgate

Gunnarsson, Åsa, Svensson, Eva-Maria (2009), *Genusrättsvetenskap.* Lund: Studentlitteratur

Gunnarsson, Åsa, Kvist, Elin (2011), 'Public Expenditure for Domestic Work Challenges Swedish Gender Equality.' In Motmans Joz, Cuypers Daniël, Meier Petra, Mortelmans Dimitri & Zanoni Patrizia (Eds.), *Equal is not enough: challenging differences and inequalities in contemporary societies.* Conference Proceedings. Antwerpen: Policy Research Centre on Equal opportunities, University of Antwerpen – Hasselt University, 156-172

Hayek, Friedrich, A. (1956), 'Progressive Taxation Reconsidered.' In Sennholz, Mary (Ed.), *On Freedom and Free Enterprise. Essays in Honour of Ludwig von Mises.* New

Jersey, Toronto, London Nostrands Company: Princeton, New Jersey, Toronto, London, 265-284

Hernes, Helga (1987), The Welfare State Citizenship of Scandinavian Women. In Hernes, Helga (ed.), *Welfare State and Women Power. Essays in state Feminism.* Oslo

Hirdman, Yvonne (1990) in SOU 1990: 44, SOU 1990: 44 *Demokrati och makt i Sverige* (Democracy and Power in Sweden)

Kautto, M., Heikkilä, M., Hvinden, B., Marklund, S. and Ploug, N. (eds), (1999), *Nordic Social Policy. Changing Welfare States.* London: Routledge

Kautto, M. Fritzell, J., Hvinden, B., Kvist, J., Uusitalo, H. (eds), (2001), *Nordic Welfare States in the European Context.* London: Routledge

Kileos, Katrine (2009), Flight of the Swedish bumblebee. http://www.renewal.org.uk/articles/flight-of-the-swedish-bumblebee/

Korpi, Walter & Palme, Joakim (1993), *Socialpolitik, kris och reformer: Sverige i internationell belysning.* Stockholm: Universitet, Institutionen för social forskning

Kvist, Elin (2011), 'Changing social organizations of care through tax laws – European tax reforms promoting paid domestic work.', *European Journal of Ageing* nr. 3

Lahey, Kathleen, A. (2011), 'The 'Capture' of Women in Law and Fiscal Policy: Implications for the Tax/Benefit Unit, Gender Equality and Feminist Ontologies.' In Brooks, Kim, Gunnarsson, Åsa, Philipps, Lisa and Wersig, Maria (Eds.) *Challenging Gender Inequality in Tax Policy Making: Comparative Perspectives.* Oxford: Hart Publishing

McCaffery, Edward, J. (1997), *Taxing Women.* Chicago and London: The University of Chicago Press

Mumford, Ann (2010), *Tax Policy, Women and the Law.* Cambridge: Cambridge University Press

OECD, Forum (2011), *OECD Forum on Tackling Inequality,* Paris, Monday 2 May 2011, Growing Income Inequality in OECD Countries: What Drives it and How Can Policy Tackle It? www.oecd.org/els/social/inequality

Pakarinen, L. (2011). Finland-Individual Taxation. At: http://online.ibfd.org/collections/ita/printversion/ita_fi.html.

Philipps, Lisa (2001), 'Income Splitting and Gender Equality: The case for Incentivizing Intra-household Wealth Transfers.' In Brooks, Kim, Gunnarsson, Åsa, Philipps, Lisa and Wersig, Maria (Eds.), *Challenging Gender Inequality in Tax Policy Making: Comparative Perspectives.* Hart Publishing, 235-254

Prop. 1989/90: 110, om reformerad inkomst- och företagsbeskattning

Pylkkänen, Anu (2009), *Trapped in Equality. Women as Legal Persons in the Modernisation of Finnish Law.* Jyväskyllä

Sainsbury Diane (1996), *Gender, Equality, and Welfare States.* Cambridge: Cambridge University Press

Sainsbury, Diane (1999), (Ed.), *Gender and Welfare State Regimes.* Oxford: Oxford University Press.

Skatteverket Rapport 2007: 2, *Enklare skatter för ökad jämställdhet*

SOU 1995: 104, 1990-91 års skattereform – en värdering

SOU 2000: 83, Two of a Kind?– Economic Crisis, Policy Responses and Well-being during the 1999's in Sweden and Finland

Steinmo, Sven (2010), *The Evolution of Modern States.* Cambridge: Cambridge University Press

Stewart, Miranda (2011), 'Gender Equity in Australia's Tax System: A Capabilities Approach.' In Brooks Kim, Gunnarsson Åsa, Philipps L & Wersig M, (Eds.) *Challenging*

Gender Inequality in Tax Policy Making: Comparative Perspectives. Oxford, UK: Hart Publishing

Svensson, Eva-Maria, Gunnarsson, Åsa (2012), Gender Equality in the Swedish Welfare State. feminists@law, 2(1): 1-27

Vahlne Westerhäll, Lotta (1996), 'Rättigheter som grund för social trygghet.' *Retfaerd 75*

Vahlne, Westerhäll, Lotta (2002), *Den starka statens fall? En rättsvetenskaplig studie av svensk social* trygghet 1950-2000. Stockholm: Norstedts Juridik AB

Villota de, Paloma, Ferrari, Ignacio (2004), *Reflexiones sobre el IRPF la perspectiva de género: La Discriinación fiscal del/de la segundo/a preceptor/a.* Instituto de Estudios Fiscales, Universidad Complutense de Madrid

Villota de, Paloma (2011), 'A Gender Perspective Approach Regarding the Impact of Income Tax on Wage-earning Women in Spain.' In Brooks, Kim, Gunnarsson, Åsa, Philipps, Lisa, and Wersig, Maria (Eds.), *Challenging Gender Inequality in Tax Policy Making: Comparative Perspectives.* Oxford, UK: Hart Publishing

Wennberg, Lena (2008), *Social Security for Solo Mothers in Swedish and EU law. On the constructions of normality and the boundaries of social citizenship.* Uppsala: Iustus förlag

Wersig, Maria (2011), 'Overcoming the Gender Inequalities of Joint Taxation and Income Splititing: The Case of Germany.' In Brooks, Kim, Gunnarsson, Åsa, Philipps, Lisa, and & Wersig, Maria (Eds.) *Challenging Gender Inequality in Tax Policy Making: Comparative Perspectives.* Oxford, UK: Hart Publishing

PART II

Symbolic Change and Subversive Traditions: Changing Intimate Relations, Institutions and Legal Cultures

Restructuring Intimate Relations: Marriage, Cohabitation and Same-Sex Relations – a Scandinavian Perspective

Ingrid Lund-Andersen

1. Introduction

Denmark, *Norway* and *Sweden* constitute Scandinavia, and together with *Finland* and *Iceland* they constitute the Nordic countries. These countries have a shared tradition of trying to harmonise family law as they are neighbours and their cultures and social conditions are very similar.[1] Moreover, uniform laws are a great advantage as many Nordic people moves between these five countries.

Seen in a more global perspective, the Nordic countries have played an important role in the shaping of family laws in Europe. In particular, the Nordic registered partnership model has inspired the legislators in many countries.[2] Thus, the Danish Partnership Act from 1989 did not only change the

1. See in more detail Ingrid Lund-Andersen, 'Approximation of Nordic Family Law within the Framework of Nordic Cooperation', in Antokolskaia, M., (ed.): *Convergence and Divergence of Family Law in Europe*, Intersentia, 2007, pp. 51-61; and Peter Lødrup, 'The Reharmonisation of Nordic Family law', in Boele-Woelki, K. and Sverdrup, T., (eds): *European Challenges in Contemporary Family Law*, Intersentia, 2008, pp. 17-26.
2. Registered partnership acts for homosexual couples have among others been introduced in the Nederlands in 1997, in Germany in 2001 and in England, Wales, Scotland and Northern Ireland in 2004.

attitudes towards homosexual people in Denmark,[3] but also changed the attitudes all over the Western world.[4]

Contrary, the division of property between unmarried cohabitants on the termination of cohabitation is completely different in Denmark, Sweden and Norway. One important difference between the countries is whether a solution is based on the principles of property or whether special family law rules have been introduced for unmarried cohabitants. Likewise, there is a difference as to whether the legal status of unmarried cohabitants corresponds in whole or in part to that of married couples, or whether cohabitees are given a less extensive legal status. These differences are found elsewhere in Europe and in other places in the world. The legal regulations in the Scandinavian countries illustrate three of the most common approaches to the division of the property of cohabiting couples.

In this article, I will describe the recent changes in family law in Scandinavia as regards legislation on same-sex relations.[5] Further, I will give a review of the current state of the legal position of cohabitants in each of the three countries. In my conclusion, I will reflect on whether it would be possible to harmonise the law concerning cohabitants to a greater extent allowing each country to retain its special character.

2. Regulation of same-sex relations

	Registered Partnership Acts Introduced:	Registered Partnership Acts Repealed:	Gender neutral marriage Introduced:
Denmark:	1989	2012	2012
Norway:	1993	2009	2009
Sweden:	1994	2009	2009

3. Ingrid Lund-Andersen, "The Danish Registered Partnership Act, 1989: Has the Act Meant a Change in Attitudes?" in Wintemute, R. and Andenæs, M. (eds): *Legal Recognition of Same-Sex Partnerships*, Hart Publishing, 2001, pp. 417-426.
4. Eg. also in US, Canada, New Zealand and Australia.
5. The legal situation of same-sex relations and cohabitation in Finland and Iceland is described by Ingrid Lund-Andersen, "The Nordic Countries: Same Direction – Different Speeds", in Boele-Woelki and K., Fuchs, A., (eds): *Legal Recognition of Same-Sex Relationhips in Europe*, Intersentia, 2012, pp. 3-17.

2.1. Registered Partnership Acts

Denmark was the first of the Nordic countries to introduce a Registered Partnership Act for same-sex couples in 1989.[6] With a few exceptions, namely the right to get married in church, the right to adopt a child, and the right to joint custody of children, a registered partnership had the same legal consequences as marriage. The gender-specific provisions of Danish law applying to one of the parties in a marriage did not apply to registered partnerships.[7] Further, the provisions of international treaties did not apply to registered partnerships, unless the other parties to a treaty agreed to their application.

Similar Registered Partnership Acts followed in *Norway* in 1993,[8] in *Sweden* in 1994,[9] in *Iceland* in 1996,[10] and in *Finland* in 2001.[11] None of the Registered Partnership Acts has opened the door to heterosexual couples.

2.1.1. Adoption

The exceptions concerning children have been repealed by amendments to the Registered Partnership Acts.

In *Denmark*, as from 1 July 1999, it became possible to adopt a child of the other partner provided the child has not been adopted from abroad.[12] The consequence of such stepchild adoption is that the registered partners will have joint custody. Similarly to a spouse, a registered partner does not need approval from the authorities to adopt. The reason why the possibility of adopting a stepchild was introduced was because of the emergence of a new understanding of "the best interests of the child." First, it was pointed out that if a person living in a registered partnership has a child, that child might effectively have only one biological parent, either because the mother has not disclosed the name of the father to the authorities, or because the other parent has died. In these cases, the child will be in a less advantageous legal position than children in a marriage, both with regard to inheritance and divorce. Sec-

6. Act No 372/1989, with effect from 1 October 1989. The Act is described by Ingrid Lund-Andersen, 'The Danish Registered Partnership Act', in Boele-Woelki, K. and Fuchs, A., (eds.): *Legal Recognition of Same-Sex Couples in Europe*, Intersentia, 2003, pp. 13-23.
7. This refers to provisions concerning filiation and to a provision from the time when matrimonial law was based on a family pattern with a male breadwinner and a female housewife.
8. Act No 40/1993.
9. Act No 1117/1994.
10. Act No 87/1996.
11. Act No 95/2001.
12. Act No 360/1999.

ond, in those circumstances in which the bringing up of a child requires contact with the authorities, it would be important for the child that the registered partners should have the same legal status as other parents.

Four years later, *Sweden* took a major step when both stepchild adoption and joint adoption were allowed for registered partners. The reason for opening up joint adoption for homosexual couples was that an extensive study of children in homosexual families could not point to any differences with regard to development and the formation of gender identity between children growing up in homosexual families and those growing up in heterosexual families.[13] Consequently, couples that have entered into a registered partnership may be considered as adoptive parents in the same way as married couples. This means that two partners can adopt a child jointly, and one partner can adopt the other partner's child – whether biological or previously adopted. The same requirements for personal eligibility apply for registered partners as for married couples who wish to adopt. As regards international adoptions, the restrictions and conditions imposed by the child's country of origin apply.[14]

In *Norway*, since 2009 it has been possible for registered partners to apply to adopt according to the same rules as apply to heterosexual spouses. However, the adoption of a child of the other partner is not allowed if the child has been adopted from a country that does not allow adoption by same-sex partners.

And finally, in 2010, *Denmark* made it possible for registered partners to adopt jointly.[15] As with married couples, registered partners cannot adopt as a single person, apart from stepchild adoption. It is a condition that the foreign country agrees to the adoption of children by partners of the same sex.

2.2. Gender-neutral marriage

Since 2009, Denmark has been overtaken by developments in Norway and Sweden, as these two countries introduced gender-neutral marriage from 2009.

13. See Government Committee Report SOU 2001:10 on *Barn i homosexuella familjer* (Children in Homosexual Families).
14. See Family Law, *Information on the rules*, Regeringskansliet, 2009, p. 25.
15. See Act No 537/2010. During the preceding years, the possibility of allowing registered partners to adopt jointly had been discussed several times in Parliament. On the 17 March 2009, a majority voted in favour of a resolution ordering the Government to introduce a bill on foreign adoption by registered partners.

After a lengthy debate in the *Norwegian* Parliament, an amendment to the Marriage Act was enacted on 17 June 2008.[16] The amendment was adopted by 84 votes to 41. The new law gives homosexual couples the formal right to marry on the same basis as heterosexuals. According to Section 1 of the Marriage Act, two persons of opposite sexes or of the same sex may contract marriage. Previously registered partners can have their partnerships converted into a marriage. In such a case the partners must submit an application to the National Population Register. On the basis of the application the Register must register the partners as married and provide them with dated confirmation.[17] A registered partnership that is not converted remains in force, though the Registered Partnership Act has been repealed as being no longer necessary. It is no longer possible to establish a new registered partnership in Norway.

The amended Marriage Act entered into force on 1 January 2009, and in the first year 658 same-sex couples converted their registered partnerships into marriage. In the following year the number had declined significantly, and only 68 registered partners converted their registered partnerships into marriage. In 2010, 264 same-sex couples entered into marriage. More women (167 couples) than men (97 couples) contracted a marriage. The number of same-sex marriages was only a little higher in the year before. As regards the dissolution of same-sex marriages, in 2010, 29 couples were separated and 4 couples were divorced.[18]

Sweden was the next Nordic country to introduce gender-neutral marriage, and the amendment to the Marriage Act was adopted by 261 votes to 16.[19]

16. See Ot.prp. No 33 2007-2008 Om lov om endringer i ekteskapsloven, barneloven, adopsjonsloven, bioteknologiloven mv. (felles ekteskapslov for hetereofile og homofile par) (Common Marriage Act for heterosexual and homosexual couples). See John Aslan and Peter Hambro, "New Developments and Expansion of Relationships Covered by Norwegian Law", In Atkin, B. (ed.): *The International Survey of Family Law, 2009*, pp. 377-378.
17. See Section 95 of the Norwegian Marriage Act.
18. See http://www.ssb.no/ekteskap.
19. The grounds for the reform were laid down in a report of a government commissioned investigation, under the leadership of a specially appointed Commissioner, see Government Committee Report SOU 2007:17 on *Ätenskap för par med samma kön, Vigselsfrågor* (Same-sex marriage, the marriage ceremony). See more in detail Maarit Jäntera-Jareborg, "Sweden: The Same-Sex Marriage Reform with special Regard to Concerns of Religion", in *FamRZ 2010*, vol. 18, pp. 1505-1508; and Anna Singer, 'Equal Treatment of Same-Sex Couples in Sweden', in Atkin, B. (ed.): *The International Survey of Family Law, 2010*, pp. 397-399. See also about the development in

The new rules of the Marriage Act came into effect on 15 May 2009. The wording of Section 1 of the Swedish Marriage Act differs from the wording in the Norwegian Marriage Act, as the sex of the spouses is not mentioned. The Swedish Marriage Act states that two persons who enter into marriage with one another become spouses.

Previously registered partnerships may be converted into marriage. For this the partners have to apply jointly to the Swedish Tax Agency.[20] Instead of applying to convert a registered partnership into a marriage, a couple can choose to be married under Chapter 4 of the Marriage Code. No examination of the impediments to a marriage is required for marriage for this special ceremony. There is no period of limitation for converting a registered partnership into a marriage. In Sweden, 774 same-sex couples – more women (445 couples) than men (329 couples) – married in the first year, and 455 couples converted their registered partnership into marriage.

With regard to *Denmark*, there have been several proposals by non-government political parties favouring the extension of marriage to same-sex partners.[21] In autumn 2011, there was a shift in political power and the centre-right parties lost their majority. A Social Democrat was appointed prime minister and she supported a proposal for same-sex marriage. In June 2012, the Danish parliament passed a bill on same-sex marriage by 85 voters to 24.

The new rules came into force on 15 June 2012. The wording of Section 1 of the Marriage is nearly the same as the Norwegian. As in Norway and Sweden previously registered partners can have their partnerships converted into a marriage and the Registered Partnership Act was repealed. However, for the time being the legal consequences of a marriage between two persons of the same sex is the same as a registered partnership. The government has appointed a committee assigned to investigate the consequences of introducing same-sex marriage, especially concerning the rules on paternity.

3. Cohabitation

In the Scandinavian countries, unmarried cohabiting partners constitute about a quarter of all cohabiting relationships (married and unmarried) and about half of all children born have parents who live together without being mar-

general Anders Agell and Margareta Brattström, *Äktenskap Samboende Partnerskap*, Uppsala, 2011, pp. 290-295.

20. See Family Law, *Information on the rules*, Regeringskansliet, 2009, p. 25.
21. The latest proposal L 123 of 5 February 2010 was rejected 3 June 2010.

ried. In contradiction to the development in relation to legal recognition of same-sex partnerships, the legal situation concerning division of property between cohabitants is very different in the three countries.

3.1. Denmark

The solution in *Denmark* is based on case law and principles of property law. In 1980, the first case came before the Supreme Court.[22] The Court concluded that co-ownership cannot be established in cohabitation beyond the general rules on co-ownership. To protect the financially weaker party the Court ruled that the weaker party can make a claim for compensation if the stronger party has obtained enrichment. This includes both a property law assessment and a family law assessment.[23] According to a later decision from the Supreme Court the cohabitation cannot have been less than two and three – quarter years.[24] In a decision from 1984, the Supreme Court has established that compensation will require an extraordinary situation if a cohabitant has exclusively worked in the home bringing up children of the relationship.[25]

In a decision from 1985[26] the Supreme Court has synthesized its view on how to assess these cases in a sort of "rule":

> "Based on Supreme Court decisions in similar cases, especially those quoted in *Ugeskrift for Retsvæsen* (the Weekly Law Journal) 1980 p. 480 and 1982 p. 93, it must be considered as established law that when a long-lasting cohabitation is dissolved, a partner who, by contributing to the partners' shared expenses – or in other ways – has, to a considerable degree, made it possible for the other partner to create or maintain a not inconsiderable fortune, may be granted an amount, the size of which will be based on an assessment taking into consideration the length of the cohabitation, the partners' economic conditions etc."

In some cases a principle of reasonable expectations can support such an assessment.[27] The case law will also be relevant for homosexual couples who are not married or have registered their partnership.

22. See Ugeskrift for Retsvæsen (Weekly Law Journal) 1980.480 H.
23. See Ingrid Lund-Andersen, "The Legal Status of Cohabitants in Denmark", in Scherpe, J. and Yassari, N. (eds), *Die Rechsstellung nichtehelicher Lebensgemeinschaften, the Legal Status of Cohabitants*, Tübingen, 2005, pp. 459-463. See also Jørgen Nørgaard, "Højesteret og de ugifte samlevendes formueforhold", in special issue of Ugeskrift for Retsvæsen 1986, pp. 97-113, and Ingrid Lund-Andersen and Irene Nørgaard, *Familieret*, Copenhagen, 2012, pp. 327-332.
24. See Ugeskrift for Retsvæsen 1982.93 H.
25. See Ugeskrift for Retsvæsen 1984.166 H.
26. See Ugeskrift for Retsvæsen 1985.607 H.
27. See Ugeskrift for Retsvæsen 1984.166 H.

Apart from making this special family law claim for compensation, the financially weaker party can make a claim on the basis of the general property law such as on loan, gift and unjust enrichment.[28] A claim for enrichment may be possible if the claimant has made payments that are significantly different from the parties' allocation of their obligations, for example if one of them has repaid a large loan taken out by the other.[29] The amount will be allocated by a discretionary calculation. As a maximum it will be equal to the enrichment, and it may not exceed the loss of the person making the payment.

3.2. Sweden

Sweden introduced provisions for cohabitees when the Cohabitees (Joint homes) Act from 1987 was implemented.[30] The aim of the Act was to give the financially weaker party certain minimum rights as regards property and taking over a dwelling.[31] Law 1987: 813 on Homosexual Cohabitants refers to the Cohabitees (Joint homes) Act and puts homosexual couples on the same footing as heterosexual couples in many respects.

The Cohabitees (Joint homes) Act was replaced in 2003 by the new Cohabitees Act.[32] According to Section 1 of the Cohabitees Act "cohabitees" means two people who live together on a permanent basis as a couple and who have a joint household. The definition in the Act was changed in 2003. The new definition also allows for homosexual relationships, and there is a requirement that there should be joint housekeeping. In addition to the parties having to have certain common financial arrangements, there will also be an emphasis on whether there are children of the relationship, and whether they have the same address in the civil register. The couple should also have lived together for more than a short period, which is normally assumed to be more than 6 months.

28. See and Ingrid Lund-Andersen and Irene Nørgaard, *Familieret*, Copenhagen, 2012, pp. 326-327.
29. See Tidsskrift for Familie- og Arveret (Journal of Family and Succession law) 1999.185 Ø. See also Ugeskrift for Retsvæsen 1993.620 V.
30. Act No 232/1987 entered into force 1 January 1988.
31. For more detail on this Act see Eva Ryrstedt, "Legal Status of Cohabitants in Sweden", in Scherpe, J. and Yassari, N. (eds.): *Die Rechsstellung nichtehelicher Lebensgemainschaften, The Legal Status of Cohabitants*, Tübingen, 2005, pp. 415-428, and Margareta Brattström, "The Protection of a Vulnerable Party when a Cohabitee Relationship Ends – An Evaluation of the Swedish Cohabitees Act", in Verschagen, B. (ed.): *Family Finances*, Austria, 2009, p. 345 ff. See also Anders Agell and Margareta Brattström, *Äktenskap Samboende Partnerskap*, Uppsala, 2011, pp. 262-289.
32. Act No 376/2003 Cohabitees Act (Sambolagen).

Section 8(1) of the Cohabitees Act provides that if a cohabiting relationship comes to an end other than by the marriage of the cohabiting partners to each other, the value of the joint property is to be divided between them by a division of the estate if so requested by one of the parties within one year of the termination of the relationship.[33] It is not relevant for this purpose which of the parties owns the home.[34] According to Sections 4-7 of the Act, the joint property consists of the joint home and the household property of the cohabiting partners which is acquired during the cohabiting relationship for joint use. The basis for the division of these assets is that in establishing the joint home there is a financial community between the cohabitees. On the other hand, a holiday home, car, boat and bank deposits are not covered by the law. Real property that is inherited or received as a gift or in other circumstances linking the property to the recipient is not included in the division of the estate. Assets acquired prior to entering into the cohabiting relationship are also outside the scope of the Cohabitees Act. This can mean that a person who moves in with their partner does not acquire a share in the value of their property even after a long period of cohabitation. If real property is acquired prior to cohabitation, and if during the period of cohabitation a large extension is built, the extension is regarded as accessory to the property, and the whole of the property will still not be treated as part of the joint property.[35]

The general rules of property law apply in parallel with the Cohabitees Act. The arrangement of "covert joint ownership" (dold äganderätt) is particularly relevant. The courts can find that there is covert joint ownership of property that is acquired only in the name of one of the parties (the overt owner), if there is presumed to be an agreement, either express or tacit, to the effect that both partners are owners of the property. This does not concern an agreement in the ordinary sense, but rather a claim on the other party to be nominated as formal co-owner of the property. In theory, on the basis of the existing case law there are the following preconditions for assuming the existence of a covert agreement: 1) the property is acquired for joint use; 2) the covert owner has made a financial contribution for the acquisition; and 3) the

33. For further on the division of the estate, see Sections 12-14 of the Cohabitees Act.
34. The division of the estate does not cover substitutions, if for example there is a sale of household property and the proceeds are deposited in a bank account. This can seem inconsistent and allow the possibility of avoiding the intention of the law.
35. See the decision of the Supreme Court in Nytt juridisk arkiv (New legal records) 2004 p. 542.

formal owner recognizes that the financial contribution has been made out of a desire to be co-owner.[36]

The decisions on covert joint ownership are based on both property law and family law considerations. In the decided cases financial contributions have included obtaining a loan or a parcel of land at a favourable family price. It is not sufficient that the married or cohabiting partner who is not the formal owner merely pays other joint expenses.[37] Work which takes place exclusively in the home is also not regarded as being equivalent to a direct financial contribution.

Covert joint ownership can be relevant to property that falls outside the scope of the Cohabitees Act, for example a holiday home, or if a cohabitee has agreed not to be bound by the rules of the Cohabitees Act; see Section 5(2).

There are no reported cases in Sweden in which a cohabitant has been allocated an amount on the basis that the other partner has obtained an unjust enrichment.[38]

3.3. Norway

The *Norwegian* Joint Household Act was enacted in 1991.[39] The Act does not regulate the division of property, but gives a member of a household the right to take over the dwelling and household goods when the community dissolves. The market value of the property has to be paid. A household community is assumed to exist between two or more adults who, without being married, live under the same roof and jointly contribute for the necessities of

36. See Eva Ryrstedt, "Legal Status of Cohabitants in Sweden", in Scherpe, J. and Yassari, N. (eds): *Die Rechsstellung nichtehelicher Lebensgemainschaften, The Legal Status of Cohabitants*, Tübingen, 2005, pp. 429-430. Covert joint ownership is discussed in detail by Anders Agell, *Äganderätten til fastighet för maker och samboende*, 1985. See also Anders Agell and Margareta Brattström, *Äktenskap Samboende Partnerskap*, Uppsala, 2011, pp. 78-82. See the judgments in Nytt juridisk arkiv 1980.705, 1981.693 and 1982.589.
37. It is different with the acquisition of movable property, see the ruling of the Supreme Court in Nytt juridisk arkiv 1992.163, according to which joint ownership can be assumed to exist even where payment is made towards joint expenses and not directly for the purchase of the movable property in question.
38. See Anders Agell and Margareta Brattström, *Äktenskap Samboende Partnerskap*, Uppsala, 2011, p. 257.
39. Act No 45/1991.

life.[40] The Act applies to cohabiting couples who have, have had or expect a child together, or who have lived together for two years in the same residence.

According to the case law of the Supreme Court, since the mid 1970s the cohabitant who is not the formal owner of the family home and household property can be regarded as the co-owner, when the relationship ends. Co-ownership can be stated either on the grounds of their work in the home ('housewife co-ownership') or as a result of payment to the joint expenses.[41] If there are minor children of the relationship it will generally be assumed to be a sufficient measure of housewife contribution for there to be joint ownership. If the couple does not have children, there can be other factors that can lead to a finding of joint ownership, such as an unusually high degree of housewife contribution, or significant payments towards the joint expenses. In many cohabiting relationships the family's home and household goods will therefore be jointly owned.[42] This practice on joint ownership also applies to married couples. With the reform of the Marriage Act in 1991, a provision was included which confirmed the practice of the courts.[43] The Norwegian Committee on cohabitation has proposed that a similar provision should be introduced for cohabiting couples.[44]

In addition, a cohabitant can bring proceedings to be awarded an amount (a compensation claim) based on the general principles of unjust enrichment, restitution and equity. In order for a compensation claim to be recognized, some significant financial advantage must have been given to the cohabiting partner, and it must be judged reasonable to grant compensation.[45] The greater the financial advantage given, the more likely it is that compensation will be awarded.[46] Work in the home and work on the joint home will generally be regarded as a natural part of living together, and thus it will not lead to an

40. See Eva Ryrstedt, "Legal Status of Cohabitants in Norway", in Scherpe, J. and Yassari, N. (eds): *Die Rechsstellung nichtehelicher Lebensgemainschaften, The Legal Status of Cohabitants*, Tübingen, 2005, p. 442.
41. See Norsk Retstidende (Norwegian Law Journal) 1975.220 and 1977.533.
42. See Peter Lødrup and Tone Sverdrup, *Familieretten*, Oslo, 2011, pp. 339-345., Eva Ryhrstedt, "Legal Status of Cohabitants in Norway, in Scherpe", J. and Yassari, N. (eds.), *Die Rechsstellung nichtehelicher Lebensgemainschaften, The Legal Status of Cohabitants*, Tübingen, 2005, 443-446.
43. Section 31(3), Ekteskapsloven.
44. See NOU 1999:25 *Samboerne og Samfundet* (The Cohabitants and the Society) p. 24.
45. The conditions of unjust enrichment and reasonableness are cumulative, as stated in Norsk Retstidende 2000.1089.
46. Peter Lødrup and Tone Sverdrup, *Familieretten*, Oslo, 2011, pp. 348-355.

award of compensation. However, the performance of extensive care work can, in special circumstances, be considered significant, since the other cohabitant will thereby be saved the costs of professional care.[47] The assessment of reasonableness can include elements of family law, such as whether a cohabitant needs means to re-establish themselves. Conversely, the award of compensation would be less likely if a cohabitant has received some benefit from their contribution, such as living for a long period in a joint home after having contributed to the restoration of the home.[48] Two new judgments from the Supreme Court have stated that the requirements are high.[49] The Norwegian Committee on cohabitation proposed the introduction of a legislative rule on compensation claims for cohabiting couples.[50]

3.4. An example

In the *Danish* High Court, in a case in 2009, a woman was granted DKK 25,000 as compensation after 28 years of cohabitation during which she had paid for the housekeeping and for the two children of the relationship. She had also done the household tasks and cared for the children. In the District Court the woman had been awarded DKK 200,000.[51] The man had assets of DKK 2.2 million, consisting mainly of the property (DKK 1.7 million) in which the family had lived. The man had bought the property two years after the establishment of the cohabiting relationship.

If the case had been decided under *Swedish* law the woman would have been entitled to half the value of the joint home – DKK 850.000 – since it had been acquired during the period of cohabitation, cf. Sections 3 and 4 of the Cohabitees Act.

Under *Norwegian* Law, it must be assumed that, on the basis of an overall assessment, the woman would have been regarded as a co-owner of the property and would have received DKK 850.000.

3.5. Closing considerations

The Scandinavian countries have a long tradition for harmonizing their family laws. This is also the case with regard to the regulation of the same-sex relationships. Although the speeds have been different, the countries have been moving in the same direction.

47. See Norsk Retstidende 2000.1089.
48. See Norsk Retstidende 1984.497.
49. See Norsk Retstidende 2011.1168 and 2011.1176.
50. See NOU 1999:25 p. 24.
51. See Tidsskrift for Familie- og Arveret 2010.221 V.

Many conservatives have found that homosexual couples should not have legal rights concerning children. Therefore, the introduction of stepchild adoption in Denmark in 1999 was a giant step, as it became accepted that a child can have two mothers or two fathers. This step prepared the way for homosexual couples to have access to joint adoption.

The introduction of gender-neutral marriage in the three Scandinavian countries has not so much been a legal change as a change in terminology. However, gender-neutral marriage has been important as a symbol of full equality.

Comparing the legal situation of cohabitants in the three countries, it can be seen that in most cases the financially weaker party will be worst off in *Denmark*. This is illustrated by the above mentioned example in 3.4. Thus, in Danish law less account is taken to the community of the parties, so that from a family law point of view there must be said to be a minimum of protection. In Danish case law housework and care work are only coned significant in unusual situations, and there must generally be a significant financial contribution before a compensation claim will be granted.

The *Swedish* Cohabitees Act can be criticized for being too inflexible in focusing only on the date of acquisition of the property. The law also seems too narrow in only covering the joint home and household goods.

The *Norwegian* practice of joint ownership is the most family friendly, where consideration for the community of the parties is given decisive importance. In 1975 one of the justices of the Supreme Court justified his voting in favour of "housewife co-ownership" by stating that "to argue otherwise would be contrary to modern views of society and the sense of justice."

In viewing the future legal position of cohabitees from a Scandinavian perspective, harmonization in the form of identical rules is not likely. On the other hand, a greater degree of harmonization would be a realistic goal where, from an overall view, the considerations are the same. I suggest that this could be done in the following ways.

Norway and Denmark should introduce rules dealing with the financial relations between cohabitants upon the termination of their cohabitation. This has been proposed by both of the expert committees which have dealt with this question in the two countries.

This would mean that the *Norwegian* practice of joint ownership would be laid down in legislation, while clarifying some problems of definitions that have arisen in practice, so that the legal status of cohabitees would be more predictable. Moreover, rules on compensation should be introduced which would apply when joint ownership is not found to exist. These rules should be framed with regard to family law, starting from the position of the community of the parties and the special circumstances of families, including care for the children of a relationship.

The introduction of a rule on the division of property in *Denmark* could most naturally take the form of an equitable assessment, as was also proposed by the Committee on marriage in 1980.[52] This also corresponds to the approach adopted by the Supreme Court, where a claim for compensation is granted on the basis of an overall assessment and on the principles of unjust enrichment and reasonable expectations. In 1985, the Supreme Court formulated guidelines for such an assessment in the form of an equitable rule. In my view a rule should be framed on the basis of equitable criteria of family law and not, as in the case of the Supreme Court's rule, primarily on the basis of property law criteria. Regard for the community of the parties and the needs of children should therefore be central, which would mean that the amounts awarded would often be higher than they are today.

As for the situation under *Swedish* law, the financially weaker party could be in a better position if the Swedish Cohabitees Act were extended to cover additional kinds of property, as proposed by the Swedish Committee on cohabitation in 1999. Among other things, the Committee proposed that cars and boats should be within the scope of the law. The Cohabitees Act should also include a rule on equitable discretion, so that on the basis of family law considerations of the community of the parties, the financially weaker of the parties could be awarded a sum if that person does not obtain a share of the assets that are regarded as being the joint property.

The intention behind these proposals is to get away from the idea that only minimum rights for cohabitants should apply upon the termination of a cohabiting relationship. If legislation is based on family law concepts, then the interests of children of the relationship will also be protected so that an assessment can also ensure that they are given good conditions for growing up with both parents after the end of the cohabitation. In my view the protection of such interests means that the self-determination of the parties, in the form of freedom of contract, should be limited, at least so that the parties cannot contract out of the rules that are based on a discretionary assessment based on family law considerations. Finally, the introduction of a clearer definition of which cohabiting couples can rely on as regards the rules on the division of property could be considered. A possible definition could be that legislation could apply to cohabiting couples who have, have had or expect a child to-

52. Report No. 915, *Samliv uden ægteskab I* (Cohabitation without marriage I), Copenhagen, 1980.

gether, or who have lived together for two years in the same residence. This definition is known in other legislation in Norway[53] and in Denmark.[54]

Through these proposals the developments in the three Scandinavian countries would be harmonized to a much greater degree and harmonized more with developments in other parts of Europe (for example Scotland[55]), and countries such as New Zealand[56] and Australia[57] – countries which can be compared with Scandinavia culturally and socially.

53. See e.g. Section 1 of the Household Community Act 1991.
54. See e.g. Section 88 of the Succession Act 2007.
55. Family Law (Scotland) Act 2006, Sections 25-29, under which on several points cohabitants obtain a legal position that corresponds to that of married couples, including a presumptive rule on joint ownership of assets that are acquired for the joint household, and a rule on a discretionary division of the property upon termination of the cohabiting relationship or upon death. Cohabitants are defined on the basis of an assessment of the duration and nature of the cohabitation, the level of financial independence, and whether the couple has children together.
56. In 2001, the Matrimonial Property Act 1976 was changed to the Property (Relationship) Act 1976, so that the family property rights of cohabitees to a large extent correspond to those of married couples. The normal requirement is for the cohabitation to have lasted three years, unless there are children of the relationship, or unless one of the parties has made significant contributions to the relationship.
57. In 2008, the Federal Family Law Act 1975 was amended so that the rules on the division of property and matrimonial maintenance also apply to cohabitees who have lived together for two years or there are children of the relationship. In most Australian states cases are decided according to the Family Law Act 1975.

Legal Recognition of Same-Sex Couples in Denmark: from the First Debates to the Enactment of the Registered Partnership Act of 1989

Jose María Lorenzo Villaverde

Introduction

Denmark has introduced same-sex marriages recently, by the Act No. 532 of 12th June 2012. This is the latest step in the process of legal recognition of same-sex[1] couples. They may now marry, and that involves not only the practical effects (most of them already achieved with the registered partnership) but all the symbolism attached to the institution of marriage. Moreover, a religious ceremony in the Danish National Church is also available. This process started some decades before, when new family models different from the traditional heterosexual marriage for the purposes of procreation began to have presence in society. This article is aimed to provide an overview of this process, until the passage of the Registered Partnership Act (RPA) in 1989.

1. The expressions "same-sex marriage" or "gender-neutral marriage" are used indistinctly, acknowledging that the notion of "sex" refers to a biological category whilst "gender" is a social construct. See further Schuster, A.: "Gender and Beyond: Disaggregating Legal Categories" in Schuster (Ed.): *Equality and Justice: Sexual Orientation and Gender Identity in the XXI Century*, Editrice Universitaria Udinese srl, Udine, Italy, (2011), p. 31 ff.

Homosexuality as a matter of criminal law and the beginning of the LGBT[2] movement

In Denmark, like in most Northern Europe,[3] homosexual sexual acts were decriminalized during the 20th Century. This happened in the 30s by the Criminal Code No. 127 of 15th April 1930, entering into force in 1933. However, this Code set a different age of consent for heterosexual and homosexual sexual activities: 15 years old for the former and 18 years old for the latter.[4] Besides, there was a backlash in 1961, when the Parliament passed an Act popularly named as "Ugly Law"[5] which condemned the client of a same-sex prostitute under 21 to up to one year imprisonment. This provision caused a significant social reaction and was considered counterproductive, with no positive influence in homosexual prostitution[6] and hence, it was repealed in 1965. Finally, equalization of the age of consent for same and opposite-sex sexual acts was achieved in 1976, 15 years old.[7]

In the achievement of this decriminalization, the role and influence of the LGBT movement was decisive. The main association, *Landsforeningen for Bøsser og Lesbiske* (LBL),[8] was founded as early as 1948 with the name of Society of 1948 and registered in 1969, as National Association for Gays. It created offices in Norway and Sweden and launched magazines combating discrimination and fighting for visibility. However, LBL was not the only association. It is noteworthy to mention the existence of, on the one hand, the Gay Liberal Front, created in 1971 as a movement with socialist roots which supported an alternative lifestyle, collective families and social families as well as a feminist left-oriented movement which came to fill the space left by the more male/gay-based LBL.

2. Acronym for Lesbian, Gay, Bisexual and Transsexual people.
3. As opposed to those countries influenced by the Napoleonic Penal Code which decriminalised sodomy a century earlier. As Von Rosen points out, sodomy was considered "an unmanly <weakness> in the South, a biblical <abomination> in the North", Von Rosen, W.: "Denmark 1866-1976: From Sodomy to Modernity" in Rydström and Mustola (Ed.): *Criminally Queer: Homosexuality and Criminal Law in Scandinavia 1842-1999*, Aksant, Amsterdam, (2007), p. 84. As it is seen, focus was mainly on male homosexuality.
4. § 225.2 of the Criminal Code. The general age was, thus, 18, unless both persons were of similar age and understanding, where the penalty could be lifted.
5. Act No. 163 of 31st May 1961, amending the Criminal Code.
6. Von Rosen, W.: *Denmark 1866-1976: From Sodomy to Modernity, op.cit.* pp. 76-77.
7. Act No. 195 of 28th April 1976, amending the Criminal Code.
8. Now LGBT Denmark.

The LGBT movement was not united on what direction should be taken in order to combat discrimination within the field of family law. There were, basically, three possible alternatives.[9] The first one would be fighting in favour of total equality between same and opposite-sex couples. This option could be developed in two different and opposed ways: either by demanding gender-neutral marriage legislation or by completely abolishing marriage, which was seen by lesbian and leftist LGBT movements as a bourgeois legal institution. Both ways would seek the same result, but both responded to different ways of thinking. Fighting for marriage would involve an acceptance of an institution which, in spite of its transformations and modernization, still represented the traditional family and had a symbolic value. On the other hand, the abolishment of marriage responded to an alternative way of conceiving family life, in the wave of the left-wing movements in the 60s and 70s.

The second option involved a framework that would provide same-sex couples with the same rights married couples enjoyed, with some minor exceptions (a registration scheme). Finally, the third option would involve a piecemeal reform in some areas of law such as social law, tax law and inheritance law, etc.

LBL opted for the second option since 1973.[10] Same-sex marriage meant full equality but possibly strong opposition, and not only outside but also inside the LGBT movement by those who saw marriage as a patriarchal old-fashioned institution. A piecemeal approach or a regulation of cohabitation was also dismissed, as it would not solve most practical problems same-sex couples would face and it could be seen as a "compulsory marriage" for those who consciously wished to avoid the legal effects of the institution.[11] A registration scheme would diminish resistance and it would provide most of the legal effects of marriage to registered partners. This approach differed from that taken by the main Swedish LGBT association, *Riksförbundet för homo-*

9. See Hansen, B. and Jørgensen, H.: "The Danish Partnership Law: Political Decision Making in Denmark and the National Danish Organisation for Gays and Lesbians" in Hendriks, Tielman and Van Der Veen (Ed.): *The Third Pink Book*, Prometheus Books, Buffalo, New York, (1993), p. 90 ff and Skridge, W.N. and Spedale, D.R.: *Gay Marriage, for Better or for Worse? What We Have Learned from the Evidence*, Oxford University Press, Oxford, (2007), p. 47.
10. Skridge, W.N. and Spedale, D.R.: *Gay Marriage, for Better or for Worse? What We Have Learned from the Evidence, op.cit.* p. 47 and Søland, B.: "A Queer Nation? The Passage of the Gay and Lesbian Partnership Legislation in Denmark, 1989", *Social Politics*, Vol. 5, 1 (1998), p. 53.
11. Dahlsgård, I.: *Women in Denmark Yesterday and Today*, Det Danske Selskab, Copenhagen, (1980), p. 93.

sexuellas, bisexuellas och transpersoners rättigheter, (RFSL), supporting a maximalist position and full marriage as its goal.[12]

First attempts and the Marriage Committee of 1969

In the wave of the movements of 1968 and with growing interest in new forms of family life, like the collective families, but also same-sex couples, the Socialist People's Party (*Socialistisk Folkeparti*) introduced a proposal to regulate these other forms of family life different from marriage. The Socialist People's Party's proposal did not make a distinction between same-sex and opposite-sex couples and defined a "stable relationship" (*samlivsforhold*) as either a marriage, a marriage-like relationship or a big family.

The main features of this proposal were contained in its articles 21 and 22.[13] When two people over 21 years were cohabiting in a stable relationship for at least three years without any interruption of longer duration, either of the parties would be entitled to require recognition of such relationship by the Chief Administrative Officer. If there were opposition by one of the parties, recognition should be granted or denied by judgment. In order to provide evidence of the existence of the relationship, aspects like the existence of common property and household or the presence of common children would be taken into consideration. Recognition would not be granted in case of the existence of impediments to marry laid down in articles 4-6 of the proposal. However, the regulation was gender neutral. The effects of recognition were the same as married couples. The term "spouse" should be understood as including a partner in a cohabiting couple, unless otherwise provided.

The proposal aimed at providing a response to new family forms. It involved a departure from the words attributed to Napoleon that "*les concubines ignorant la loi, donc la loi ignore les concubines*", present in different Civil Codes in the 19th Century. In fact, the Socialist People's Party linked its proposal of regulation of cohabitation to the "common-law marriage."[14] The purpose was both protecting the weaker party and providing a legal frame-

12. Rydström, J.: "Legalizing Love in a Cold Climate: The History, Consequences and Recent Developments of Registered Partnership in Scandinavia", *Sexualities*, Vol. 11, 1-2 (2008), p. 197 ff.
13. *Folketingstidende 1968-69, Tillæg A,* sp. 966.
14. General comments to the proposal, *Folketingstidende 1968-69, Tillæg A*, sp. 971.

work for those couples who were not able to marry, namely "homophile couples", same-sex couples.[15]

The proposal was turned down. The main arguments against a comprehensive regulation of cohabitation were: 1) It would involve a "forced marriage", for those who do not wish to marry;[16] 2) It would undermine individual choice;[17] 3) the position of cohabitants may be improved by the amendment of specific legislation.[18] However, there were special references to the recognition of same-sex couples. The Minister rejected the idea of same-sex marriage as such, but other parties, like the Social Democrats (*Socialdemokratiet*), the Left-Socialists (*Venstresocialisterne*) and the Social-Liberals (*Radikale Venstre*), stressed the fact that same-sex couples, by not having access to marriage, could enjoy a more comprehensive regulation of their cohabitation, which would also have a symbolic value in order to undermine rejection and reinforce tolerance towards those couples and homosexuality as a whole.[19]

In spite of its rejection, the proposal had the effect of introducing same-sex couples into the political and legal debate as early as in 1968. The need of any sort of regulation had a positive response among some political groups, mainly on the left.

A Marriage Committee was established in 1969. It worked for more than a decade and issued nine reports from 1973 to 1983. In its very first report,[20] the Committee discussed the possibility of amending marriage law in order to include same-sex couples within its scope. Its answer was negative. It pointed out that, in its overwhelming opinion, marriage "must be between a man and a woman."[21] Some reasons were given.[22] First, they claimed that marriage is connected with tradition and same-sex marriages would involve a sharp rupture. Second, the possibility of lack of recognition abroad was also mentioned, as well as the possible negative impact on the consideration of Danish family law by other jurisdictions. Finally, it was argued that the problems of

15. Ibid, sp. 971-972.
16. In this way, the Minister of Justice Knud Thestrup and the rapporteurs of the parties in Government Social-Liberal Party (*Radikale Venstre*), Liberal Party (*Venstre*) and Conservative Party (*Konservativ*). *Folketingstidende, Forhandlinger I*, sp. 647, 656, 657, 659, 661 ff.
17. Venstre and Radikale Venstre, ibid, sp. 657-664.
18. Minister of Justice Knud Thestrup and the Social Democrats, ibid. sp. 636.
19. Ibid, pp. 650 and 659 ff.
20. Report 691/1973 (no. 1) *Ægteskababs indgåelse* (formation of marriage)
21. Ibid. p. 9.
22. Ibid. p. 19.

same-sex couples could be better solved by concrete amendments of the existing law (as couples who do not wish to make their relationship public would not get the benefits of marrying). There was a dissenting opinion in favour of allowing same-sex couples to marry. In summary, the arguments were: (religious) tradition,[23] international (private) law issues, possible forced "outing" for same-sex couples and numerical considerations about the amount of existing people in homosexual relationships.

The Committee rejected the possibility of opening marriage. However, the need for any kind of regulation for same-sex cohabitants, parallel to the regulation of opposite-sex *de facto* unions, was discussed. Two reports were issued on cohabitation, one in 1980[24] and another one in 1983.[25] The first one dealt with same-sex cohabitation.

The Committee expressly mentioned that LBL requested the modification of the rules on inheritance tax and housing with regards to same-sex couples and that LBL reported that the association was no longer interested in a "heterosexual pattern" marriage but in a registration scheme for partnerships.[26] Indeed, LBL sent a letter to the Marriage Committee on 15th July 1976[27] expressing their interest in a registered partnership for two people which would take place as suggested in the letter, regardless of their sex (hence, such registration scheme could be open to opposite-sex couples as well).[28] This LBL suggestion was due to practical considerations, as demanding marriage as such would face more obstacles and reluctance by parliamentary members, media and society as a whole.

23. The traditional Christian religious conception of marriage has undoubtedly left its footprint in the civil regulation of marriage, as one between a man and a woman with the major purpose of procreation. In a similar way, with regards to Sweden and the influence of the Church's values on marriage conceptions, see Sörgjerd, C.: *Reconstructing Marriage in a Changing Legal and Societal Landscape: Challenges of New Cohabitation Models in Sweden*, Uppsala Universitet, Uppsala, Sweden, (2011), p. 193 ff.
24. Report 915/1980 (no. 8) *Samliv uden ægteskab I* (cohabitation without marriage I).
25. Report 989/1983 (no. 9) *Samliv uden ægteskab II* (cohabitation without marriage II).
26. Report 915/1980 (no. 8) *Samliv uden ægteskab I* (cohabitation without marriage I), pp. 25-26.
27. *Skrivelse af 15. juli 1976 fra Forbundet af 1948 til Ægteskabsudvalget* (letter of 15th July 1976 from the Society of 1948 to the Marriage Commitee), as included in the appendix I of the Report 915/1980 (no. 8) *Samliv uden ægteskab I* (cohabitation without marriage I), p. 140.
28. And following their reluctance to the "economic relationship" marriage involves, LBL also suggested individual taxation for the proposed scheme.

The Committee, however, emphasized that solving those individual issues regarding inheritance tax and housing would diminish to a great extent the need for a comprehensive regulation of same-sex cohabitation.[29] The Committee made some general considerations[30] with regards to the need of any kind of regulation for cohabiting couples. In this sense, it reinforced the idea of marriage as the "best legal framework for family life" and hence, marriage should be made more attractive and cohabitation out of wedlock should not be more advantageous than marrying, particularly for tax purposes and social benefits. A comprehensive regulation of cohabitation would also have the consequence of imposing a statutory framework on couples who do not wish to, creating a "second-class marriage." Moreover, the Committee points out the difficulties of proving cohabitation. In this sense, any regulation on cohabitation, the Committee suggested, should be carried out by amending specific legislation, particularly in social and tax law.[31] In any case, these statements appear to apply to opposite-sex couples only because the "right not to marry" may only be invoked if the right to marry as such is applicable, and that was not the case for same-sex couples. However, the Committee, in spite analyzing them separately at times, did not distinguish between both kinds of couples in its conclusions: basically, the modification of specific legislation to improve the conditions of cohabitants, regardless their sex.

LBL's proposal on registered partnerships

LBL prepared a proposal on registered partnerships by a commission of experts.[32] LBL's proposal[33] was made up of ten chapters with seventy-six diffe-

29. Report 915/1980 (no. 8) *Samliv uden ægteskab I* (cohabitation without marriage I), p. 26.
30. Report 915/1980 (no. 8) *Samliv uden ægteskab I* (cohabitation without marriage I), pp. 48-51.
31. As Lund-Andersen has pointed out, amendments in specific legislation would not create a "second-class" marriage but, instead, a "third-class" one, Lund-Andersen, I.: "Legal Status of Cohabitants in Denmark" in Scherpe and Yassari (Ed.): *Die Rechtsstellung nichtehelicher Lebensgemeinschaften*, Mohr Siebeck, Tübingen, (2005), p. 456
32. It included lawyers, members of LBL, and other members of the organisation. Hansen, B. and Jørgensen, H.: *The Danish Partnership Law: Political Decision Making in Denmark and the National Danish Organisation for Gays and Lesbians, op.cit.* pp. 90-92 and Skridge, W.N. and Spedale, D.R.: *Gay Marriage, for Better or for Worse? What We Have Learned from the Evidence, op.cit.* p. 48

rent provisions. This gives an idea of the different conception of the proposal as compared to the brief final RPA which would finally be passed in 1989, with only seven articles referring to marriage law unless otherwise stated. Conversely, LBL's proposal was very detailed, with some relevant exceptions as compared to marriage law, particularly regarding the "economic relationship" between the partners. Hence, instead of deferred community of property, the general property regime would be separate property, unless agreed otherwise by the partners.[34] Moreover, no maintenance obligations would arise.[35]

Certainly, one of the reasons for this approach of "pick and choose" among the legal effects of marriage may have been not to undermine the heterosexual monopoly over marriage.[36] However, the main reason was linked to the above mentioned ideological position from some sectors within the LGBT movement against the economic dependency between spouses/partners and, as the comments to the proposal expressed, "we (the LBL) do not find common ownership compatible with the desire of emphasizing that there are two independent persons in a registered partnership."[37]

This "pick and choose" approach, the internal structure of the proposal and the detailed description of the provisions, in number and length, resemble the same technique that would be used more than two decades later in the United Kingdom when the Civil Partnership Act of 2004 was passed.[38] Such technique has the advantage of providing a comprehensive regulation for same-sex couples, but it has the inconvenience of its lack of flexibility, as any amendment of marriage legislation would probably lead to an amendment of the legislation on registered partnerships.

This technique was finally dismissed in Denmark. In this way, the bill introduced by the Social-Liberal Party in 1984[39] contained only four provisions referring to marriage legislation with no distinctions with regards to registra-

33. The proposal is found in the Appendix 2 of the Report 1127/1988 *Homoseksuelles Vilkår* (The conditions of homosexuals), pp. 169-185.
34. Cfr. § 5 and 16 of the proposal.
35. § 8 of the proposal.
36. Hansen, B. and Jørgensen, H.: *The Danish Partnership Law: Political Decision Making in Denmark and the National Danish Organisation for Gays and Lesbians, op.cit.* p. 92
37. Comments to Chapter 4, Report 1127/1988 *Homoseksuelles Vilkår* (The conditions of homosexuals), p. 172.
38. For a detailed overview of the British Civil Partnership Act of 2004, see Gray, N. and Brazil, D.: *Blackstone's Guide to the Civil Partnership Act 2004*, Oxford University Press, Oxford (2005).
39. *Folketingstidende, tillæg A*, 1983-84, sp. 3489-3492.

tion, legal effects and dissolution. The content of the proposal of a registration scheme by the Social-Liberals would be exactly the same as marriage, save in name, in an "equal but different" outfit.[40] In any case, LBL's proposal opened a debate and influenced the establishment of a commission "to elucidate the circumstances of homosexuals in the society in Denmark"[41] (the HomoCommission).

The Report on "The Conditions of Homosexuals" of 1988 and the RPA

The HomoCommission was proposed by parties from left and centre of the parliamentary spectrum, the Social Democrats, the Socialist People's Party and the Social-Liberals. It was composed of public servants representing the relevant ministries, two representatives from LBL, one from the Danish Women's Society, the judge Svend Danielsen as vice-chairman and the former spokesperson of the Socialist People's Party, Poul Dam, as chairman.[42]

Its mandate was broad:[43] carrying out research on legal, social and cultural conditions of homosexuals and proposing measures and amendments in the law with the aim of eliminating discrimination and improving the situation of homosexuals.

The HomoCommission had in mind the experience of the Swedish commission to investigate the conditions of homosexuals, appointed by the Swedish government in 1978, as an example to follow. Its results, published

40. In a similar way, Søland, B.: "A Queer Nation? The Passage of the Gay and Lesbian Partnership Legislation in Denmark, 1989", *op.cit.* p. 55
41. *Folketingstidende, Tillæg A*, 1983-1984, sp. 3677-3682.
42. Hansen and Jørgensen point out that the Minister, the conservative Ninn-Hansen, used a series of strategies to secure a majority in a commission which was not considered desirable by the conservative government in power at that time, see Hansen, B. and Jørgensen, H.: *The Danish Partnership Law: Political Decision Making in Denmark and the National Danish Organisation for Gays and Lesbians, op.cit.* p. 94. However, it is significant to mention that Poul Dam was member of the Socialist People's Party. See further, Scherpe, J.M.: "The Nordic Countries in the Vanguard of European Family Law", *Scandinavian Studies in Law*, Vol. 50, (2007), pp. 267-268.
43. *Folketingstidende, Tillæg A*, 1983-84, sp. 3677-3678.

in 1984,[44] were the starting point of the Swedish Homosexuals Cohabitees Act of 1987.[45]

The main report issued by the HomoCommission is the one on "the conditions of homosexuals" in 1988,[46] but it was not the only one. Some interim reports were published: one on homosexual lifestyles, problems and proposals;[47] a chapter on discrimination which led to an Act amending some pieces of legislation[48] and, also, a report on inheritance tax,[49] suggesting that a same-sex surviving partner should pay the same as a the survivor spouse which led to an amendment of the inheritance tax legislation.[50]

The HomoCommission, in its report of 1988, considered that the starting point of any proposal of registered partnership should be marriage law. In this way, the HomoCommission's idea of a registered partnership was closer to the Social-Liberal Party's proposal in 1984 as opposed to the detailed "pick and choose" LBL's proposal, though with more restrictions than the former. The HomoCommission prepared two drafts for an eventual introduction of a registered partnership: one for an act introducing a registration scheme and another one for an act adapting some provisions of marriage law in order to provide coherence to the whole system. For instance, being part of a registe-

44. Committee Report (SOU 1984:63): *Homosexuella och samhället* (homosexuals and society).
45. For further knowledge on the Swedish Committee and its approach, see Bradley, D.: *Family Law and Political Culture: Scandinavian Laws in Comparative Perspective*, Sweet & Maxwell, London, (1996), pp. 101-105; Sörgjerd, C.: "Neutrality: the Death or the Revival of the Traditional Family? Regulating Informal Partnerships in Sweden" in Boele-Woelki (Ed.): *Common-Core and Better Law in European Family Law*, Intersentia, Antwerp, (2005), pp. 341, 346 ff; Sörgjerd, C.: *Reconstructing Marriage in a Changing Legal and Societal Landscape: Challenges of New Cohabitation Models in Sweden, op.cit.* p. 202 ff; Rydström, J.: *Odd Couples: A History of Gay Marriage in Scandinavia*, Aksant, Amsterdam, (2011), p. 50 and ff; Skridge, W.N. and Spedale, D.R.: *Gay Marriage, for Better or for Worse? What We Have Learned from the Evidence, op.cit.* p. 68 ff.
46. Report 1127/1988 *Homoseksuelles Vilkår* (The conditions of homosexuals)
47. Appendix 1 of the Report 1127/1988 *Homoseksuelles Vilkår* (The conditions of homosexuals), pp. 139-168.
48. Act 357 of 3rd June 1987, amending the Criminal Code and the Act prohibiting discrimination on the grounds of race, among others [prohibition against discrimination on the grounds of sexual orientation])
49. Report 1065/1986, *Homoseksuelle og arveafgift* (Homosexuals and Inheritance Tax)
50. Act 339 of 4th June 1986 amending the Act on taxes on inheritance and gifts [relaxation of inheritance tax to cohabiting siblings and cohabiting same-sex couples]). This Act was repealed with the introduction of the RPA in 1989, see Elmer, M. and Lund Larsen, M.: "Familieretlige lovændringer i 1989", *Juristen*, Vol. 3, (1990), p. 137

red partnership would become an impediment to marriage and considered within the criminal offence of bigamy.

Some significant points were laid down in the report:

– The introduction of a registered partnership[51] involves the introduction of a new legal institute.[52] This assumption has some consequences: first, it involves a new civil status for those registered couples, and second, it means a departure from marriage, as limited to opposite-sex couples. Hence, there is not a breach of tradition but, on the other hand it does not constitute recognition of cohabitation as the Swedish Homosexuals Cohabitees Act of 1987 does. It is a *tertium genus*, different from cohabitation and marriage, with all the consequences this will have not only from a Danish internal point of view but, very remarkable, from an international private law perspective.

- A fact that reinforces the idea that a registration scheme is a *tertium genus* (different from the SF proposal of 1969, for instance) is that the registration is constitutive of the partnership, and not declarative of an existing relationship. The HomoCommission proposed that registering should not require that the couple should live together.[53]
- Marriage shall not be entered into if one of the future spouses is part of a registered partnership. The new legal institute would appear as an impediment to marry and marriage as an impediment to register.[54]
- There was a concern with regards to the eventual lack of legal recognition of a registered partnership abroad, mostly on the ground of *ordre public* in the hosting State. Private international law issues, particularly with regards to recognition and registration, were, therefore, discussed by the Commission.[55] In particular, in order to avoid sham registrations, it was suggested that at least one of the partners should be domiciled in Denmark (as opposed to marriage where such connecting factor has never existed).[56]
- A Church ceremony, it was suggested, should be excluded for registered partners and, consequently, also the mediation by a priest used.[57]

51. Term that the HomoCommission support because LBL had been used it for a long time and because it was a short and easy term.
52. Report 1127/1988 *Homoseksuelles Vilkår* (The conditions of homosexuals), p. 114.
53. Ibid, p. 115.
54. Ibid. pp. 112-113, 115 and 117.
55. Ibid, pp. 115-116.
56. Ibid. pp. 118.
57. Ibid, p. 120.

- As for the dissolution, and taking into account that the new legal institution was not known in any other country, a *forum necessitatis* was established so that, regardless the rules on procedure applicable to marriage, a Danish court would always be competent to dissolve a Danish registered partnership.[58]

Arguments in favour and against the registered partnership within the HomoCommission

The HomoCommission rejected the idea of a partnership for six votes (including Poul Dam, the chairman) against five.[59]

In favour,[60] the minority pointed out that:

- It would favour visibility of homosexual people in society because of its symbolic value, impossible to achieve by specific cohabitation legislation or by general amendments in antidiscrimination law
- The introduction of a registered partnership dos not change the status of those couples wishing to cohabit without registering. Hence, the minority did not support an act on cohabitation similar to the Socialist People's Party's proposal of 1969 because it would undermine freedom of choice. To this extent, a registration scheme was intended to be closer to marriage than to cohabitation.
- Specific amendments in certain laws are unable to achieve the same results and they would involve more bureaucracy and paperwork than a simple registration.

Against,[61] the following arguments were used by the majority:

58. Ibid, pp. 111 and 120.
59. The majority consisted of Ville Budtz (Ministry of Social Affairs), Poul Dam (member of Parliament), Svend Danielsen (judge), Marianne Levy (Ministry of Justice) Kamma Struwe (Ministry of Education) and Lone Ømann (Ministry of Cultural Affairs). The minority was composed by Per Kleis Bönnelycke, Mikkel Emborg (LBL), Preben Hertoft (consultant), Helle Jarlmose (Danish Women's Society) and Henning Jørgensen (LBL). Those who voted against were, mostly, members of the Government.
60. Ibid, pp. 122-125.
61. Ibid, pp. 125-128.

- The need for a registered partnership was not proven because the number of homosexuals was unknown.
- The need for a registered partnership was not proven because one could assume that many same-sex couples wished to hide their relationship and would not benefit from a registration scheme.
- The need for a registered partnership was not proven because it was assumed that different gender roles in opposite-sex marriages have no parallel in same-sex couples and, therefore, there is no relevant need to protect the weaker party.
- The problems same-sex couples face may better be solved by legislation on cohabitation, a situation "about 20 % of all heterosexual couples have voluntarily subjected themselves [to]."[62]
- Finally, the possibility of foreign reactions against Danish registered partnerships (and against the Danish family law as a whole) was emphasized.

The three first arguments are easily challengeable as they are based on presumptions, as the majority actually admits, instead of based on a thorough research on those areas.[63] With regards to the fourth argument, Denmark, unlike Sweden, did not and does not have a comprehensive regulation on cohabitation and, in any case, opposite-sex couples would still enjoy a choice same-sex couples would not. Regarding the last argument, no further explanations were given on how those reactions against Danish law could eventually be shaped in practice.

The introduction of the RPA in 1989

As mentioned, the HomoCommission rejected the introduction of a registration scheme. However, LBL continued to lobby in favour of it among the political parties more keen on the proposal: the Social Democrats, Socialist Pe-

62. Report 1127/1988 *Homoseksuelles Vilkår* (The conditions of homosexuals), p. 127.
63. In this sense, it is interesting to point out that the Swedish Commission of 1978 achieved the conclusion that "the only certain difference between homosexuals and heterosexuals is that homosexuals are emotionally drawn to persons of the same sex. In the light of this it is self-evident that homosexuals shall not be discriminated against", Committee Report (SOU 1984:63): *Homosexuella och samhället* (homosexuals and society), p. 19, as translated by Caroline Sörgjerd, cfr. Sörgjerd, C.: *Reconstructing Marriage in a Changing Legal and Societal Landscape: Challenges of New Cohabitation Models in Sweden, op.cit.* p. 202.

ople's Party and the Social-Liberals. Those three parties held the majority in the Danish parliament.

The proposal[64] was similar to the model prepared and rejected by the HomoCommission.[65] It resembled marriage with some main exceptions. Church ceremonies were excluded and at least one of the partners should be domiciled in Denmark. Regarding the legal effects, no rights on adoption were granted. Finally, a *forum necessitatis* was established if a registered couple wished to dissolve their partnership and rules on priest mediation were also excluded. Moreover, the Act would not be applicable to Greenland and the Faroe Islands, unless brought into force in those territories by Royal Decree.

The bill was introduced twice in 1988, due to the call for the elections the very same year, and the debates in the Parliament were heated and passionate.[66]

It is relevant to note two things: first, the role of the minority party Christian People's Party (*Kristelig Folkeparti*), and its role in the passage of the bill. The fiercest opposition came from this small party which represented fundamental Christian views and the rejection of the bill was its main issue in the campaign of 1988.[67] Following its Christian ideology, marriage should be reserved for opposite-sex couples. However, it is noteworthy that such legislation would introduce a completely new legal institute and, hence, the institution of marriage would not comprehend same-sex couples, in spite of the similarities between both. In any case, and regardless of its importance as a party in the governmental coalition, it only held four seats in Parliament.

Second, it is also important to take into account the role of another political party, the Progress Party (*Fremskridtsparti*)[68] in the passage of the bill. The original proposal's requirement for a couple to register in Denmark was that at least one of them should be domiciled in the country. However, FP proposed that both of them should be Danish citizens. Even though Social

64. *Lovforslag nr. L. 117, Folketingstidende 1988-89, Tillæg A*, sp. 2937-2938.
65. *Lovforslag nr. L. 117, Folketingstidende 1988-89. General Remarks*, sp. 2941.
66. For detailed account of the political debates around the partnership, see Skridge, W.N. and Spedale, D.R.: *Gay Marriage, for Better or for Worse? What We Have Learned from the Evidence, op.cit.* pp. 50-57; Albæk, E.: "Political Ethics and Public Policy: Homosexuals between Moral Dilemmas and Political Considerations in Danish Parliamentary Debates", *Scandinavian Political Studies*, Vol. 26, 3 (2003), pp. 251-256; Søland, B.: "A Queer Nation? The Passage of the Gay and Lesbian Partnership Legislation in Denmark, 1989", *op.cit.* p. 56 ff.
67. Albæk, E.: "Political Ethics and Public Policy: Homosexuals between Moral Dilemmas and Political Considerations in Danish Parliamentary Debates", *op.cit.* p. 252.
68. The current right-winged nationalist Danish People's Party (*Dansk Folkeparti*) is a split from the Danish Progress Party in 1995.

Democrats were keen on that requirement, LBL maintained a strong position: if the double requirement of nationality was to be kept, they would lobby against the proposal among the other political parties.[69] Finally, the requirement included in the Act was that at least one of the parties should be Danish citizen domiciled in Denmark (the situation of the other party would not be taken into consideration in this regard). The reason behind these requirements was preventing Denmark from becoming a new Las Vegas,[70] but also the possible lack of recognition of registered same-sex couples abroad.[71] Such requirement, which was copied, *mutatis mutandis*, in the registered partnership acts of the other Nordic countries, it was argued, may be connected with considerations of "national identity."[72] Whatever the case, it could have amounted to discrimination on the grounds of nationality from an EU law perspective.[73] More than twenty years after the RPA was approved, the fear of a "Danish gay heaven" has proven to be unrealistic.

Finally, the RPA was passed with 71 votes in favour, 47 against, 5 abstentions and entered into force the 1st of October of 1989.[74] As above mentioned, it resembled marriage with the following main exceptions (as a summary):

- Registration: at least one of the partners should have Danish nationality and domicile in Denmark; no registration in the Church was allowed.

69. I want to thank Steffen Jensen, spokesperson of LGBT Denmark, for providing me with this information.
70. See, *inter alia*, Albæk, E.: "Political Ethics and Public Policy: Homosexuals between Moral Dilemmas and Political Considerations in Danish Parliamentary Debates", *op.cit.* p. 256; Lund-Andersen, I.: "Cohabitation and Registered Partnership in Scandinavia: The Legal Position of Homosexuals" in Eekelaar and Nhlapo (Ed.): *The Changing Family. International Perspectives on The Family and Family Law*, Hart Publishing, (1998), p. 399.
71. See, *inter alia*, Pedersen, M.H.: "Denmark: Homosexual Marriages and New Rules Regarding Separation and Divorce", *Journal of Family Law*, Vol. 30, (1991-1992), p. 290; Jeppesen De Boer, C.G. and Kronborg, A.: *Registered Partnership in Denmark: Danish National Report*, IVIIIth Congress of the International Academy of Comparative Law, Washington, (2010), p. 4.
72. Rydström, J.: *Odd Couples: A History of Gay Marriage in Scandinavia, op.cit.* p. 11.
73. See, *inter alia*, Broberg, M.P.: "The Registered Partnership for Same-Sex Couples in Denmark", *Child and Family Law Quarterly*, Vol. 8, 2 (1996), pp. 151-152; Sloane, C.A.: "A Rose by Any Other Name. Marriage and The Danish Registered Partnership Act", *Cardozo Journal of International and Comparative Law*, Vol. 5, (1997), p. 205
74. Act No. 372 of 7th June 1989 on register partnership. Members of Parliament from the different political parties were given free vote, which is very seldom and it only happens when discussing issues related to ethics and morals.

- Legal effects: the whole regulation regarding children and parenthood would not be applicable to registered partners; provisions referring to the spouses by their gender, as husband and wife, would not be applicable to registered partners: provisions on international treaties would not be applicable to registered partners, unless otherwise provided.
- Dissolution: a *forum necessitatis* was established and, some months later, priest mediation in case of separation and divorce was also excluded.[75]

Conclusions

Since 1989, the exceptions regarding children, requirements of nationality and domicile and religious ceremonies have been lifted. Registered partners were allowed stepchild adoption ten years after the passage of the RPA, in 1999[76] and joint adoption eleven years later.[77] The requirements of nationality and domicile were softened with the passage of the time[78] but not totally eliminated with regards to the RPA. Only the introduction of gender-neutral marriage law equalized those requirements and now not only opposite-sex but also same-sex couples who are lawfully present[79] in the country are allowed to marry. The same may be said regarding a religious ceremony, only possible once same-sex marriage was introduced in 2012, although registered partners were able to have a blessing in the Danish National Church since 1997.[80]

The Act No. 532 of 12th June 2012 on same-sex marriages repealed the RPA. However, even though same-sex couples may no longer register, but

75. Act 821 of 19th December 1989 amending the Act on registered partnerships. In the general comments to this Act, it was stated that: "it is thus reasonable to assume it was not intended that priests should assist in the dissolution of registered partnerships. Moreover, on religious grounds some priests feel that they cannot or should not participate in the mediation between two registered partners. Thus, in the view of the Ministry of Justice it is not reasonable for society to put priests in such a situation where there is a conflict of conscience."
76. Act No. 360 of 2nd June 1999.
77. Act No. 537 of 26th May 2010.
78. Thus, Act No. 360 of 2nd June 1999 and Act No. 446 of 9th June 2004.
79. § 11.a and §11.b of the Consolidated Act on Formation and Dissolution of Marriage No. 38 of 15th January 2007.
80. Report on Registered Partnerships, Cohabitation and Blessings, Århus, May 1997 and Report on the Danish National Church and Registered Partnership, Ministry for Ecclesiastical Affairs, 2010.

only marry, the RPA is still in force for those couples already registered who do not wish to convert their register partnership into marriage. However, it is still possible to register in Greenland.[81] Same-sex marriages are only possible in mainland Denmark, although Greenland is likely to implement the new legislation. The current picture of the Realm is: same-sex marriage is in force in mainland Denmark (and also the RPA for those couples already registered); RPA is in force in Greenland (but same-sex couples are not yet able to marry there); no legislation recognizing homosexual couples is in force in Faroe Islands. This situation may lead to practical problems of private interprovincial/interregional law.

Denmark started the debate on legal recognition of same-sex couples early if compared to other European countries. The new legal institute created in Denmark, the "registered partnership", was exported to the rest of the Scandinavian and some European countries. It has played a major role in combating discrimination on the grounds of sexual orientation in Denmark and it has been an example for many other jurisdictions. In this sense, it has been a first milestone, the fire which switched on the engine of the process of legal recognition of same-sex couples in the (Western) World.

Reference list

Albæk, E.: "Political Ethics and Public Policy: Homosexuals between Moral Dilemmas and Political Considerations in Danish Parliamentary Debates", *Scandinavian Political Studies*, Vol. 26, 3 (2003)

Bradley, D.: Family Law and Political Culture: Scandinavian Laws in Comparative Perspective, Sweet & Maxwell, London, (1996)

Broberg, M.P.: "The Registered Partnership for Same-Sex Couples in Denmark", *Child and Family Law Quarterly*, Vol. 8, 2 (1996)

Dahlsgård, I.: *Women in Denmark Yesterday and Today*, Det Danske Selskab, Copenhagen, (1980)

Elmer, M. and Lund Larsen, M.: "Familieretlige lovændringer i 1989", *Juristen*, Vol. 3, (1990)

Gray, N. and Brazil, D.: *Blackstone's Guide to the Civil Partnership Act 2004*, Oxford University Press, Oxford, (2005)

Hansen, B. and Jørgensen, H.: "The Danish Partnership Law: Political Decision Making in Denmark and the National Danish Organisation for Gays and Lesbians" in Hendriks, Tielman and Van Der Veen (Ed.): *The Third Pink Book*, Prometheus Books, Buffalo, New York, (1993)

81. The RPA was implemented in Greenland by Royal Decree No. 320 of 26th April 1996.

Jeppesen De Boer, C.G. and Kronborg, A.: *Registered Partnership in Denmark: Danish National Report*, IVIIIth Congress of the International Academy of Comparative Law, Washington, (2010)
Lund-Andersen, I.: "Legal Status of Cohabitants in Denmark" in Scherpe and Yassari (Ed.): *Die Rechtsstellung nichtehelicher Lebensgemeinschaften*, Mohr Siebeck, Tübingen, (2005)
Lund-Andersen, I.: "Cohabitation and Registered Partnership in Scandinavia: The Legal Position of Homosexuals" in Eekelaar and Nhlapo (Ed.): *The Changing Family. International Perspectives on The Family and Family Law*, Hart Publishing, (1998)
Pedersen, M.H.: "Denmark: Homosexual Marriages and New Rules Regarding Separation and Divorce", *Journal of Family Law*, Vol. 30, (1991-1992)
Rydström, J.: "Legalizing Love in a Cold Climate: The History, Consequences and Recent Developments of Registered Partnership in Scandinavia", *Sexualities*, Vol. 11, 1-2 (2008)
Rydström, J.: Odd Couples: A History of Gay Marriage in Scandinavia, Aksant, Amsterdam, (2011)
Scherpe, J.M.: "The Nordic Countries in the Vanguard of European Family Law", *Scandinavian Studies in Law*, Vol. 50, (2007)
Schuster, A.: "Gender and Beyond: Disaggregating Legal Categories" in Schuster (Ed.): *Equality and Justice: Sexual Orientation and Gender Identity in the XXI Century*, Editrice Universitaria Udinese srl, Udine, Italy, (2011)
Skridge, W.N. And Spedale, D.R.: Gay Marriage, for Better or for Worse? What We Have Learned from the Evidence, Oxford University Press, Oxford, (2007)
Sloane, C.A.: "A Rose by Any Other Name. Marriage and The Danish Registered Partnership Act", *Cardozo Journal of International and Comparative Law*, Vol. 5, (1997)
Søland, B.: "A Queer Nation? The Passage of the Gay and Lesbian Partnership Legislation in Denmark, 1989", *Social Politics*, Vol. 5, 1 (1998)
Sörgjerd, C.: Reconstructing Marriage in a Changing Legal and Societal Landscape: Challenges of New Cohabitation Models in Sweden, Uppsala Universitet, Uppsala, Sweden, (2011)
Sörgjerd, C.: "Neutrality: the Death or the Revival of the Traditional Family? Regulating Informal Partnerships in Sweden" in BOELE-WOELKI (Ed.): *Common-Core and Better Law in European Family Law*, Intersentia, Antwerp, (2005)
Von Rosen, W.: "Denmark 1866-1976: From Sodomy to Modernity" in Rydström and Mustola (Ed.): *Criminally Queer: Homosexuality and Criminal Law in Scandinavia 1842-1999*, Aksant, Amsterdam, (2007)

Same-Sex Marriage in Denmark and Legal Culture

Theis Munthe-Brun

Despite being the first country in the world to legally recognize same-sex couples, Denmark is dragging its legislative feet in abolishing the legal difference between opposite-sex marriage and same-sex partnership. This stands in contrast to opinion polls from as far back as 2003 that show a large majority in favour of same-sex marriage.[1] Also, several countries that Denmark usually compares itself with have already adopted same-sex marriage legislation such as Sweden, Norway and The Netherlands. It would be tempting to conclude that being the first to legally acknowledge same-sex couples, Denmark would also be among the first to legalize same-sex marriage. This, however, has turned out not to be true. Instead, a political and public debate has slowly been simmering for ten years on whether the church should be forced to perform same-sex weddings and whether the meaning of the traditional word for marriage, 'ægteskab', should be reserved for opposite-sex couples. Contrary to expectations, the new centre-left government that took power in the fall of 2011, whose parties have traditionally been supporters of gay and lesbian rights, did not swiftly pass same-sex marriage but instead compelled the Danish Lutheran Church to begin formulating a ritual for same-sex weddings.

Danes often see themselves at the vanguard of social justice, as a country where progressive secular thinking ensures not just equal rights but equal rights to a decent living standard.[2] Although Denmark in some ways is, the

1. 'Homosexual marriage, child adoption by homosexual couples: Is the public ready?' *EOS Gallup Europe* http://www.rklambda.at/dokumente/news_2003/News-PA-031015-Gallup-Umfrage-Text.pdf
2. Rydström, Jens, *Odd Couples. A History of Gay Marriage in Scandinavia* (Aksant: Amsterdam, 2011) p. 28, l. 27-28.

same-sex marriage situation reveals that it is not always the case and that legal rights do not necessarily follow popular support even in a supposedly progressive Scandinavian state. This supposed inconsistency merits a closer look at the legal culture in Denmark in relation to same-sex marriage.

The Legal System as a Process & Feminist Legal Theory

Lawrence Friedman presents in his article, 'Legal Culture and Social Development', a definition of the legal system as a process that proposes a general analytical framework for examining law and social change. Friedman explains how a conventional understanding of the legal system classified according to families of law with similar traits stresses a historical-evolutionary method which only yields typology.[3] In order to study how legal systems work, he argues, we need to look instead at 'what legal institutions do and how they do it'[4] and not scrutinize an unchanging set of traits.

In studying this process, according to Friedman, we need to look at the demands on the legal system in relation to the system's three main components; its substantive, structural and cultural components. The first two components refer to the output of the legal system and the forms and processes of the legal institutions themselves. The final component, legal culture, is recognized as the key concept[5] and defined as that which determines "when and why and where people turn to law and government, or turn away."[6] One simple but paramount distinction this definition makes is between a society's view of justice and that society's legal system. Obviously, not every social rule is codified in law and neither is every notion of what is just. A rule or injustice has to be considered a subject for law in order for it to be codified in law.

Another equally important distinction is demonstrated by Friedman's analysis of how the formal distinctions of a legal system are insufficient, sometimes inconsequential, to the outcomes of that system. Forms and processes of legal systems may be different yet have the same outcomes and vice versa.[7] Instead, the process of law, or a legal system, and its outcome is de-

3. Friedman, Lawrence, 'Legal Culture and Social Development', *Law & Society Review*, Vol. 4, No. 1 (August, 1969) pp. 32-33.
4. Friedman (1969) p. 33, l. 30-31.
5. Friedman (1969) p. 34, l. 41.
6. Friedman (1969) p. 34.
7. Friedman (1969) p. 36, l. 21-22.

termined by a culture's understanding and interpretation of law. The 'when, why and where' are thus both encoded into the structure of a legal system and function as the foundation on which the interpretation and use of the system is performed.

Same-sex marriage is a minority issue that challenges traditional gender roles and sexual morals, and it is very likely that the supposed inconsistency in the Danish legal system is influenced by a normative bias. As a result, Danish legal culture requires not only clarification on this issue but necessitates a problematization of the values that the legal culture consists of.

Feminist engagement with law reveals in legal culture the invisible determinant 'who' and the relationship between 'who' and, in Friedman's terminology, the 'when, why and where.' In problematizing what Bourdieu calls doxa, the "sum of social beliefs or practises which are seen as normative, as going unsaid, as being outside the framework of challenge and criticism",[8] feminist critique of law and the legal profession aims to make visible the inherent biases of a legal system. Because the doxa of a culture justifies the 'when, why and where' on a normative basis it renders itself and the 'who' or the 'who not' invisible. In her article 'Feminist Legal Theory', Ruth Fletcher describes this in terms of challenging the objectivity or neutrality of law and the values of equality, justice and freedom that underpin it.[9] When we examine how Danish Marriage Law is biased, according to feminist legal theory, we need to expose how doxa shapes the process and outcome of the legal system.

In applying the general analytical framework suggested by Friedman, I turn first to an examination of Danish marriage law and the legal culture that has shaped it, and then to the current status of same-sex marriage legislation in the Danish Parliament, the legal culture that directs it, and its relationship to public opinion. This will enable us to conclude and reflect on both the specific situation of same-sex marriage and more broadly on feminist legal theory in relation to legal culture.

8. Bourdieu, Pierre, p. 4, footnote 2.
9. Fletcher, Ruth, 'Feminist Legal Theory', *An Introduction to Law and Social Theory*, Reza Banakar and Max Travers (eds.) (Hart Publishing: Oxford, 2002) p. 136.

Danish Marriage Law and Registered Partnership Law

The formulation of Danish Marriage Law is, in fact, gender neutral.[10] It is only in its complimentary laws and its function that gender is specified. This clearly reflects the doxa of the original law, written at a time when there was no legal need to specify the gendered conditions of marriage. When the Registered Partnership Law was adopted in May 1989 it gave same-sex couples many of the same rights that opposite-sex couples received in marriage yet reinforced the gendered conditions. The law referred to the Marriage Law with exceptions in relation to, for example, adoption, nationality and church weddings.[11] Since then, the gap between the two has slowly narrowed. In June 2010, restrictions on adoption were abolished leaving a few but important exceptions.

One significant restriction that I will mention only shortly is the limitations on who are allowed to enter a partnership. The partnership law states that one of the parties must have Danish citizenship and domicile, 'bopæl' in Denmark, or that both parties must have resided in Denmark in the two consecutive years prior to being registered.[12] Today, persons who have citizenship from and domicile in either the Nordic countries, The Netherlands, Belgium and Spain are equated with Danish citizenship and domicile. The law is further restricted in that other governments are not obliged to recognize Danish registered partnerships. This nationalist aspect was originally connected to apprehensions in relation to giving foreign couples marriage rights in Denmark when those rights would not be applicable in their home country, and a concern for Denmark's international reputation. A report, for example, on the conditions of homosexuals in Denmark, commissioned by the Danish Justice Department and published in 1988, expresses fears of strong negative reactions towards an adoption of a same-sex partnership law from foreign authorities.[13] Simultaneously, however, a majority was in favour of the law and saw its adoption as something to be proud of.[14]

10. 'Bekendtgørelse af lov om ægteskabets indgåelse og opløsning', https://www.retsinformation.dk/forms/r0710.aspx?id=31944
11. Rydström (2011), p. 52, l. 27-32.
12. § 2 of the Law on Registered Partnership. https://www.retsinformation.dk/forms/r0710.aspx?id=31533
13. Homoseksuelles vilkår: Afgivet af Kommissionen til belysning af homoseksuelles situation i samfundet. 1988. Betænkning 1127. (Statens informationstjeneste: Copenhagen) p. 128, l.12-17. http://www.statensnet.dk/betaenkninger/vis.cgi?nummer=1127-1988
14. Rydström (2011) p. 11.

The restriction on who is allowed to enter a registered partnership and its jingoistic concerns are particularly interesting in relation to an international perspective and from a family reunification perspective of same-sex marriage law, two aspects I will not be including. It is important to observe, however, the connection between the legal system and national character, and the erroneous conclusions this conflation potentially creates. People of a nation are not necessarily tolerant or occupied with minority rights simply because its legal system momentarily is. Neither does legal recognition eradicate prejudice in that same legal system, and certainly not in society at large.

The most visible exception is the restriction that bars same-sex couples from being wed in a religious congregation. Proponents of the registered partnership law in the late 1980s accepted this exception mainly because it would enable the legislation to be passed.[15] Despite that same-sex couples are bared from being wed in all religious congregations, same-sex marriage is rarely, if ever, discussed publicly except in relation to the Danish Lutheran Church.

Being a state Church, it is regulated by the Danish Constitution, and as the only religious nomination in the country it is supported in matters of 'holiday law', ecclesiastical law, and is subsidised financially and administratively.[16] Even though few Danes go to church more than a couple of times a year, and one-fifth never does,[17] it enjoys a huge membership of 80,1 percent of the Danish population.[18] These numbers suggests a non-reflexive relationship to the values of the church and what consequences its membership has in government legislation. The reason is found in the close connection between the values of the Church and the State. In her article, 'Women, Secular and Religious Laws and Traditions: Gendered Secularization, Gendering Shari'a',

15. Rydström (2011) p. 75, l. 1-3.
16. 'Danmark – kirkelige og religiøse forhold', *denstoredanske.dk* (Gyldendals åbne encyklopædi).
http://www.denstoredanske.dk/index.php?title=Samfund%2C_jura_og_politik/Religion_og_mystik/Danske_folkekirke/Danmark_(Kirkelige_og_religiøse_forhold
17. 'Historisk krise i forholdet mellem stat og kirke', *information.dk* (December 5, 2001) http://www.information.dk/287022
'Nye tal på kirkegang og moskébesøg', *kristlig-dagblad.dk* (March 19, 2007).
http://www.kristeligt-dagblad.dk/artikel/267241:Statistik-om-religion--Nye-tal-paa-kirkegang-og-moskebesoeg
18. Member percentage 2011
http://www.km.dk/folkekirken/statistik-og-oekonomi/kirkestatistik/folkekirkens-medlemstal.html

Hanne Petersen explores the close relation between the Danish State and the Danish State Church, and this relationship's subsequent consequences to gender relations in legal culture. Petersen stresses the findings of the Finish feminist legal historian, Anu Pylkkänen, who claims that "secular law has been so much intertwined with religious norms and understandings that it does not make sense to discuss the relation of law and religion as if such a bind did not exist."[19] Pylkänen further concludes that Lutheran ideas and social welfare have fused and that family is an issue with deep religious roots where "often unconscious and unacknowledged religious values still play a very important role."[20]

This is confirmed by Anette Jensen, who in her Ph.d. *Fra selvfølge til symbol – ægteskabet mellem stat kirke og befolkning i 1800-tallet*, describes how the concept of Lutheran marriage is considered part of the structure of society but created by God. Particularly, Lutheran marriage prescribed proper sexual behaviour, no pre- or extramarital sex, and formalised an exceedingly patriarchal gender order. Marriage in the Lutheran tradition, then, traverses family, society and religion and proscribes the gender roles in them.[21] A quote-worthy line from the Lutheran catechism states that: 'As the church subordinates itself to Christ, so shall you women too subordinate yourself to your men in everything.'[22] This parable pictures not only the subordination of women to men but overtly illustrates the Lutheran patriarchal megalomania.

The result of the synthesis of state and church is that the Lutheran legal culture of marriage is understood as secular, and that its social norms in relation to, for example, fidelity, procreation and gender roles seem unconnected to religion. This seeming secularism will in turn ensure little critique from a population that does not see itself as religious and its values as mired in religious doctrine.

19. Petersen, Hanne, 'Women, Secular and Religious Laws and Traditions: Gendered Secularization, Gendering Shari'a', *Shari'a s Discourse. Legal Traditions and the Encounter with Europe*, eds. Jørgen S. Nielsen & Lisbeth Christoffersen(Ashgate Series: Cultural Diversity and Law, 2010) p. 83, l. 12-15.
20. Petersen (2010) p. 84, l. 1-4.
21. Jensen, Anette, *Fra selvfølge til symbol – ægteskabet mellem stat kirke og befolkning i 1800-tallet*, Ph.d. afhandling (IHKS Syddansk Universitet: 2003) p. 31-33.
22. Jensen (2003) p. 31, l. 12-13.

The Institution of Marriage

Ruth Fletcher sets down in her article three particular conceptual paradigms that have assisted in organising feminist study of law;[23] sex/gender, public/private and equality/difference. These three paradigms each address different aspects of the more or less visible doxa of the legal institution of marriage that excludes same-sex couples.

The sex/gender paradigm highlights the continued gender essentialism that is used to limit marriage to, and to preserve special status for, opposite-sex couples. The critique of gender essentialism, that gender does not define what you do and desire, is what initially led to an acceptance of same-sex desire.[24] Yet it is still the basis for denying same-sex couples access to marriage. In 2009, the then Minister of Justice, Lars Barfod, described how marriage was understood from a legal, traditional and historical perspective as a special relationship between a man and a woman, and that the government did not wish to simply change this definition with the stroke of a pen by including same-sex couples in that definition. He furthermore explained that the government found it natural that there are two different definitions for two different kinds of partnerships.[25] With a plea to tradition and history, and the law that has codified them, Barfoed insisted that the sex of two people having a relationship will define that relationship, and that the two partnerships will be markedly different from another and therefore need different definitions in the eyes of the state.

This understanding of relationships carries with it two assumptions; one, that same-sex relationships are valid and therefore worthy of public recognition, and another which, in the same breath, defines opposite-sex couples as real couples, a blueprint of relationships that same-sex couples are unable to achieve. The essentialist understanding of gender and relationships, what Barfoed defines as 'natural', is connected to a particular comprehension of what marriage is. A married couple is not merely a partnership but a family or the start of one. Although 'rainbow families' are increasingly accepted in the legislative body, reflected in the government's decision in May 2010 to

23. Fletcher (2002) p. 138, l. 1-2.
24. Fletcher (2002) p. 141, l. 33-34.
25. "L 123 Forslag til lov om ændring af lov om ægteskabs indgåelse og opløsning og forskellige andre love samt ophævelse af lov om registreret partnerskab" http://www.ft.dk/samling/20091/lovforslag/l123/beh1/2/forhandling.htm?startItem=

allow registered partners full adoption rights,[26] Barfoed's insistence on the definition exemplifies the justification of those who oppose same-sex marriage.

In giving an example of the second paradigm, equality/difference, Fletcher points out that same-sex marriage, if achieved, is an assimilation that fails to question marriage as a social institution.[27] Thomas Søbirk Petersen[28] adequately demonstrates in his article on the discrimination of homosexuals how Danish legal culture in relation to marriage is heterosexist and chauvinistic. He reminds his readers that the Danish government banned artificial insemination in 1997 for both lesbians and women who were not married or living in a de facto relationship with a man.[29] Although later revoked, it shows how marriage as a legal institution exemplifies and enforces a particular patriarchal social order that, in the words of Virginia Held, bases justice, freedom and equality on the contractual society, a society modelled on 'equal men' where women and children are excluded.[30] Conforming to marriage will position the patriarchal heterosexist relationship as a comparator and normalise male heterosexual experience. Instead, "[e]quality must value and accommodate difference if it is to be meaningful."[31]

This is not a new aspect of the same-sex marriage debate but was also discussed prior to the registered partnership law being adopted. In his book, *Odd Couples*, Jens Rydström explains how the legal regulation of same-sex partnerships primarily was a project formulated by gay men, and that lesbians were mainly uninterested because of its patriarchal foundation and its lack of custody rights.[32] Only radical gay men joined the lesbians' opposition.

26. 'Homoseksuelle får lov til at adoptere', *berlingske.dk* (May 4, 2010) http://www.b.dk/politik/homoseksuelle-faar-lov-til-adoptere
27. Fletcher (2002) p. 148, l. 29-31.
28. Petersen, Thomas Søbirk, 'Diskrimination af homoseksuelle ved adoption, ægteskab og kirkelig vielse', *Født og forbliver lige og frie? Om diskrimination og etik*, eds. Kasper Lipper-Rasmussen og Jesper Ryberg (Museum Tosculanums Forlag: København, 2007) p. 184.
29. 'Lesbiske og enlige betaler prisen', *lgbt.dk* (October 2nd, 1997) http://www.lgbt.dk/372/
30. Held, Virginia, Chapter 10: Noncontractual Society: The Postpatriarchal Family as Model', *Feminist Morality. Transforming Culture, Society and Politics* (The University of Chicago Press: 1993) p. 198-199.
31. Fletcher (2002) p. 152, l. 11.
32. Rydström (2011) p. 167, l. 14-32.

"If the feminist argument against gay marriage or registered partnership was based in a materialist critique of patriarchy, radical gay men's standpoint focused on the capitalist modes of production and the crippling mechanism of a homophobic environment."[33]

Rydström suggests that there might be a connection between the stronger financial position of gay men and their support for legal regulation, whereas lesbians and radical gay men wanted to change society before entering it.[34] The opposing arguments are as relevant today as they were then. According to Görel Granström the heterosexist framework of law, religion and economy does not only normalise heterosexism but legitimizes discrimination and ultimately violence.[35] This backside of the legal culture of marriage contains potential detrimental consequences to same-sex couples.

This brings us to the third paradigm, public/private, and to its paradoxical position in relation to the equality/difference paradigm. Being recognized in heterosexist society means having access to what is considered the public sphere where the 'equal men' have justice, freedom and equality, to use Virginia Held's words again. In order for same-sex couples to gain legal rights they need to be accepted by the legal establishment as recipients of relationship rights. In effect, accepting those rights places on same-sex couples the expectation to submit to the legal culture of marriage.[36] Refusing to submit results in being kept in the private sphere where same-sex couples are denied rights and marginalized. On the other hand, this non-inclusion into a legal framework potentially protects the difference of the same-sex couple from heterosexist and chauvinistic normalizing influence. Either way will ensure the status quo of heteronormative society because the public sphere will only grant rights to same-sex couples under the condition that they conform.

Today, the oppositional voices made against marriage equality from within the gay and lesbian community are much fewer, as the majority sees the issue as a personal choice and a landmark in the fight for diversity.[37] This supports Dr. David Paternotte's claim in his lecture on same-sex marriages in a transnational perspective at Amsterdam Research Centre for Gender and Sexuality, in December 20011, that legal discourse is today considered the

33. Rydström (2011) p. 79, l. 15-18.
34. Rydström (2011), p. 81, l. 15-16.
35. Granström, Görel, 'Challenging the Heteronormativity of Law', *Exploiting the Limits of Law. Swedish Feminists and the Challenge to Pessimism*, eds. Åsa Gunnarsson, Eva Maria Svensson & Margaret Davies (Ashgate: 2007) p. 128, l. 34-36.
36. Rydström (2011) p. 125.
37. Rydström (2011) p. 138, l. 34-36.

main referent in defining equality.[38] With a legal framework constitutive of heterosexist and chauvinistic values, this view of the legal system is highly problematic.

The Legislative Process, Public Opinion and the Role of Secularism

A member of the Copenhagen City Council demonstrated in the summer of 2011 that the legislative body itself has failed to enforce Danish Marriage Law. On the 7th of August, Lars Aslan Rasmussen of the Social Democrats was reprimanded by the Danish Justice Department and threatened to have his authority to perform marriages revoked. Since being elected to the Council in 2005, Rasmussen had pronounced same-sex couples for 'ægtepar', (married), instead of 'registered partners.' He had done this intentionally, fully aware of the illegality in protest against the state having different legal names for marriages between opposite-sex couples and same-sex couples.[39]

Rasmussen's actions reflect the opinions of the centre-left part of the legislative body in Parliament, which at the time had been out of power for almost a decade. When the centre-left regained power in early autumn 2011, the newly appointed Church and Equality Minister, Manu Sareen, who shares party membership with Rasmussen, did not, contrary to expectations, immediately proclaim clear proceedings for implementing marriage equality. Through the following autumn the press reported a series of 'one step forward, one step back' proceedings on Sareen's commitment to using the same definition for same-sex couples and on his negotiations with the bishops.[40] In

38. Paternotte, David, 'Global 'Times, Global Debates? Same-sex Marriage Worldwide', Amsterdam Research Center for Gender and Sexuality (Amsterdam, December 16, 2011)
http://www.arcgs.uva.nl/arcgs_events/calendar.cfm/19E70161-FCC5-4E09-AD0C0910DB366EFF
The presentation is available here
http://www.youtube.com/watch?v=92ZJ9dyNDHE
39. 'Borgerrepræsentant får homoreprimande', *information.dk* (August 7, 2011) http://www.information.dk/telegram/275244
40. 'Homoseksuelle skal vies i kirken hurtigst muligt' *politikken.dk* (November 10, 2011) http://politiken.dk/debat/ECE1446336/homoseksuelle-skal-vies-i-kirken-hurtigst-muligt/
'Minister: Homoer kan blive livsfæller, ikke ægtefæller', *information.dk* (October 31, 2011) http://www.information.dk/283679
'Biskopper nægter at arbejde med homovielser', *Politikken* (December 8, 2011) http://politiken.dk/indland/ECE1474177/biskopper-naegter-arbejde-med-homovielser/

the negotiation process with the Church, it has become clear that Sareen is not really concerned with the aspect of equality in the wording or the ritual but mainly with the ceremony being performed in the church. This he considers a 'historical' moment and 'the greatest thing since allowing women priests in the church.'[41] Although a news article from the Danish newspaper *Politikken* reports that the definition will be the same for same- and opposite-sex couples, and that the expression 'total equality'[42] is used to describe what is instigated, it is obvious that the meaning of this concept of 'total equality' has not been the subject of contemplation in the legislative body nor in the press. The concept of equality is assumed to be known already and of no further concern. Besides the uncertain support for the issue of the definition, another major indication is that Sareen will not demand a gender-neutral marriage ritual. Same-sex couples will be pronounced 'ægtepar', the same as opposite-sex couples, but will have their own ritual.[43] What stands out is the continuation of gender essentialism reflected in the different rituals, and the lack of attention to those same-sex couples who want freedom *from* religion or freedom *of* religion. Sareen and Parliament are primarily concerned with the engagement with the Lutheran State Church and the internal and inter-relational tensions that are generated in the process. In this narrowed focus is an utter lack of legislative debate on and attention to the rights of same-sex couples as well as the wider legal implications.

Friedman's observation that legal culture is not merely an opinion poll is amply demonstrated by public opinion in Denmark on gay marriage. When a large majority is in favour of reforms that have few economic and bureaucratic consequences, it should spell a political incentive. Why this is not so in relation to same-sex marriage in Denmark is the subject of Marie Ulf-Møller's thesis, *Det er så Yndigt? Ægteskab for homoseksuelle i Danmark og Holland – Et komparativt studie i policy-forskelle.* Ulf-Møller explains how the lack of policy initiative is caused by a lack of public attention to the issue, which in turn results in an apathetic majority in Parliament.[44] In other words, even though a majority is in favour of a particular issue, the legislative body will not necessarily act on it unless it generates enough or the right kind of public attention. The key to the Dutch success in passing marriage for same-sex

41. 'Homoer får lov til at sige ja i kirken', *politikken.dk* (November 23, 2011) l. 5-6 http://politiken.dk/indland/ECE1458707/homoer-faar-lov-til-at-sige-ja-i-kirken/
42. 'Homoer får lov til at sige ja i kirken' (2011) l. 9.
43. 'Homoer får lov til at sige ja i kirken' (2011).
44. Jensen, Anette, *Fra selvfølge til symbol – ægteskabet mellem stat kirke og befolkning I 1800-tallet*, Ph.d. afhandling (IHKS Syddansk Universitet: 2003) p. 106.

couples lies, in Ulf-Møller's findings, on the policy's attachment to another important issue, one that engages the entire population and not just the small homosexual minority. This is what she calls the 'religious line of conflict.' Because of Holland's pluralistic religious history, same-sex marriage was carried on the back of the issue of secularism and the division of church and state, a historical issue that is important to the majority and not just the minority.[45] In Denmark, the blurred distinction between the Danish State, society and Church seems to lead, on this issue, to apathy. There is apparently no awareness of the complexity of the issue in the legislative body where the State Church is allowed to define the debate, and the Danish majority in favour of same-sex marriage has proven inconsequential to the legislative process.

Conclusions and Reflections

The distinction that Friedman makes between the substantive, structural and cultural components of the legal system have shown themselves not to be so distinctive. The cultural component permeates the substantive and structural and the three are in a constant revolving relationship with each other. Furthermore, an issue's relationship with another, as Ulf-Møller has shown, has the potential to guaranty success or spell failure. What seems particularly difficult is to separate legal culture from culture that is not legal culture. Because legal culture includes doxa that only becomes visible in examination and analysis of interpretation, it is near impossible to define its borders and consequently its content. Even misconceptions about national character have the potential to influence the legal process.

Danish Lutheran marriage law was obviously not a direct attempt to bar people of the same sex from entering marriage. Foremost it was a divinely ordained regulation of gender roles and a positioning of the family in society. Same-sex considerations in relation to marriage were not relevant until homosexual relationships were a viable option. Now that they are, legal culture has changed among both the homosexual minority and the heterosexual majority from being one that governs specific relationships to one that also encompasses and becomes a marker of cultural understandings of equality.

The symbolic content of marriage is in itself certainly not unimportant. This has been a problem from the beginning of the discussions on whether

45. Jensen (2003) p. 106-108.

same-sex couples should have access to partnership or marriage. Only those who deem the symbolism drastically less important, those who see themselves as having different legal needs, oppose the legalization of same-sex couples. Not because same-sex couples should be barred from marriage but because marriage is a patriarchal heterosexual institution. When the registered partnership law was adopted opposition came from lesbians and radical gay men. Today opposition is nearly just found among the queer conscious radical left, and certain feminist and sexual studies scholars. It is, on the other hand, more than understandable that the homosexual minority either consciously or unconsciously sacrifices certain legal needs to gain rights, recognition and protection. Submission to the majority seems a necessary and only possible step for a minority who is seeking to change the legal culture of the society they are subjected to.

With the disappearance of the need for a community, with specific legal needs due to its incorporation into the majority, also disappears its collective experience of reality and the specific political concerns that are created within it. In relation to marriage equality in Denmark, the result seems to be that political identification rather than one's sexuality defines one's view on legal culture.

The result of equality from the perspective of law is not difference but sameness and Justice is truly blind when she believes that everyone is the same. The singularity of law in combination with the understanding that law is the main referent of justice seems to have two possible outcomes. Either law will have to become less singular or marginalization will increase. Rydström notes that the more gays and lesbians are part of the value system of normative culture, the harder it is for them to criticise it. This, he concludes, has the potential to "strengthen heteronormativity and impoverish the conceptual reality of same-sex couples."[46] Marie Ulf-Møller's observation that minority rights may have to, so to speak, ride on the back of issues important to the majority furthermore indicates that minority rights issues needs a normative frame in order to be taken seriously. Yet, the institution of marriage is continuously changing and, as Anette Jensen reminds us, it is not the first time it is part of the political agenda.[47] The difficult question to answer is whether the minority is allowed to participate or is actually involved in the changing at all.

46. Rydström p. 14.
47. Jensen (2003) p. 2, l. 1.

The concern for patriarchal heterosexist legal culture is both the most important aspect of same-sex marriage and the most overlooked in the debate in Denmark today. This concern is not just mirrored in considerations on marriage legislation but in legal culture in general on an international scale. Fletcher talks about making law more gender sensitive,[48] Margaret Thornton about the technocentrism of the law profession and its political underpinnings,[49] and Virginia Held about looking to refashion society and law in the image of the relationship between mother and child.[50] Hanne Petersen goes one step further by including the environment and sustainable masculinities.[51]

Feminist critique is, to a great extent, political, and radical politics in relation to the legal culture of the majority. In her examination of Swedish legislation on domestic violence and hate crimes, Görel Granström finds that both gender-specific and gender-neutral legislation has its disadvantages.[52] The ideal situation for proponents of a pluralistic legal culture seems to be the possibility that same-sex marriages, regardless of definition, will change legal culture slightly and result in a more inclusive Law, and that the enforcement of patriarchal heteronormativity inherent in marriage will fail to penetrate same-sex couples too deeply.

Bibliography

Fletcher, Ruth, 'Feminist Legal Theory', *An Introduction to Law and Social Theory*, Reza Banakar and Max Travers (eds.) (Hart Publishing: Oxford, 2002) p. 135-154

Friedman, Lawrence, 'Legal Culture and Social Development', *Law & Society Review*, Vol. 4, No. 1 (August, 1969) p. 29-44

Granström, Görel, 'Challenging the Heteronormativity of Law', *Exploiting the Limits of Law. Swedish Feminists and the Challenge to Pessimism*, eds. Åsa Gunnarsson, Eva Maria Svensson & Margaret Davies (Ashgate: 2007) p. 127-140

Held, Virginia, Chapter 10: Noncontractual Society: The Postpatriarchal Family as Model', *Feminist Morality. Transforming Culture, Society and Politics* (The University of Chicago Press: 1993) p. 192-214

48. Fletcher (2002) p. 154, l. 18-20.
49. Thornton, Margaret,'Commentary. Technocentrism in the Law School: Why the Gender and Colour of Law Remain the Same', *Osgoode Hall Law Journal*, Vol. 36, No 2 (1998).
50. Held (1993) p. 214.
51. Petersen, Hanne, 'Gender and Environmental law and justice: thoughts on sustainable masculinities', *Environmental Law and Justice in Context*, eds. Jonas Ebbesson & Phoebe Okawa (Cambridge: 2009).
52. Granström (2007) p. 137, l. 31-32.

Jensen, Anette, *Fra selvfølge til symbol – ægteskabet mellem stat kirke og befolkning I 1800-tallet*, Ph.d. afhandling (IHKS Syddansk Universitet: 2003)

Petersen, Hanne, 'Gender and Environmental law and justice: thoughts on sustainable masculinities', *Environmental Law and Justice in Context*, eds. Jonas Ebbesson & Phoebe Okawa (Cambridge: 2009) p. 98-113

Petersen, Hanne, 'Women, Secular and Religious Laws and Traditions: Gendered Secularization, Gendering Shari'a', *Shari'a s Discourse. Legal Traditions and the Encounter with Europe*, eds. Jørgen S. Nielsen & Lisbeth Christoffersen(Ashgate Series: Cultural Diversity and Law, 2010) p. 77-87

Petersen, Thomas Søbirk, 'Diskrimination af homoseksuelle ved adoption, ægteskab og kirkelig vielse', *Født og forbliver lige og frie? Om discrimination og etik*, eds. Kasper Lipper-Rasmussen og Jesper Ryberg (Museum Tosculanums Forlag: København, 2007) p. 179-203

Rydström, Jens, *Odd Couples. A History of Gay Marriage in Scandinavia* (Aksant: Amsterdam, 2011)

Thornton, Margaret, 'Commentary. Technocentrism in the Law School: Why the Gender and Colour of Law Remain the Same', *Osgoode Hall Law Journal*, Vol. 36, No 2, p. 369-398

Ulf-Møller, Marie, *Det er så yndigt? Ægteskab for homoseksuelle i Denmark og Holland – Et komparativt studie i policy-forskelle* (Speciale på Institut for Statskundskab, Københavns Universitet, Vejleder Henrik Jensen: 2007)

Internet Sources

'Bekendtgørelse af lov om registreret partnerskab' (Law on Registered Partnership) https://www.retsinformation.dk/forms/r0710.aspx?id=31533 (last visited December 17, 2011)

'Bekendtgørelse af lov om ægteskabets indgåelse og opløsning', https://www.retsinformation.dk/forms/r0710.aspx?id=31944 (last visited December 17, 2011)

'Biskopper nægter at arbejde med homovielser', *politikken.dk* (December 8, 2011) http://politiken.dk/indland/ECE1474177/biskopper-naegter-arbejde-med-homovielser/

'Borgerrepræsentant får homoreprimande', *information.dk* (August 7, 2011) http://www.information.dk/telegram/275244

Bourdieu, Pierre, 'On Male Domination', *Le Monde Diplomatique*, English Edition (October, 1998) http://mondediplo.com/1998/10/10bourdieu

'Danmark – kirkelige og religiøse forhold', *denstoredanske.dk* (Gyldendals åbne encyklopædi) http://www.denstoredanske.dk/index.php?title=Samfund%2C_jura_og_politik/Religion_og_mystik/Danske_folkekirke/Danmark_(Kirkelige_og_religiøse_forhold) (last visited December 17, 2011)

'Historisk krise i forholdet mellem stat og kirke', *information.dk* (December 5, 2001) http://www.information.dk/287022

'Homoer får lov til at sige ja i kirken', *politikken.dk* (November 23, 2011) http://politiken.dk/indland/ECE1458707/homoer-faar-lov-til-at-sige-ja-i-kirken/

'Homoseksuelle får lov til at adoptere', *berlingske.dk* (May 4, 2010) http://www.b.dk/politik/homoseksuelle-faar-lov-til-adoptere

'Homoseksuelle skal vies i kirken hurtigst muligt' *politikken.dk* (November 10, 2011) http://politiken.dk/debat/ECE1446336/homoseksuelle-skal-vies-i-kirken-hurtigst-muligt/

'Homosexual marriage, child adoption by homosexual couples: Is the public ready?' *EOS Gallup Europe* http://www.rklambda.at/dokumente/news_2003/News-PA-031015-Gallup-Umfrage-Text.pdf Last visited

"L 123 Forslag til lov om ændring af lov om ægteskabs indgåelse og opløsning og forskellige andre love samt ophævelse af lov om registreret partnerskab" http://www.ft.dk/samling/20091/lovforslag/l123/beh1/2/forhandling.htm?startItem= (last visited December 17, 2011)

'Lesbiske og enlige betaler prisen', *lgbt.dk* (October 2nd, 1997) http://www.lgbt.dk/372/

'Manu Sareen sender stat of kirke mod skilsmisse', *politikken.dk* (December 3rd, 2011) http://politiken.dk/indland/ECE1469683/manu-sareen-sender-stat-og-kirke-mod-skilsmisse/

'Minister: Homoer kan blive livsfæller, ikke ægtefæller', *information.dk* (October 31, 2011) http://www.information.dk/283679

'Nye tal på kirkegang og moskébesøg', *kristlig-dagblad.dk* (March 19, 2007) http://www.kristeligt-dagblad.dk/artikel/267241:Statistik-om-religion--Nye-tal-paa-kirkegang-og-moskebesoeg

From Decriminalisation to Marriage: Changing Judicial, Political and Religious Attitudes in the United Kingdom to Gay and Lesbian Families

Kenneth McK. Norrie

Introduction

In 2012, the year that Denmark opened marriage to same-sex couples, and as this paper is being written, the legal systems of the United Kingdom are moving closer towards the removal of the existing limitation on marriage to opposite-sex couples. This chapter will explore the remarkable cultural and legal change that has allowed, within barely more than a single generation, gay men and lesbians to move from their previous position of criminality, immorality and social exclusion to one of protected and legitimate full citizenry. The embracing of a human rights perspective in legal culture at the turn of the 21st Century is one of the important elements in explaining why this revolution of social and political attitudes has come about but it is not, as we will see, the only one and a shift of attitudes was clearly evident before then. This paper will also examine the attitudes of mainstream religion in the United Kingdom to modern legal norms that require non-discrimination principles to be extended to gay men and lesbians, and to same-sex couples. For it is organised religion that is, in 2012 and 2013, providing the main focus of opposition to governmental plans to extend marriage to same-sex couples. Before doing so, however, it is as well to remind ourselves that, unlike most other vulnerable groups who have suffered centuries and even millennia of discrimination and social exclusion, gay men (in particular) faced the ultimate legal sanction of criminality for living their lives according to their own nature.

The Importance of Decriminalisation

The acceptance that Mr Justice Scalia of the United States Supreme Court is right on a matter of sexual orientation jurisprudence does not come easily to legal commentators who support sexual orientation equality and non-discrimination. Even more difficult to accept is that he was right in *Lawrence v. Texas*[1] when he dissented from the decision of the Supreme Court that struck down, as contrary to the US Constitution, the criminalisation of male-male sexual activity. Yet right he was, if in his reasoning though not his conclusion. "Today's opinion" he states, with insight, "is the product of a Court, which is the product of a law-profession culture, that has largely signed on to the so-called homosexual agenda, by which I mean the agenda promoted by some homosexual activists directed at eliminating the moral opprobrium that has traditionally attached to homosexual conduct."[2] The decision of the majority, to strike down all anti-sodomy laws in the US, "dismantles the structure of constitutional law that has permitted a distinction to be made between heterosexual and homosexual unions, insofar as formal recognition in marriage is concerned. If moral disapprobation of homosexual conduct is 'no legitimate state interest' for purposes of proscribing that conduct ... what justification could there possibly be for denying the benefits of marriage to homosexual couples exercising '[t]he liberty protected by the Constitution'? ... The Court today pretends that ... we need not fear judicial imposition of homosexual marriage, as has recently occurred in Canada ... Do not believe it."[3]

Though his motives were malign, his point is undeniable. Criminalisation of same-sex sexual activity, in a society that no longer unquestioningly takes its moral guidance from religious texts, provides the only sustainable firewall against claims for equality and non-discrimination, and removing that firewall therefore exposes discriminatory laws to the harsh spotlight of rationality. Moral disapprobation may well have virtually disappeared from judicial and political discourse in the UK (as elsewhere), but the fear of crime, as a subversion of society itself, remains and politicians continue to feel able to cast criminals in the role of other, of outsider, of wrongdoers who do not deserve the civic entitlements that full members of society take for granted.[4]

1. (2003) 539 US 558.
2. (2003) 539 US at p. 602.
3. *Ibid.*
4. As shown by the political furore that followed the European Court of Human Rights' decision that the UK's blanket ban on prisoners from voting in elections was an infringement of Protocol 1, art. 3 of the European Convention on Human Rights: *Hirst*

Removing criminality as well as moral disapprobation from same-sex sexual conduct becomes not only the start of the process towards equality and non-discrimination but is also the catalyst that, sooner or later, makes relationship recognition, as the ultimate expression of civic entitlement, inevitable.[5]

Changing Social Attitudes

It is not the purpose of this paper to identify whether legal developments have driven changes in social attitudes towards gay men and lesbians and to same-sex relationships or whether, instead, it is changing social attitudes that have created an environment in which legal changes can be effected. The two have, in all likelihood, gone hand in hand, the one feeding off, supporting and encouraging, the other. Legal developments will be discussed in detail later, but the change in social attitudes towards homosexuality has been traced by the British Social Attitudes Survey since 2000.[6] This shows a continuous fall in the number of people in the United Kingdom who consider same-sex relationships to be always or mostly wrong (48 % in Scotland and 46 % in England in 2000; 40 % in both Scotland and England in 2005; and 27 % in Scotland and 29 % in England in 2010), together with a concomitant rise in the number of those who consider same-sex relationships to be not wrong at all (29 % in Scotland and 34 % in England in 2000; 35 % in Scotland and 37 % in England in 2005; and 50 % in Scotland and 44 % in England in 2010). The Scottish Social Attitudes Survey 2010[7] breaks the Scottish figures down in terms of gender, age and attendance at religious services.[8] Unsurprisingly there is a significant age disparity and the natural demographics of population replacement can only serve to speed the rate of increase of the acceptability in (or indifference to) homosexuality. 46 % of those over 55 held the view in 2010 that same-sex relationships are always or mostly wrong, but only 19 % of those aged between 35 and 54 did so, falling to 13 % for those aged be-

v. United Kingdom (2006) 42 EHRR 411 and, particularly, *Greens v. United Kingdom* (2011) 53 EHRR 21. See for example "David Cameron Backs Prison Rebels" *The Telegraph* February 10, 2011.

5. A point made by K. Waaldijk, "Civil Developments: Patterns of Reform in the Legal Position of Same-Sex Partners in Europe" (2000) 17 Rev. Can. Dr. Fam. 62 at p. 86.
6. See *28th British Social Attitudes Report*, National Centre for Social Research, 2010, Table 2.6.
7. Published by the Scottish Government at www.scotland.gov.uk/socialresearch .
8. *Scottish Social Attitudes Survey 2010*, Table 7.3.

tween 18 and 34. 57 % of those who attend a religious service at least once a week considered same-sex relationships to be always or mostly wrong; but only 24 % of those who attend religious services at least once a month did so. These figures had fallen from 64 % and 48 % respectively in 2005.

It is implausible to imagine that this fall since the beginning of the 21st Century in the number of people opposed to same-sex relationships began only when these Surveys first asked the question in 2000, and it is likely that the trend started rather earlier, as decriminalisation removed an important inhibition on gay men and lesbians living openly.[9] Throughout the 1980s and 1990s gay men and lesbians became much more visible in the community, in the mass media, and even in politics.[10] This increased visibility helped to lessen the fear of the unknown[11] (homophobia, properly, being fear of rather than hatred towards, homosexuals[12]). The very normality of gay people, and their lives and relationships, helped to remove the preconception that gay people were deliberately seeking to subvert social and ethical norms,[13] and this allowed an environment to develop in which law- and policy-makers felt able, and then obliged, to extend equality imperatives to gay men and lesbians, and to same-sex couples.

9. An opinion poll reported in *The Economist* March 3, 2012, traces the fall in disapproval of same-sex relationships to 1990, after a sharp increase in the mid-1980s, explained, the article suggests, by the HIV-AIDS panic at that period.
10. It was a major news story in 1984 when Chris Smith MP became the first member of the British House of Commons to openly admit that he was gay (becoming, in 1997, the first openly gay minister in a British Cabinet). By 2010, the fact that the winning candidate, Ruth Davidson, MSP, to become the Leader of the Conservative Party in Scotland is a lesbian was barely worth mentioning in the press.
11. The *Scottish Social Attitudes Survey 2010* (n.7 above) shows (Table 7.5) that people who personally know a gay man or lesbian are around twice as likely to support same-sex marriage as people who do not themselves know any gay or lesbian people.
12. From "phobia", defined in the *Shorter Oxford English Dictionary* as "(A) fear, (a) horror, (an) aversion: *esp.* an abnormal and irrational fear or dread aroused by a particular object or circumstance."
13. See further M. McCormack, *The Declining Significance of Homophobia* (Oxford, OUP, 2012).

Changing Judicial Attitudes

Decriminalisation of male-male sexual conduct occurred at different points throughout the United Kingdom,[14] with England and Wales leading the way in 1967,[15] Scotland following in 1980,[16] and Northern Ireland being (with deep reluctance) required to follow suit two years later[17] after the European Court of Human Rights decision in *Dudgeon v. United Kingdom.*[18] It was not to be expected that the lives of gay men and lesbians (most of whom were never charged with any criminal offence) would change immediately on decriminalisation, and for some years thereafter social attitudes to homosexuality remained profoundly negative and served to ensure a continuing reluctance on the part of gay men and lesbians to live their lives openly and honestly. These social attitudes were reflected in the attitudes of judges who, when gay men or lesbians came to their attention (even beyond the confines of the criminal law), treated them with suspicion at best and contempt at worst. In, for example, *R v. Bishop,*[19] eight years after decriminalisation in England and Wales, a witness in a trial for burglary was revealed to be a homosexual and the legal question this gave rise to was whether it would have any effect on his credibility as a witness. The Court of Appeal held that the witness's homosexuality, being a matter that indicated immorality, did indeed compromise the reliability of the witness. A person such as that was more likely than the "normal" person to tell lies and even to commit the criminal offence of perjury. A similarly attitude is shown in the child adoption case of *Re D (An Infant) (Adoption: Parent's Consent),*[20] where the House of Lords held that a

14. Though it is as well to note that decriminalisation was only partial, with a variety of provisions making criminal acts which, had they been heterosexual in nature, would be legally innocuous, such as advertising or soliciting for sex. Another difference was that decriminalisation did not extend to members of the armed services, who remained subject to court martial for any "homosexual offence": see for example *Secretary of State for Defence v. Warn* [1970] AC 394. The most noticeable difference, however, concerned the age of consent, which was originally 21 (as opposed to 16 for non-gay sex); after being reduced to 18 in 1994 the age of consent became 16 with the Sexual Offences (Amendment) Act 2000. Sexual orientation neutrality in criminal law was achieved in England and Wales by the Sexual Offences Act 2003 and in Scotland by the Sexual Offences (Scotland) Act 2009.
15. Sexual Offences Act 1967, s. 1.
16. Criminal Justice (Scotland) Act 1980, s. 80.
17. Homosexual Offences (Nothern Ireland) Order 1982.
18. (1981) 3 EHRR 40, (1982) 3 EHRR 149.
19. [1975] QB 274.
20. [1977] AC 602.

father's consent to the adoption of his child could be dispensed with because, as a homosexual, he had nothing to offer the child.[21] The father's influence, in the court's view, was not likely to be other than harmful: a reasonable father would do all he could to protect his son from contact with homosexuals.[22] It was pointed out[23] that Parliament in 1967 had only partially decriminalised "male homosexualism" and could not therefore be said to have taken a morally neutral view of that phenomenon. That homosexual conduct remained immoral, in the eyes of the law, even after decriminalisation is seen again in a case in which a newspaper that carried advertisements in its personal columns for men to meet other men, potentially for sexual purposes, was convicted of conspiracy to corrupt public morals and conspiracy to outrage public decency.[24]

The issue arose with far sharper focus in the 1980s and early 1990s, when the courts were required to assess the impact of sexuality on the welfare of children in the context of child custody disputes. At this time, a mother's lesbianism was treated as a strongly negative factor in her claim to custody of her child. In *Re P (A Minor) (Custody)*[25] the Court of Appeal in England rejected a father's claim that his children, currently living with their mother, should be removed from her and placed in public care because the mother was a lesbian, but the Court expressed concern about the dangers to the child posed by the mother's lifestyle: allowing children to live "in proximity to sexual deviance", they said, could "only be countenanced by the courts when it is driven to the conclusion" that there was no acceptable alternative. Eight years later, the terminology of "deviance" had been dropped but it was still assumed that a parent's homosexuality was a strongly negative factor in a child custody dispute. In *B v. B*[26] custody was awarded to the lesbian mother after the judge examined the literature and found no evidence that children brought up by such mothers suffered harm, yet even in light of that lack of evidence the judge felt obliged to assert that it was important to distinguish

21. Per Lord Simon of Glaisdale at p. 639 and Lord Kilbrandon at p. 642. It passed without comment in the case that the mother had obtained a divorce against the father on the basis of the latter's "cruelty" which was constituted by his homosexuality.
22. Per Lord Wilberforce at p. 628.
23. Per Lord Simon of Glaisdale at p. 637.
24. *Knuller (Publishing, Printing and Promotions) Ltd v. Director of Public Prosecutions* [1973] AC 435 (House of Lords). This is not surprising since sexual acts between males that fall short of the penetration needed to constitute the act of sodomy (buggery, in English law) were legally characterised as "gross indecency between males."
25. [1983] 4 FLR 401.
26. [1991] 1 FLR 402.

between, on the one hand, lesbians like the mother in the present case "who were private persons who did not believe in advertising their lesbianism" and, on the other hand, "militant lesbians who tried to convert others to their way of life." Homosexuality was acceptable to the judge, but only if it was discreet and conforming, and there was no better option. In *Early v. Early*[27] the Scottish court removed an eight year old child from his mother who had always looked after him when she entered into a relationship with another woman, and transferred custody to the father with whom he had never stayed and who had two convictions for child neglect in respect of his other children. In *C v. C*[28] the judge at first instance had awarded custody of the child to the mother but was overruled by the English Court of Appeal for giving wholly inadequate weight to the fact that she had entered into a lesbian relationship.

In most of these cases, as it happens, the mothers were able to retain custody of their children, which may indicate that the rhetoric of societal disapproval will readily give way to the judicial recognition of reality that children thrive in a stable and loving environment even when that environment fails to meet society's perception of the "ideal" – as, in truth, most families do, to some extent. A thawing in judicial attitudes is evident in *R v. Gray,*[29] which concerned a conviction for "importuning." The Court of Appeal held that whether an invitation to engage in homosexual conduct was "an immoral purpose" was a question for the jury to answer depending on the circumstances rather than a question of law that always demanded a positive answer. And in *Re D (An Infant) (Adoption: Parent's Consent),*[30] already considered, Lord Kilbrandon was at pains to emphasise that the decision laid down no rule of law that homosexuals could never offer their children anything.[31]

27. 1989 SLT 114; 1990 SLT 221.
28. [1991] 1 FLR 223.
29. (1982) 74 Cr. App. Rep. 324.
30. [1977] AC 602.
31. "It could easily be productive of injustice if one were to attempt any hard and fast rule as to the attitude which the courts ought to adopt, in custody, access or adoption matters, towards those whose sexual abnormalities have denied them the possibility of a normal family life. This is because it is not possible to generalise about homosexuals, or fair to treat them as other than personalities demanding the assessment appropriate to their several individualities in exactly the same way as each heterosexual member of society must be regarded as a person, not as a member of a class or herd. Naturally, in a family law context, the fact of homosexual conduct cannot be ignored, but no more can the consequences of taking it into account be standardised. The kind of influence, in this type of problem, which the fact may have will be infinitely variable" *per* Lord Kilbrandon at pp. 641-642.

The gradual softening of social attitudes to homosexuality throughout the 1980s and 1990s is given concrete expression in the watershed decision for judicial attitudes, *T, Petitioner.*[32] In this Scottish case a gay man sought to adopt the child he had been looking after for some years. He had a male partner, and the judge at first instance, Lord Gill, refused the adoption order (which was, in fact, being opposed by no-one) on the ground that there was a fundamental question of principle as to whether the law permitted an adoption order to be made in favour of a man living in an admittedly homosexual relationship with another man. On appeal, however, the Inner House of the Court of Session overturned this decision holding, dismissively, that there was no such question of principle. The matter turned solely on the best interests of the child and it was open to anyone who objected to the adoption to bring evidence to the court to show that living with this applicant would be harmful to this child. But it was simply not open to a court, exercising a proper judicial discretion, to start off with a negative preconception about the dangers of homosexuality. A judge must base his decision strictly on the evidence that is put before him, and what he must *not* do "is to permit his own personal views, or his own private beliefs, to affect his judgment." The English court made a similar decision soon afterwards.[33]

It is of some significance that this change in judicial attitudes was first evidenced in cases involving children, where there tends to be the strongest political resistance to accepting the moral neutrality of sexual orientation.[34] The decision in *Fitzpatrick v. Sterling Housing Association,*[35] a case of fundamental importance, was perhaps made easier by the fact that it did not involve children. Here the House of Lords was faced with the question of whether a same-sex couple could be regarded as a "family" for the purposes of succession to a tenancy. The same question had been raised and answered negatively, both by the domestic court and at Strasbourg, some fifteen years previously.[36] By a narrow 3-2 majority, the House of Lords held that such a couple could indeed, for statutory purposes, come within the concept of "family."

32. 1997 SLT 724. For comments on this case, see K. Norrie, "Parental Pride: Adoption and the Gay Man" 1996 SLT (News) 321; M. Ross, "Attitudes to Sexual Orientation in Adoption Law" (1997) 1 Edin. L.R. 370.
33. *Re W (Adoption: Homosexual Adopter)* [1997] 2 FLR 406.
34. Parenting rights are frequently excluded from civil partnership legislation (see n.63 below) – though they were not from the UK legislation.
35. [1999] 4 All ER 707.
36. *Simpson v. Harrogate Borough Council* (1984) 17 Housing Law Rep. 205; *S v. United Kingdom* (1986) 47 D & R 274.

Once it had been accepted that a family could include a couple who were not married, there was no rational basis upon which a limitation of the concept to opposite-sex couples could be imposed. Though the immediate significance of the case was its extension of a particular, and statutorily limited, right to same-sex couples, its importance is far more profound for it shows that, even before the coming into force of the Human Rights Act 1998, the judges in the highest court in the United Kingdom were analysing a claim of right in terms of rational justification for limiting the right at issue to one sexual orientation rather than another.[37]

Two months after *Fitzpatrick* the European Court of Human Rights held, for the first time, that sexual orientation discrimination came within the ambit of article 14 of the European Convention on Human Rights,[38] and within a very few years had declared that where states attempt to differentiate treatment of individuals according to their sexual orientation "there is a need for particularly convincing and weighty reasons to justify" such difference.[39] The European Court now stresses that "discrimination based on sexual orientation is as serious as discrimination based on race, origin or colour."[40] The Human Rights Act 1998 came into force in 2000, and the strong statutory instruction that that Act gave British courts to interpret and apply all legal rules in a way that is consistent with the ECHR and Strasbourg jurisprudence had immediate effect.[41] The Civil Partnership Act 2004 was not only accepted, but embraced, by the judiciary. Lord Walker may be found in 2006 saying "the enactment of the 2004 Act was possible only because of the profound cultural change which has occurred in most of Europe, within the last two generations, in attitudes towards homosexuality. Many people (and not only homo-

37. It was more than ten years after *Fitzpatrick* before the European Court of Human Rights finally accepted that same-sex couples could claim "family life" as protected by Art. 8 of the European Convention: *Schalk v. Austria* (2011) 53 EHRR 20.
38. *Da Silva Mouta v. Portugal* (2001) 31 EHRR 47.
39. *Karner v. Austria* (2004) 38 EHRR 24 at para. 37 (raising exactly the same issue as faced the House of Lords in *Fitzpatrick*). See also *EB v. France* (2008) 47 EHRR 509 at para. 91; *Kozak v. Poland* (2010) 51 EHRR 16 at para. 92.
40. *Vejdeland v. Sweden* (App. 1813/07) 9th February 2012, at para. 55.
41. *Fitzpatrick* had refused to go as far as to hold that a same-sex couple were "living together as husband and wife" – the formulation used in a large number of UK statutes granting rights and responsibilities to unmarried couples – but as a direct result of the non-discrimination requirements in the ECHR the House of Lords reversed that position only five years later and held that any statute that gave benefits or imposed obligations on unmarried couples now had to be interpreted, in light of the Human Rights Act 2008, in a way that would include same-sex couples: *Ghaidan v. Mendoza* [2004] 2 AC 557.

sexuals) would say that that change has taken far too long, and they would be right."[42] Lord Hope, a few years afterwards, deprecates the "rampant homophobic teaching that right-wing churches indulge in throughout much of sub-Saharan Africa",[43] in a case that involved a claim for asylum made by a gay man whose life would be in danger in his own country. The Supreme Court rejected (with some contempt, it may be noted) the argument of the immigration authorities that he could avoid the risk of harm by hiding his sexuality and living his life discreetly:[44] this less than 20 years after the English courts were requiring of lesbian mothers such discretion if they wished to retain custody of their own children.

Changing Political Attitudes

Responding to the same social changes in attitudes to homosexuality as the courts, the UK Parliament has similarly shifted from one of outright hostility towards, to one of embrasure of, gay men and lesbians and of same-sex relationships. It started badly. Only one year before Denmark introduced the world to the concept of a legally created status, separate from marriage, for same-sex couples,[45] the UK Parliament deliberately expressed profound antipathy towards such relationships by passing legislation of doubtful grammar but clear malign intent, prohibiting the promotion of the "acceptability of homosexuality as a pretended family relationship."[46] This legislation was a reaction to what a majority in Parliament at that time regarded as an unwelcome social development: the palpable lessening of the social hostility faced by gay men and lesbians, and the encouraging of children to be tolerant of different ways of life. It is in the context of an increasing acceptance of homosexuality, an increasing understanding that gay men and lesbians were not deliberately choosing to subvert social norms but instead simply living their lives according to their own natures, that the passing of "section 28" is to be

42. *M v. Secretary of State for Work and Pensions* [2006] UKHL 11 at para. 92.
43. *HJ and HT v. Secretary of State for the Home Department* [2010] UKSC 31 at para. 21.
44. An argument that had already been rejected by the United Nations High Commission for Refugees *Guidance Note on Refugee Claims Relating to Sexual Orientation and Gender Identity* (UNHCR, 2008) at paras. 25-26.
45. Denmark's Act on Registered Partnership was enacted on 7th June 1989.
46. Local Government Act 1988, s. 28, inserting s.2A into the Local Government Act 1986. I explore the (legal) meaninglessness of this provision in "Symbolic and Meaningless Legislation" (1988) 33 *Journal of the Law Society of Scotland* 310.

understood. That provision was intended as a replacement to the firewall protecting against relationship recognition that decriminalisation had removed: its aim was a Parliamentary attempt to counter the growing belief in the moral equivalence between gay and straight, same-sex relationships and opposite-sex relationships. Rather pleasingly, it had exactly the opposite effect since the passing of "section 28" proved a catalyst for gay rights activists: its very malignity attracted friends to the gay-rights movement from across the political spectrum.

It is not, however, surprising that little legislative progress was made while the Conservative Government responsible for "section 28" remained in power but that, and everything else, changed in 1997 when the Labour Government took over. Within a year, the Human Rights Act 1998 had been passed, together with a constitutional restructuring of the United Kingdom itself with the establishment of devolved legislatures in Scotland, Northern Ireland and Wales. The Scottish Parliament may lay claim to be the first legislature within the United Kingdom that enacted legislation that, in dealing with family relationships, deliberately included same-sex couples to the same extent as opposite-sex couples,[47] and since then the statutory imperative for all the UK legislatures has been to do so, without discrimination. "Section 28" was repealed by the Scottish Parliament in 2000[48] and by the UK Parliament in 2003.[49] Throughout the Labour Government's time in power (1997 – 2010) political hostility to same-sex relationships became confined to the far right and even the party responsible for "section 28", the Conservative Party, did not oppose the civil partnership legislation in 2004 and, since 2010 in coalition government with the Liberal Democrats (long supporters of equality legislation), have promoted an equality agenda that moves beyond civil partnership for same-sex couples.

Relationship equality within family law was further advanced when same-sex couples were given parity with opposite-sex couples in the new adoption legislation which removed the restriction on couple adoptions to married couples.[50] The extension of cohabitants' rights in Scotland (not replicated

47. The Adults with Incapacity (Scotland) Act 2000, s. 87(2) defines "nearest relative" within the mental health legislation to include members of conjugal same-sex couples.
48. Ethical Standards in Public Life (Scotland) Act 2000, s. 34.
49. Local Government Act 2003, Sched. 8 Pt 1.
50. See the Adoption and Children Act 2002, s. 144(4) (for England and Wales) and the Adoption and Children (Scotland) Act 2007, s. 29 (for Scotland). For Northern Ireland, see *Re P (A Child) (Adoption: Unmarried Couples)* [2008] UKHL 38.

elsewhere in the United Kingdom) embraced same-sex couples.[51] And the Human Fertilisation and Embryology Act 2008, which applies throughout the United Kingdom, replaced its 1990 predecessor and removed the provision that allowed clinics and hospitals to limit their services to married women and heterosexual couples.[52] It also extended the definition of parenthood, in circumstances when artificial reproductive technology had been used, to include same-sex couples: now a child may have a mother and another "parent" who is the same sex as the mother[53] and parental orders (conferring parenthood by order of the court) can be granted to couples of any gender mix after a surrogacy arrangement has been given effect to.[54]

The Civil Partnership Act 2004

These legislative developments, important as they are, did nothing more than equate same-sex couples with opposite-sex *unmarried* couples. The ability to access the universal rights and responsibilities available to opposite-sex couples through the institution of marriage came with the passing, again without significant political opposition, of the Civil Partnership Act 2004. Opposition came mainly from religious bodies, who have long claimed to have a special voice in relation to the institution of marriage, and the 2004 Act was deliberately designed in a way that it was hoped would neutralise opposition from that source. So for example it excluded opposite-sex couples, to prevent civil partnership from being seen as a secular alternative to marriage.[55] Instead, its aim was to provide a means by which all the rights and responsibilities currently available to opposite-sex couples through the institution of marriage could become available to same-sex couples through an equivalent, but quite

51. Family Law (Scotland) Act 2006 which not only created new rights (and liabilities) for both types of couple but also extended all existing rights (and liabilities) to same-sex couples.
52. This was the aim (though in truth not the legal effect) of s.13(5) of the Human Fertilisation and Embryology Act 1990 which originally required providers to take account of the need of the child for a father. This was amended in 2008 to read that account had to be taken of the need of the child for supportive parenting.
53. Human Fertilisation and Embryology Act 2008, ss. 42-47.
54. Human Fertilisation and Embryology Act 2008, ss. 54-55.
55. There are long and tedious rules designed to ensure that this gender mix is not affected by the fact that one of the parties changes sex, something finally permitted in UK law only months before the Civil Partnership Act 2004 was passed, with the Gender Recognition Act 2004.

distinct, institution. For the same reason, civil partnership was deliberately designed to be an entirely secular institution which could not be brought into existence, as marriage can, through religious ceremony. Only a state official, the district registrar, is able to bring a civil partnership into existence by registration. Also, as originally passed for all three jurisdictions in the United Kingdom, it was explicitly forbidden to use places that are (or were in the past) used solely or mainly for religious purposes.[56] These rules remain as originally enacted in Northern Ireland, but were amended for England and Wales when the Equality Act 2010 allowed for the approval of religious premises in which civil partnership registrations may take place, so long as the religious body that owns or controls the premises wishes.[57] For England and Wales, at least, the complete secularity of civil partnership has been broken, though there remain rules against the participation of religious officials in the registration process. In Scotland the Marriage and Civil Partnership (Scotland) Bill 2013 aims to harmonise the places where marriages and civil partnerships may be conducted.

The other major difference between marriage and civil partnership is that there is no sex in civil partnership. Marriage remains, at least to some extent, a sexual relationship, that is to say one in which it is expected that the parties' relationship will be sexual, and within which sexual norms will be enforced. This perception of marriage is explained by its religious history. Most Christian religions have long seen marriage as the sole legitimation of the sexual act, and the modern law of marriage in all parts of the United Kingdom still retains vestiges of this sacramental view of marriage. So for example the canon law crime of adultery – sexual intercourse by a married person with someone he or she is not married to – is deemed to constitute the irretrievable breakdown of the marriage and so provide a ground for divorce.[58] This is not, however, a ground for dissolving a civil partnership, though all the other (non-sexual) grounds for divorce are replicated as grounds for dissolving a civil partnership. Another manifestation of the importance of the sexual act within marriage is seen in the still extant rules relating to consummation and impotency. In England and Wales a marriage is voidable (that is to say can be

56. Civil Partnership Act 2004, section 6, as originally passed (England and Wales), section 93 (Scotland), section 144 (Northern Ireland).
57. Equality Act 2010, s. 202, given effect to by Marriages and Civil Partnerships (Approved Premises) (Amendment) Regulations 2011/2661, which came into force on 5th December 2011.
58. Divorce (Scotland) Act 1976, s. 1(2)(a); Matrimonial Causes Act 1973, s. 1(2)(a) (England and Wales).

annulled and treated as if it never had been) if it is not consummated;[59] in Scotland a marriage is voidable if one or other of the parties is, at the date of the marriage, incurably impotent (that is to say unable to consummate the marriage).[60] Neither of these rules was replicated for same-sex couples in the civil partnership legislation.[61]

However, other than these peculiarities concerning the creation of a civil partnership, which serve to differentiate the concept from marriage – and isolate civil partnership from the sphere of religion – the actual consequences of both relationships, once created, are virtually identical. It is for this reason that civil partnership in the United Kingdom might legitimately claim to be "marriage in all but name."[62] There are fewer distinctions made in UK law between marriage and civil partnership than in most other jurisdictions that have introduced a marriage-equivalent as the means of achieving gay and lesbian equality in family law.[63] It follows that any human rights challenge on

59. Matrimonial Causes Act 1973, s. 12(a) (inability to consummate) and (b) (wilful refusal to do so). Consummation of marriage is constituted by full penile penetration of the vagina at some point after the parties have been declared to be husband and wife. If this never occurs, then the marriage may be declared null by a court of law. The Roman Catholic Church will also treat the marriage as if it had never been, so providing Roman Catholics with a means of escaping from an unsatisfactory marriage without calling it "divorce."
60. In Scotland this is a common law rule that has never found its way into statute.
61. An interesting practical consequence of removing sex from the relationship is provided from Ireland where similarly civil partnership is entirely asexual. It has been reported that two elderly women, both heterosexual, entered a civil partnership with each other so that one could inherit the other's property without paying death duties. This could not be achieved by marriage as the lack of conjugal intention would render the marriage a "sham" marriage. See report at www.jillkerby.ie/blog/sundaytimes_moneycomment (5th February 2012).
62. See for example N. Bamforth, "The Benefits of Marriage in All but Name? Same-Sex Couples and the Civil Partnership Act 2004" (2007) 19 CFLQ133. The European Court of Human Rights, in *Burden v. United Kingdom* (2008) 47 EHRR 38 at para. 65 equiperated civil partnership with marriage and distinguished them both from unregistered cohabitation: "There can be no analogy between married and Civil Partnership Act couples, on the one hand, and heterosexual and homosexual couples who choose to live together but not to become husband and wife or civil partners, on the other."
63. Parenting of children by gay and lesbian people is usually the issue that legislatures draw the line at: even Denmark, when it first introduced registered partnerships for same-sex couples in 1989, excluded the parenting of children as an effect and that exclusion remains in many countries that have introduced civil partnership legislation. See, most recently, the Republic of Ireland's Civil Partnership and Certain Rights and

the basis that same-sex couples are being discriminated against by not being able to marry has less chance of success in the United Kingdom than in many other European countries where the limitation of same-sex couples to a distinct but equivalent regime limits them to a regime with less rights, obligations and liabilities than opposite-sex couples who can access marriage.[64]

Continuing Religious Opposition

Society in general and lawmakers – whether judges or legislators – have thus seemed to embrace the moral neutrality of sexual orientation. Not so religion. Religion remains, in the words of Kay Goodall,[65] "the only powerful current ethical framework in Western states which holds sexual orientation to be a relevant factor by which to make fundamental judgments about the worth of individuals." Religious opposition to the legal recognition and regulation of same-sex couples has become much more muted since the Civil Partnership Act 2004 was passed, though the mainstream religions in the United Kingdom continue to struggle to find the correct response to the profound changes in society that the Act represents.[66] Few churches actively seek the repeal of the 2004 Act, but only a very few small denominations are willing to embrace its terms. The Church of England has since 2005 (when the 2004 Act came into force) prohibited its priests from granting blessings to civil partners[67] and it reinforced that message when civil partnership registrations became possible in religious places, by prohibiting the use of Church of England premises

Obligations of Cohabitants Act 2010, which excludes civil partners from jointly adopting a child or holding joint guardianship in relation to a child.

64. In *Wilkinson v. Kitzinger* [2006] 2 FLR 397 a female couple who had married in Canada sought to have their relationship recognised in England as a marriage (rather than as a civil partnership, the 2004 Act converting all overseas formalised relationships involving same-sex couples into civil partnerships) but they failed because the judge saw no practical distinction other than the name between the two institutions. Implicit in his judgment is that there is no human right to call the relationship one thing rather than another. See R. Auchmuty, "What's So Special About Marriage? The Impact of *Wilkinson v. Kitzinger*" (2008) 20 CFLQ 475.
65. "Challenging Hate Speech: Incitement to Hatred on Grounds of Sexual Orientation in England, Wales and Northern Ireland" (2009) 13 Int. J. H.R. 211 at pp.215-216.
66. See J. Rivers, "Law, Religion and Gender Equality" (2007) 9 Ecc. L.J. 24 who, at pp. 33-39, traces the struggle that religions have had in the face of what he calls modern society's more "plastic" conception of gender.
67. House of Bishops, *Pastoral Statement* 25th July 2005.

for that purpose.[68] That church continues to suffer bitter divisions about the possibility of gay priests becoming bishops,[69] at the same time (and not accidentally) as it suffers virtually identical divisions at the idea of women bishops.[70] The Church of Scotland was deeply split in 2011 on the question of whether members of civil partnerships (ie non-celebate gay people) could be ministers of the church and the General Assembly of the Church of Scotland voted (not untypically) to postpone making a decision on the subject until 2013.[71] The Roman Catholic Church does not suffer (in public, at any rate) the same divisions, being unquestioningly opposed to any legal recognition of same-sex relationships. While preaching tolerance towards gay and lesbian individuals, it remains appalled at the very idea of gay sex,[72] and it has been at the forefront of the opposition in Scotland to the Scottish Government's plans to open marriage to same-sex couples.[73] To be fair to that church, however, its disapproval of gay sex should be seen within the context of its more general disapproval of any sexual act other than the potentially procreative. Its continuing opposition to the use of contraception is traced to the same ideology that sees sexual acts as justified solely by the role that they play in the creation of human life. Limiting access to birth control has, of course, a disproportionate effect on women, who overwhelmingly bear the costs (both physical and economic) of procreation. Thus it is that denying the legitimacy of any form of non-procreative sex is the basis both for discrimination against gay people and for the *weltanschaung* that relegates women to a secondary

68. Church of England General Synod (GS Misc 1005) 2nd December 2011.
69. "Senior Anglican condemns gay bishops as a compromise too far" *The Independent* January 6, 2013. The compromise is that an Anglican priest who is gay may become a Bishop, but only if he promises to be celebate.
70. It is as well to remember here that, the Church of England being the established (state) church, its 26 most senior bishops are guaranteed a seat in the House of Lords: the result is that even today 26 seats in the UK legislature are reserved for males who are (or claim to be) heterosexual.
71. *Report of the Special Commission on Same-Sex Relationships and the Ministry* (Report to the General Assembly of the Church of Scotland, May 2011).
72. The Cathecism of the Roman Catholic Church at 2359 demands that gay and lesbian people accept that they are "called to a life of chastity."
73. See *Sunday Telegraph* March 4, 2012, in which Cardinal O'Brien, a Scottish Archbishop and the most senior Catholic cleric in the United Kingdom, described the plans as "a grotesque subversion of a universally accepted human right" and (somewhat bemusingly) likened the proposal to allow same-sex couples to marry to a proposal to legalise slavery.

role of service providers for the male polity.[74] Gay people and women have a common cause against the religious traditionalism embodied in current Roman Catholic (and indeed Anglican) church doctrine.

While institutional religion has sought to influence the political debate, individual religious believers have sought to challenge particular applications of the equality norms that the 2004 Act most effectively represents. In doing so they raise starkly the question of the extent to which religion and religious believers can be exempted from secular laws that contradict their beliefs.[75] Article 9 of the European Convention on Human Rights, which attempts to strike a balance between non-discrimination and religious freedom by guaranteeing an unqualified right to freedom of thought, conscience and religion, but allowing any manifestation of religion or belief to be subjected to such limitations as are prescribed by law and are necessary in a democratic society for the protection of the rights and freedoms of others, has proved to be of very little help to those who seek to manifest their religious beliefs by treating gay men and lesbians, and same-sex relationships, differently from (inevitable, less well than) non-gay people and opposite-sex couples.[76]

In *Ladele v. Islington Borough Council*[77] the claimant, who was a district registrar, asked her employers to exempt her from having to register civil partnerships since, as "an orthodox Christian", she regarded civil partnership as an attack on (opposite-sex) marriage, which was the only form of sexual relationship sanctioned by her god. When this request was refused, she sued her employers on the ground that they had discriminated against her because of her religious beliefs. The claim was rejected by the Court of Appeal. It was her refusal to do a part of her job and not her religious beliefs that was the reason for her dismissal: anyone would have been dismissed for that reason whether their motivation was religious or otherwise. She could not be allowed to give effect to her religious beliefs when this would be contrary to the policies and practices of her employers, who were legally bound to pro-

74. See further A. Stuart, "Freedom of Religion and Gender Equality: Inclusive or Exclusive?" (2010) 10 HRL Rev. 429.
75. This question is examined more broadly, in the context of a number of legal systems' approach to gender equality, by F. Raday, "Culture, Religion and Gender" (2003) Int J. Con. Law 633. Her conclusion that women always lose out when cultural or religious norms are applied by courts in preference to human rights or equality norms is hardly surprising and sounds a clear warning for gay and lesbian people.
76. See L. Vickers *Religious Freedom, Religious Discrimination and the Workplace* (Hart Publishing, 2008).
77. [2010] 1 WLR 955. See A. Hambler, "A No-Win Situation for Public Officials with Faith Convictions" (2010) 12 Ecc. L.J. 3.

vide a public service without discrimination on the basis of sexual orientation.

The same result was reached in *McFarlane v. Relate (Avon) Ltd*[78] where an employee of a company that provided relationship counselling services was dismissed for refusing to provide these services to same-sex couples. The case is eloquent in its defence of secularism as the correct – indeed only legitimate – approach to judicial reasoning. It rejected out of hand the notion that individuals can claim exemption from the general law based solely on their religious beliefs. Laws LJ said this:

> "The conferment of any legal protection or preference upon a particular substantive moral position on the ground only that it is espoused by the adherents to a particular faith, however long its tradition, however rich its culture, is deeply unprincipled. It imposes compulsory law, not to advance the general good on objective grounds, but to give effect to the force of subjective opinion."[79]

The Court of Appeal returned to the issue in *Bull and Bull v. Hall and Preddy*[80] where hoteliers were held to have acted unlawfully in refusing a same-sex couple a double room in their hotel. They had argued that, following an orthodox Christian belief that sexual relations were legitimate only within the context of marriage, they were entitled to insist that only married couples be allowed double rooms in their hotel for to do otherwise would require them to be complicit in the "promotion of sin." The court had little difficulty in holding that, since opposite-sex couples were able to marry while same-sex couples were not, the effect of putting into practice a belief that only married couples could legitimately have sexual relations was to discriminate against same-sex couples and was therefore unlawful.[81] Article 9(1) of the European Convention provided no defence, since Article 9(2) allowed the state to prevent the hoteliers from manifesting their religious beliefs in the moral superiority of heterosexuality over homosexuality by refusing a double room to a

78. [2010] IRLR 872.
79. At para. [23]. The European Court of Human Rights decided, on January 15, 2013, that UK domestic law did not fail to adequately protect Ms Ladele's and Mr McFarlane's rights to manifest their religious beliefs, contrary to Art. 9 of the Convention, taken alone or in conjunction with Art. 14. The actions of their employers were a proportionate response to legitimate non-discrimination policies: see *Ladele and McFarlane v. United Kingdom* App Nos. 51671/10 and 36516/10.
80. [2012] EWCA Civ. 83, [2012] 2 All ER 1017. See also *Black v. Wilkinson* (County Court, Reading, October 18, 2012).
81. Under the Equality Act (Sexual Orientation) Regulations 2007 (now replaced by the Equality Act 2010).

same-sex couple, because such a limitation was necessary in a democratic society for the protection of the rights and freedoms of same-sex couples not to be discriminated against.

The result in all these cases was relatively easy for the courts to reach. The Civil Partnership Act 2004 was so deliberately structured to differentiate civil partnership from marriage that the lawyer's answer to Ms Ladele (for example) was easy: civil partnership has nothing to do with marriage but is a secular means by which the state effects the legal regulation of some couples, so her objection that it attacked marriage was simply mistaken.[82] Likewise, the lawyer's answer to the hoteliers in *Bull and Bull v. Hall and Preddy* was easy – providing access to a double room does not "promote" sin.[83] But these answers do not address the real complaint of such religious traditionalists, which is the message of tolerance and moral equivalence that the Civil Partnership Act so powerfully represents. The state is saying loud and clear what religious traditionalists vehemently deny: that gay and lesbian people are no longer to be seen as morally inferior to heterosexual people. The "moral disapprobation" that Scalia J wanted the US Supreme Court to preserve is officially and comprehensively rejected in the United Kingdom.

The battle, in truth, is between secularism and faith, between universally applicable law and religiously mandated personal law, but this is a battle that, in western Europe at least, was lost long ago. All the legal systems in the developed western world are based, more or less, on the Enlightenment principles of secular democracy.[84] One of the most important practical consequences of that – so self-evident that it seldom requires to be explicitly stated – is that courts operate through a system of testing evidence, not only of facts but

82. Another argument, of course, is that since there is such disagreement amongst Christians as to how they should regard homosexuality there was, in fact, no "requirement" of Ms Ladele's faith to discriminate against same-sex couples. In *R (Playfoot) v. Millais School Governing Body* [2007] EWHC 1698 (Admin) the court held that a school rule banning the wearing of rings did not interfere with the religious freedom of a pupil who wished to wear a ring to symbolise her commitment to pre-marital purity: there was no religious *requirement* to wear such a ring which was therefore a matter of personal choice, merely influenced by religious considerations and so not covered by Article 9.
83. Just as a nurse's supervision of a labour ward is not the involvement of that nurse in the termination of pregnancy carried out on patients in that ward: *Doogan and Woods, Petitioners* [2012] CSOH 32, where ward supervisors were held not entitled to claim the conscientious objection to the "participation" in the termination of pregnancy provided for in s.4(1) of the UK's Abortion Act 1967.
84. See A. Sajo, "Preliminaries to a Concept of Constitutional Secularism" 2008 Int J. Con. Law 605.

of propositions. No moral conclusion is today accepted axiomatically and any stated proposition will gain judicial credence only by being justified either by factual evidence or by human rationality. Since at least the Human Rights Act 1998, all UK legislation has been subject to judicial oversight of its (secular) rationality.[85] Religions, on the other hand, work quite differently and, at least with the Abrahamic religions (or "religions of the book"[86]), operate through revelatory texts.[87] Religious reasoning starts from "the truth", being the revealed word of God, as recorded in immutable texts, and human propositions and moral judgments are deduced from the text. Different strands of each religion give more or less flexibility in interpreting these texts, but it is a definitional feature of religious belief that the text itself is the foundation of any moral position and cannot itself be challenged. This is the very reverse of the secular rationalism applied by courts of law where truth is the end point, the rationally deduced conclusion from evidence or reasoning against which all propositions of social good are tested.[88] There is no longer any legal assumption, traced to a foundational text (such as a law criminalising gay sex), that gay people are less worthy of respect than non-gay people. Secular rationalism would have no problem in allowing differential treatment if social evidence showed that gay people do in fact constitute some risk to society. It was the realisation that such social evidence simply does not exist that has persuaded most western countries to reject their previous assumptions about the social and moral inferiority of gay and lesbian people. Religious traditionalists, however, by adhering to revelatory truths, reject the need for social evidence and rely instead on divine text for their moral guidance. "We walk by faith, not by sight"[89] is the crucial, definitional, characteristic of religious belief, but it is a proposition that any court of law (at least one operating within the parameters of secular rationalism) is bound to reject. To do otherwise would allow any individual to claim exemption from any legal rule on the ba-

85. Baroness Hale, in *Ghaidan v. Mendoza* [2004] 2 AC 557 at para. 132, talked of "the rational behaviour we now [since the coming into force of the Human Rights Act 1998] expect of government and the state", adding, "If distinctions are to be drawn, particularly on a group basis, it is an important discipline to look for a rational basis for those distinctions."
86. That is to say Judaism, Christianity and Islam.
87. See F. Raday, "Culture, Religion and Gender" (2003) Int J Con. Law 663.
88. I explore this clash between the secular rationalism of modern jurisprudence and what I call the "revelatory rationalism" of theology more fully in "Accommodating Religion to the Gay Equality Imperative in Family Law" in J. Mair and E. Orucu (eds) *The Place of Religion in Family Law: A Comparative Search* (Intersentia, 2011).
89. II Corinthians 5:7.

sis solely of their own religious or philosophical conviction that they ought not to be subjected to that rule. Law, however, enforced through the police power of the state, must apply to everyone, whether they agree with it or not. That is, quite simply, the definition of "law."

The Coming of Marriage

This battle between secularism and faith as the guiding principle for legal development has now moved to the political stage and religious traditionalists hope to find it easier to persuade politicians than judges that the law should continue to reflect moral propositions traced ultimately to religious texts. The mainstream religions in the UK have long claimed a special voice in the way family life is regulated by the law and, in 2013, they are united in their opposition to changes to one family law concept – marriage – that is claimed to be, though a legal concept, one that is of uniquely religious import.[90] Both the Scottish Government[91] and the British Government[92] (representing England and Wales) have issued public consultations on the question of opening marriage to same-sex couples. Though the details of each consultation differ,[93] both are responses to claims from gay rights supporters that, the content of marriage and civil partnership being (in the United Kingdom) virtually identical, the withholding of the name "marriage" from same-sex couples

90. Indeed marriage is a concept that both defines and differentiates various Christian traditions. Changes to marriage laws – and in particular the introduction of divorce – was characteristically one of the first manifestations of the legal effects of the Reformation: see J. Witte, "Church, State and Marriage: Four Early Modern Protestant Models" (2012) 1 Ox. J. Law and Rel. 151.
91. *The Registration of Civil Partnerships: Same-Sex Marriage: A Consultation*, Scottish Government, Edinburgh 2011.
92. *Equal Civil Marriage: A Consultation*, Government Equalities Office, March 2012.
93. The Anglo-Welsh consultation was limited to civil marriage while the Scottish consultation included both religious marriage and religious civil partnership. The Anglo-Welsh consultation disclaimed any need to amend civil partnership in any way at all and so excludes from consideration the question of whether to open civil partnership to opposite-sex couples, while the Scottish consultation asked whether there would be any need to retain civil partnership at all if marriage were opened to same-sex couples. The Scottish Government announced on September 4, 2012 that it would include a bill to open marriage to same-sex couples in its 2012-13 legislative programme and it published its bill on 12 December 2012. The British Government is likely to follow a similar timetable: see "Gay Marriage Could be Approved within Weeks", *Telegraph* November 23, 2012.

achieves nothing other than to deny them the dignity and respectability that (it is said) is uniquely conferred by the status of marriage. This profoundly secularist argument persuaded the United States Court of Appeals for the Ninth Circuit to strike down "Proposition Eight",[94] which was a constitutional amendment, approved by plebiscite in 2008, that removed the right of same-sex couples in California to marry.[95] The court based its conclusion on the fact that Californian law (like UK law) granted to same-sex couples all the substantive rights of married couples through the institution of domestic partnership and that the only effect of Proposition Eight was to remove the name "marriage" from same-sex relationships. Though this imposed no substantive legal loss, it served "to lessen the status and human dignity of gays and lesbians in California, and to officially reclassify their relationships and families as inferior to those of opposite-sex couples."[96] As such, the court held that Proposition Eight was unconstitutional since it achieved no legitimate state purpose. It is this thinking that lies behind both the Scottish and the UK Governments' proposals.

The responses of the mainstream churches in the United Kingdom have been uniformly negative. Both governments took pains to emphasise that no religious organisation will be forced to conduct marriage ceremonies that are contrary to their own doctrinal beliefs – and indeed the English proposals were originally limited to civil marriage that has no religious involvement in any case – thus allowing the Church of England to avoid an internal debate on the issue similar to the destructive debates it continues to have in relation to women bishops.[97] This makes it very difficult for the churches to oppose the Governments' plans on the basis of their doctrinal beliefs, since to embody these beliefs in law would be to impose their own beliefs on other religious bodies (and, through the state, everyone else) who do not hold these beliefs – which is the very thing that the mainstream churches want to avoid happening to themselves.

It is for this reason that the main argument being propounded by the churches opposing the opening of marriage to same-sex couples is that it is simply not open to *any* religion or state authority to alter the existing and

94. *Perry and Ors v. Brown* 671 F 3d 1052 (2012).
95. Such couples having been granted that right by judicial decision less than a year previously: *In Re the Marriage Cases* (2008) 43 Cal 4th 757.
96. *Perry v. Brown* at p. 1063.
97. On November 20, 2012, the General Synod (governing body) of the Church of England once again rejected proposals to allow women to become bishops: see "Women Bishops: A Failure of Leadership" *Telegraph* November 23, 2012.

long-standing definition of marriage.[98] This argument is ostensibly based on the assertion that marriage as an opposite-sex relationship is either a natural phenomenon or a divinely-created institution – in either case a rule of mankind cannot overturn a rule of nature or of God.[99] In truth, however, this is an argument about who has power to change marriage rules, not whether anyone can do so at all. Legal systems have frequently moved away from those rules of marriage, traced to religious texts, that no longer serve the needs of society – and many religious bodies have felt able to alter their understandings of scripture to accommodate these changes. The most obvious example in recent times in the United Kingdom is the Marriage (Prohibited Degrees of Relationship) Act 1986 which removed many of the prohibitions on (non-blood) relatives marrying each other that were traced to the Book of Leviticus.[100] The "definition" argument fails to grasp – indeed denies – that marriage has become today a legal institution through which the state identifies who is entitled to certain rights and subjected to certain obligations. This is not to say that marriage may not also be regarded as a religious sacrament, or that the state (as opposed to religious authorities) may well have no capacaity to amend the definition of any religious sacrament which is, necessarily, a self-defined idea. But in its manifestation as a legal institution, regulated in the United Kingdom by the Marriage Act 1949 (for England and Wales), the

98. This argument is made both by the Church of England and the Roman Catholic Church: see the comments of the Archbishop of York (the second most senior cleric in the Church of England) in an interview published on January 27, 2012 in the *Telegraph*, and of Cardinal O'Brien, the most senior UK cleric in the Roman Catholic Church, in an article published in the *Sunday Telegraph* on March 4, 2012. See also the Archbishop of Glasgow's "Statement on Marriage" in which he set out the Roman Catholic Church's response to the Scottish Government's Consultation: www.scottishcatholicmediaoffice.org.uk/articles/archbishop-mario-conte-issues-statement-on-marriage.html
99. Of course, in Roman Catholic theology traced to the writings of St Thomas Aquinas (particularly *Summa Theologiae*), divine law *is* natural law: see "The Natural Law Tradition in Ethics" in *Stanford Encyclopedia of Philosophy* (2002). The sense of using "nature" as the determinant of moral good is comprehensively rejected by K. Goodall in "Human Rights Pitted Against Man (II): A Response" (2010) 14 Int. J. HR 1165 at pp. 1179-1182.
100. Others had previously been removed by statutes such as the Deceased Wife's Sister's Marriage Act 1907 and the Deceased Brother's Widow's Marriage Act 1921 (both of which are limited to England and Wales where particular biblical injunctions had been accepted): see S. Cretney *Family Law in the 20th Century: A History* (Oxford, OUP 2004) at pp. 48-57.

Marriage (Northern Ireland) Order 2003[101] (for Northern Ireland) and the Marriage (Scotland) Act 1977 (for Scotland), marriage is as open to legislative change and development as (for example) is the age of majority. Any religious body remains free to set different parameters to its religious institution, currently also called "marriage", different from those applying to the legal institution and in fact there are numerous instances of such bodies having done so. The Roman Catholic Church, for example, defines marriage as a religious sacrament and therefore as an indissoluble union. But the indissolubility of marriage in the eyes of that Church has no effect in law and does not deny access to the divorce courts to those who married according to Roman Catholic rites or who even now adhere to the Roman Catholic faith. The Church of England (in many respects the Church of Rome without the Pope) refuses to marry in church ceremonies people who have been divorced and whose (ex)-spouses still live,[102] but such people remain entirely free to marry in law, either by civil ceremony or in a church that has fewer qualms about divorce.[103] Faith and its incidents may well affect the behaviour and lifestyles of individual people who choose to adhere to a particular religious group, but law and its incidents apply – by definition – to everyone. Churches that deny the distinction between the religious sacrament of marriage and the legal institution of marriage are asserting a power over the state, and this is not a power that a modern secular state can ever concede.

A more subtle – but also more dangerous – variation of the definition argument is that marriage is necessarily and by definition a reflection of the essential complementarity between men and women. There is a long theological tradition (not only in Christianity, but also in Judaism and Islam) that takes from scripture a divinely ordained separation of the roles of the genders.[104] It is the male role to lead and the female role to support; the female role to advise and conciliate, the male role to decide and fight. The genders are of equal worth, but different – they have (it is said) complementary roles.

101. S.I. 2003 No. 413.
102. Which is why the Prince of Wales, when he married his present consort whose previous husband was still alive, was required to do so in a Registry Office (though the Church was, somewhat inconsistently, happy thereafter to offer a ceremony of blessing). For the constitutional and religious oddities, see S. Cretney, "Royal Weddings, Legality and the Rule of Law" (2007) 37 Fam. Law 159 and "Royal Marriages: Some Legal and Constitutional Issues" (2008) 124 LQR 218.
103. So for example the Princess Royal (sister to the Prince of Wales) chose religious ceremony in the Church of Scotland in order to marry her second husband, her first husband still being alive.
104. See generally U. King *Religion and Gender* (Blackwell, 1995).

The very structure of many churches, the Roman Catholic Church most obviously, reflects this complementarianism and it underpins the continued opposition in the Church of England to women in leadership roles such as bishops.[105] But it goes much further and complementarity of the genders in all aspects of life is part of the Catechism of the Roman Catholic Church.[106] Applying complementarian theology to marriage allows that institution to be one that both reflects *and demands* different gender roles. Without complementarity the relationship, whatever it is, is not marriage: thus it is simply impossible for a relationship between two people of the same sex to be a "marriage."

It cannot be denied that, for many long centuries, the law reflected this understanding of the essential complementarity of the genders. Marriage in the United Kingdom (and elsewhere) was a relationship in which the man alone had legal authority to decide how, and where, the couple were to live[107] and how, and by whom, any children were to be brought up;[108] the woman's position was one of utter dependency, with all her property transferring automatically on marriage into the name (or at least control) of her husband;[109] the woman was (until as late as 1989[110]) presumed by the law to have given ongoing and non-retractable consent to her husband's sexual advances (ie could not – in law – be raped by her husband whether or not – in fact – she was raped by him). Traditionally marriage was a relationship characterised by power and dependency, with an essential complementarity between the husband's duty of support and the wife's obligation to obey, between male dominance and female subservience.

However, notwithstanding this traditional acceptance of complementarity, the law has moved away from all of these positions and today reflects the so-

105. Though the Church of Scotland has for some decades permitted women ministers, and has in recent years been headed by women, this is a relatively recent phenomenon. Its Calvinist founder, John Knox, published in 1558 the wondrously titled *The First Blast of the Trumpet Against the Monstruous* [ie unnatural] *Regiment* [ie rule] *of Women.*
106. *Catechism*, 2333-2335.
107. In Scotland this rule survived until 1984: see Law Reform (Husband and Wife) (Scotland) Act 1984.
108. Only with the Guardianship of Infants Act 1925 did the various jurisdictions in the United Kingdom accept that the claim of the father to control of his child's upbringing was not superior to the claim of the mother.
109. A rule gradually ameliorated by a series of statutes including, for England and Wales, the Married Women's Property Acts 1870, 1882 and 1893, and, for Scotland, the Married Women's Property (Scotland) Acts 1881 and 1920.
110. *S v. Lord Advocate* 1989 SLT 469 (for Scotland); *R v. R (Rape: Marital Exemption)* [1991] 4 All ER 481 (for England and Wales).

cial understanding that relations between the genders should be based on equality and partnership, not domination and dependency. The challenge for traditional theologians is to explain why complementarity should continue to govern eligibility to marry (and church structures) but not anything else – not even the consequences of marriage. For complementarity, if it makes any sense, is an all or nothing doctrine: if marriage must retain complementarity between the male head of the family and his female helpmeet,[111] then so too must the whole of society and all its laws and institutions. To say "the structure of our church, and rules for entry into marriage, requires male leadership over the female, but nothing else does" has no logic and, in truth, by delimiting the scope of complementarity concedes the point that male dominance – including in church governance and marriage – is a social construct rather than a natural phenomenon.

All social constructs change as society itself changes, and the acceptance by society of gender equality is, in itself, the denial of a literalist (or unchangeable) approach to scriptural interpretation. St Paul told the Corinthians that women had to be silent in church[112] and this is one of the major scriptural bases for the doctrine that only men may take on leadership roles in religious organisations. But modern, or liberal, theology regards St Paul's words as doing no more than reflecting the makeup of the ancient society in Corinth and denies that it sets down any divinely ordained rule that must be applied today, and forever more. If the genders are equal – and modern society, and its legal rules, strive to make that aspiration a reality – then in neither church governance nor marriage is there a need to retain gender-specific roles. Traditional marriage may well have been unable to accommodate same-sex couples because of the inherent complementarity of its patriarchal power-structure, but modern marriage, as understood (and wanted) by the vast majority of the population in the United Kingdom (and elsewhere in the western world), as a partnership of equals, can accommodate same-sex couples just as easily as opposite-sex couples, and it is good social policy for the law, through its design of marriage, to encourage that more modern view of relationships. If opening marriage to same-sex couples helps to remove once and for all an understanding that marriage involves a power-structure based on expected gender roles then that opening will have served a valuable social function that is justification enough for doing so.

111. *Genesis* 2:18.
112. 1 *Corinthians* 14: 34.

Problems with Opening Marriage

None of the arguments currently being propounded by religious traditionalists, being based on scriptural truths that are not universally accepted, or are not universally accepted to be immutable, make much sense to a secular lawyer and they should have little weight with legislators committed to providing universal laws, applicable to all citizens, whatever form of faith (if any) they adhere to. But it does not follow from the removal of religious precepts from the legal concept of marriage – as it seems to be assumed in the USA to follow – that the law should provide one institution for all couples, and that that institution should be called "marriage." Marriage today has been designed to suit the needs of opposite-sex couples and while the needs of same-sex couples very substantially overlap those of their heterosexual counterparts it would be wrong to assume that the issues facing each type of couple are identical in every respect. It has already been accepted that the rules concerning sexual behaviour within the relationship (adultery, impotency and consummation) are uniquely suited to opposite-sex couples and have no (legal) relevance to same-sex couples.[113] The practical issues facing a male couple who wish to have children are very different – and demand different legal solutions – from those facing female couples (or opposite-sex couples) with the same wish. The financial consequences of marriage and separation, designed primarily to address the structural economic imbalance in society between men and women, are not self-evidently suitable when a same-sex couple, between whom financial parity is more likely, separate.[114] The problem of forced marriages as a means of creating family alliances will simply not arise in relation to same-sex marriage.[115]

113. See the UK Government's *Responses to Civil Partnership: A Framework for the Legal Recognition of Same-Sex Couples*, (Department of Trade and Industry, 2003) at p. 36. The Marriage and Civil Partnership (Scotland) Bill 2013 proposes to limit the rules of impotency to opposite-sex marriages, and to retain the necessarily heterosexual quality of adultery. English law will deal with these matters differently but details are not yet finalised.
114. See further, K. Norrie, "Marriage is for Heterosexuals. May the Rest of Us Be Saved From It" (2000) 12 CFLQ 363.
115. A fact recognised by the Scottish Parliament when it enacted the Forced Marriage etc (Protection and Jurisdiction) (Scotland) Act 2011 providing civil remedies to those being forced into marriage but not civil partnership. The power to extend the Act in future to civil partnership is included if the issue does arise, but it is assumed that it will not.

Using marriage as the universal union for all couples also runs the risk of assimilating same-sex couples into bland and constraining heteronormativity. The effect of opening marriage is, Nancy Polikoff has long argued,[116] far less socially transformative than the creation of parallel institutions (such as civil partnership) or a series of institutions of equal worth. Marriage ensures that difference is made safe by being minimised, rather than accepted for what it is and celebrated.[117] The powerful political alliance between gay rights and feminist activists, who have a common enemy in the doctrine that sex is legitimate only when potentially procreative, has withered as marriage, previously seen by many feminists as part of the problem, comes to be seen in the LGBT community as the solution. Yet the identity of the arguments against advancing the rights of women and the rights of gay people is seen with naked clarity as the Church of England interminably debates the issue(s) of women bishops and gay bishops.

It is in any case naïve at best to see marriage as the solution to society's ills. Even if we accept that marriage is an important stabilising influence on society, it does not follow that it is more effective in providing that stability than good social welfare, parenting support, education and equal opportunities policies. The focus on marriage as a solution is, in other words, dangerously short-sighted. Homophobic hate crimes will not disappear when marriage is opened to same-sex couples. Equality and non-discrimination in employment and in the provision of goods and services is at least as important for individual gay men and women as civil partnership and marriage is for same-sex couples. The focus on marriage as a goal, in other words, adopts the utterly traditional approach of preferencing the couple over the individual, preferencing conformity over diversity. Not for nothing did the British (Conservative) Prime Minister, David Cameron say in 2011 "I don't support gay marriage in spite of being a Conservative. I support gay marriage because I am a Conservative."[118]

116. "We Will Get What We Ask For: Why Legalising Gay and Lesbian Marriage Will Not Dismantle the Legal Structure of Gender in Every Marriage" (1993) 79 Va. L. Rev. 1535; *Beyond (Straight and Gay) Marriage* (Beacon Press, Boston 2008).
117. The whole thrust of the law, both at the UK and the European level, is to extend rights and obligations to same-sex couples who seek to participate in traditional, nuclear family-style relationships: see C. Stychin *Governing Sexuality: The Changing Politics of Citizenship and Law Reform* (Hart, 2003).
118. David Cameron, MP, "Leadership for a Better Britain", speech to Conservative Party Conference October 5, 2011 (available on Conservative Party website, "speeches").

Conclusion

Marriage is likely to be opened to same-sex couples in the United Kingdom within a very few years of this book being published, and that will effect a truly remarkable transformation in the legal position of gay men and lesbians from the days of criminality, a mere generation ago. We should not, however, expect too much from the opening of marriage to same-sex couples, even with its message of tolerance, respect and equality. Opening marriage alone will not prevent hate speech and homophobic assault, nor remove individual feelings of moral superiority over those of a minority sexual orientation. These things can be reduced not only by the law deeming them unacceptable,[119] but by society in all its manifestations accepting the moral equivalence of homosexuality and heterosexuality. Today, both legislation and case law in the United Kingdom give out the unambiguous message that gay men and lesbians, and same-sex couples, pose no threat to the good of society, and are entitled to be accorded the respect and dignity that the heterosexual majority take for granted. That message, however, fails to achieve complete social transformation in attitudes because the opposing message, that same-sex relationships hurt society and its members, continues to be propounded by religious traditionalists, who still feel free to proclaim the moral superiority of heterosexuality over homosexuality, even when they would hesitate to proclaim, openly, the moral superiority of white people over black, or the superiority of Christian people (as people) over Jew or Muslim – or the superiority of the male over the female. Anti-semitism and racism have long since been expelled from the sphere of respectable political (and indeed religious) discourse and it is today limited to the extreme fringes of right-wing politics. Anti-gay sentiments are, however, not yet considered to be beyond the pale, or unacceptable in normal political discourse, almost solely because they continue to receive a legitimacy and a respectability from scriptural texts which religious leaders assert are still valid, even while they accept that other biblical injunctions (such as, for example, the Judeo-Christian God's hysterical demands for genocide in *Joshua*[120]) may, even must, be disregarded. The

119. See K. Goodall, "Challenging Hate Speech: Incitement to Hatred on Grounds of Sexual Orientation in England, Wales and Northern Ireland" (2009) 13 Int. J.H.R. 211. Limitations on free speech which prevent the distribution of leaflets that were contemptuous of and disparaging towards homosexuals are not inconsistent with Art. 10 of the European Convention on Human Rights: *Vejdeland v. Sweden* (App 1813/07), 9th February 2012. See comment at (2012) EHRLR 348.
120. Joshua 6:21 and 10:40-41.

message of homosexual inferiority, proclaimed from pulpits and bishops' palaces, is heard and translated into a message of intolerance and hatred by thugs, who then feel aggrieved when they are charged with hate crime as opposed to common assault.

Gay men and lesbians would not be the only losers if the state were to defer to religious (or cultural) traditionalism and allow religious beliefs to qualify human rights and equality norms. The risks to women, in particular, are great for patriarchy is an inescapable feature of most mainstream religions across the world. Giving priority to equality over religious beliefs and practices – even when that involves the sudden subversion of many hundreds of years of social, legal and religious discrimination against sexual minorities – is, therefore, the best guarantee that every citizen will be allowed to lead their life as a dignified human person, free to shape their life and relationships according to their own nature, and with as much opportunity to exercise choice as anyone else. It is the grand purpose of the law to minimise religion's proven capacity to hurt individuals, particularly those who are "other."[121] Preferencing equality and non-discrimination norms of gay and lesbian people over religious freedom is a powerful message that the state is willing to fulfil its duty in this regard, and is the ultimate acceptance of gender equality itself.

121. Including, of course, the "otherness" of women, in Simone de Beauvoir's sense: *The Second Sex* (1949).

Same-Sex Marriage: An Old and New Issue in Asia

Douglas Sanders[1]

An old Issue

The recognition of same-sex relationships is an old issue in Asia, not a simple copy of demands from the West.

Lesbian and gay homoerotic carvings feature on the famous medieval Indian religious temples of Kanarak and Khajuraho.[2] Male homosexual activity was accepted or tolerated at the Muslim court in Mogul India.[3]

A wealth of fiction and commentary celebrated same-sex love, often involving Samurai, in pre-Meiji Japan.[4]

Tokugawa-period (1600-1867) Japan has probably the best recorded tradition of male same-sex love in world history. Period novels, poetry, and art all provide extensive representations of the varieties of homosexual love practiced. Incidental information gleaned from biographies, news, scandals and official records as well as testimony from foreign visitors show how widely practiced was male-male eroticism through all strata of society. Tokugawa (homo)sexuality has recently been widely discussed in both English and in Japanese. These researchers amply illustrate the widespread preva-

1. Professor Emeritus, Faculty of Law, University of British Columbia, Vancouver, Canada (1977-2003); former visiting professor, Masters Program in Business Law, Faculty of Law, Chulalongkorn University, Bangkok, Thailand (1998-2008); Member of the Governing Board for the Doctoral Program in Human Rights, Mahidol University, Bangkok, Thailand.

   This is an updated version of the paper delivered at ASLI, the annual Asian law schools meeting, National University of Singapore, May 31-June 1, 2012.
2. Rakesh Ratti, A Lotus of a Different Color, Alyson, 1993, 22.
3. Ratti, 31-33.
4. See, for example, Saikaku, The Great Mirror of Male Love, Stanford University Press, 1990 (a translation of Nanshoku Okagami of 1687).

lence of homosexual relations among men of the samurai class as well as among urbanites generally.[5]

At many points in Chinese history

... homosexuality acted as an integral part of society, complete with same-sex marriages for both men and women.[6]

Prior to the introduction of Western sexology into China in the early twentieth century there were "sizable historical, literary, and legal discourses concerning male-male sexuality ...."[7]

These Asian traditions were displaced by Western colonial expansion in the late 19th century when new German sexological studies were exported to Asia as part of Western science, generally seeing sexual variation as an illness. The *Indian Penal Code* of 1860 criminalized homosexual acts. It was copied for other British colonies in Asia, Africa and Oceana.[8]

Dr. Ruth Vanita comments for India:

Notwithstanding some scholars' discomfort with ascribing to colonialism the modern erasure of earlier homoeroticisms (and other eroticisms), evidence so far available indicates overwhelmingly that a major transition did indeed occur at that historical moment.[9]

5. Mark McLelland, Male Homosexuality in Modern Japan, Curzon, 20-21 (references omitted).
6. Hinch, Passions of the Cut Sleeve: The Male Homosexual Tradition in China, University of California Press, 1990, 2.
7. Tze-ian D. Sang, The Emerging Lesbian, Chicago, 2003, 42. See also, Tan Chong Kee, Same-sex love in ancient and modern Chinese history, fridae.com, June 12, 2007 and June 19, 2007.
8. See Douglas Sanders, 377 and the Unnatural Afterlife of British Colonialism in Asia, Asian Journal of Comparative Law, Volume 4, 2009, 165-206. The adoption of the Napoleonic code decriminalized homosexual acts in half of Europe, with the result that prohibitions were enacted for British colonies, but not those of France, the Netherlands, Portugal or Spain. There had been an early criminalization by the Spanish in the Philippines, but that law was repealed when Spain adopted the Napoleonic penal code. The non-colonized states of China, Japan and Thailand entered the post WWII period with no express prohibition. Prohibitions in Central Asia have early European origins conveyed through Russian imperialism.
9. Ruth Vanita, Queering India, Routledge, 2002, 4. The industrial revolution began in Europe around 1750. It created, over time, a great technical, economic and intellectual advantage for European powers. The result was the European led globalization and colonialism of the last half of the 19th century. German 'sexology' and British criminal law spread in this context.

The High Court in Delhi ruled that the colonial-era criminal law against homosexual acts violated the Constitution of India. In the appeal before the Indian Supreme Court some history was canvassed:

The Court was quick to pick up on the argument of homophobia as a colonial legacy, and expressed a big appetite for historical material on pre-colonial acceptance of sexual and gender diversity. All of a sudden the right-wing claim to 'tradition' was unhinged.[10]

Protesting the New Homophobia

Protests against the new intolerance are scattered through local histories. Some couples defied the prevailing homophobia by staging same-sex weddings. Most were private affairs. Some got public notice. In the 1970s and 1980s newspapers in Thailand ran stories of same-sex marriages.[11] On April, 19th, 1981, two women, Jossie and Bonnie, were married in Jakarta. The reception was a lovely affair "with invitations, guests, fine clothes, and members of both families present ...." The wedding was a feature story in two national Indonesian language magazines, Liberty and Tempo. Liberty made it a front-page story.[12] The 1987 wedding of two female police constables, Leela Namdeo and Urmila Shrivastava made national headlines in India. Both were fired from their jobs.[13] Father Mickley, a Catholic Priest, has conducted same-sex marriages in the Philippines for well over ten years (without the approval of the Catholic hierarchy). While same-sex marriage is prohibited by the marriage law in Cambodia, there was considerable publicity about a 1995 marriage between two women in Kandal Province.

"The authorities thought it was strange, but they agreed to tolerate it because I have three children already (from a previous marriage). They said that if we were both single (and childless), we would not be allowed to get married because we could not produce children." The marriage appeared to

10. Akshay Khanna, activist and commentator, SOGI-List, June 8, 2012.
11. Communication from Dr. Peter Jackson, Australian National University, August 15, 2011.
12. Tom Boellstorff, The Gay Archipelago, Princeton, 2005, 62-3.
13. Geeta Patel, Homely Housewives Run Amok, (2004) 16 Public Culture, 131, at 147.

have official approval and was reportedly a popular event, with 250 attendees, including Buddhist monks and high-officials from the province.[14]

One of the best known public weddings was that of popular author Hsu Yoshen and his partner Gary Harriman in Taipei in 1996. Chen Shui-bian, then the mayor of Taipei, sent a representative to the ceremony.[15]

We know of perhaps a dozen marriages in Vietnam. In April, 1997, two men married in Ho Chi Minh City. A hundred guests celebrated the marriage at a hotel reception, provoking public controversy. Authorities said that they had broken no law. In March, 1998, two women married in the province of Vinh Long. The local People's Committee refused to register the marriage. In June, 1998, Vietnam's national assembly banned same-sex marriage.[16] In June, 2011, the internet circulated pictures of a new public marriage event of two men in a "luxurious restaurant" in Ho Chi Minh City, but used only their nicknames. Weddings have continued in Vietnam:

A gay couple in the Mekong Delta province of Kien Giang recently exchanged wedding vows at a ceremony attended by their parents and hundreds of guests; a lesbian couple in Ca Nau Province only halted their wedding in February after authorities objected; a lesbian couple in the Ha Noi and a gay couple in Sai Gon too grabbed headlines after photos of their weddings and celebrations went viral online.[17]

A public same-sex marriage took place in Taipei in 1996. Other marriages followed. In August, 2011, one of the couples who had staged a marriage in 2006, applied for a marriage license. After a refusal they began a lawsuit. On April 10, 2012, the couple, and their respective mothers, appeared in court for a pre-trial hearing. The two mothers publicly stated their support and love.[18]

Both People's Daily and Shanghai Daily covered a Beijing wedding of two men in January, 2011. They celebrated the "comparatively open" event with 50 guests at a restaurant in the capital city.[19]

14. Cambodian Center for Human Rights, Coming Out in the Kingdom: Lesbian, Gay, Bisexual and Transgender People in Cambodia, December, 2010, 20. The story in the Phnom Penh Post bore the title "Gay marriage: not completely illegal after all."
15. A stomach ailment, he said, prevented his attendance, but he sent a representative.
16. Erick Laurent, Sexuality and Human Rights: An Asian Perspective, Journal of Homosexuality, 2005, 163 at 192.
17. A Change Brewing, July 24, 2013, circulated on the AP Rainbow list July 26, 2012.
18. See two stories on www. fridae.asia: Taiwanese gay couple to appeal unsuccessful marriage registration in court, 5 April 2012; Mothers of Taiwanese gay couple appear in court to show support, 12 April, 2012.
19. Gay men 'marry' in Beijing, fridae.com, January 25, 2011. This story gives links to the Shanghai Daily and Peoples Daily stories.

In December, 2011, there was extensive coverage of a civil partnership ceremony involving a Malaysian man and an Irish national in Dublin. The Malaysian, who was studying medicine in Ireland, had broken off contact with his parents, who asked police to trace him as a missing person. Pictures of the partnership ceremony surfaced on U-Tube. In response to questions, Malaysia's acting law minister Nazri Aziz said the country would not legalize same-sex marriage:

The similar gender marriage will not happen in our country. Full stop![20]

In January 2012, The Nation newspaper in Bangkok had a front page story and picture of a 'gay marriage' in front of parents and 200 guests. The story told how the two met on Facebook.[21] It was no private affair. There was television and print coverage.

... the parents were not only smiling but also talking enthusiastically about how happy they were. ... Smiles also adorned the faces of the 200 or so guests. Many called out funny remarks. The emcee got the newlyweds to kiss.[22]

Video footage and news reports spread across Thailand. Thai gay activist Vitaya Saeng-Aroon followed up with a background story of the January wedding, occupying most of the front features page in The Nation newspaper on, appropriately enough, February 14th.[23]

Malaysian born Christian pastor, the Reverend Oyoung Wen Feng, married his partner in New York and announced plans for a wedding banquet back home.[24] The banquet took place in Kuala Lumpur on August 4th, 2012,

20. AFP, Gay man threatened over 'same sex union, Bangkok Post, December 23, 2011, 7. The Malaysian opposition leader, Anwar Ibrahim, who had been charged twice with homosexual acts (the first involved a conviction, reversed on appeal, the second dismissed at trial) testified in August, 2012, that marriage should not be extended to homosexuals in order to uphold the sanctity of marriage between a man and a woman. He was testifying in a libel case he brought against a newspaper that said he was a gay rights proponent. See Anwar agrees to discrimination against gays to protect sanctity of marriage, July 20, 2012, ILGA Asia e-letter, accessed August 6, 2012.
21. Trifa Saekhow, Facebook friendship blossoms into gay marriage in Trang, The Nation (Bangkok), January 8, 2012, 1A.
22. Brave hearts in Trang, The Nation (Bangkok), Friday, January 13, 2012, 2B.
23. Vitaya Saeng-Aroon, Love for a new age, The Nation, XP, February 14, 2012, 1B. Vitaya hosts the gay variety show "Pink Mango" on Nation Broadcasting's Mango TV.
24. Keep coming out, urges Malaysia's gay pastor, Bangkok Post, Spectrum, August 14, 2011, 15; Malaysian pastor to register marriage on Aug 31, Malaysia's independence day, www. fridae.com, August 17, 2011. The latter story was accompanied by a pic-

with 200 guests, including the pastor's mother. There were public kisses and karaoke singing. Chinese-language journalists were asked not to file stories in advance of the event.

... Malayasia's cabinet minister for Islamic affairs voiced fears that his nuptials could promote "extremism" among Malaysia's 28 million people ... Banquet guests ushered to their seats at a Chinese restaurant in Kuala Lumpur found small heart-shaped chocolates wrapped in Chinese-language notes that translated into "God loves gays."[25]

These marriages have often been done in compliance with local heterosexual religious customs. A marriage in Bihar, India, in 2004, involved a sacred vow in a Hindu temple.[26] In 2010 a lesbian couple in Johor, Malaysia, married with the blessings of their families in a traditional Chinese marriage ceremony.[27] Associated Press gave international coverage to the marriage of two American women at a Hindu temple in Nepal in June 2011. The traditional ceremony was conducted by a Hindu priest at a major temple.[28] In August, 2012, two women in Taoyuan, Taiwan, married in a Buddhist ceremony.

Fish Huang and her partner You Ya-ting, both wearing traditional white bridal gowns, said "I do" in front of a Buddha statue and exchanged prayer beads rather than rings in a monastery in Taoyuan, in northern Taiwan. Nearly 300 Buddhists chanted sutras to seek blessings for the couple, both aged 30. Shih Chao-hui, a female Buddhist Master who presided over the ritual, hailed it as a historic moment.[29]

ture of a poster, based on the famous film "The Wedding Banquet", showing Oyoung and his partner with a blank space for a female bride.

25. AP, Gay couple hold wedding banquet in Kuala Lumpur, Bangkok Post, August 7, 2012, 5.
26. Lesbian couple arrested in Bihar, Indo Asian News Service, December 24, 2004.
27. Buddhist groups in Malaysia hold public talk about homosexuality, August 15, 2011, www. fridae.com.
28. AP, First lesbian wedding as country drafts new laws, Bangkok Post, June 21, 2011, 8. "According to Member of Parliament and gay rights activist Sunil Babu Pant, this is the first public wedding of a lesbian couple in Nepal. 'There were many closet lesbian weddings in the past but this wedding encourages the community to honor their relationships and think of themselves as normal as straight people,' he said." Shitu Rajbhandari, American couple gives Nepal its first lesbian wedding, My Republica, June 21, 2011.
29. AFP, Same-sex couple 'marry' in Taiwan, Bangkok Post, August 12, 2012, 9.

Ms Shih, who presided, is a well-known advocate for social justice in Taiwan. The couples parents had agreed to attend, but when they realized that media would cover the event, they stayed away.

In 2004, King Sihanouk, while still on the throne in Cambodia, watched television coverage of the same-sex weddings that Mayor Gavin Newsom had allowed in San Francisco. The King was moved by the joy he saw expressed, particularly as pioneer activists Del Martin and Phyllis Lyon, now around 80, were married after five decades of living together. He said such marriages should be allowed in Asia. He later abdicated in favor of his gay son, who had trained and performed in ballet.

No one has been able to pull all the local wedding stories together. Dr. Ruth Vanita sets out many of the Indian stories in a book rich in Indian religious and social history.[30] The dark sides of these stories in India are the frequent accounts of joint suicides by young women after being forcibly separated or required to marry men.[31]

Marriage Activism

Most same-sex marriages have been private affairs, though often shared with many friends, and sometimes covered by the media. Increasingly we see some marriage events staged by activists as political theatre. The participants need not be couples in real life.

In March, 2002, a showy wedding took place in a Hong Kong registry office.

The bride wore a black tuxedo and sported a fake moustache; the groom was resplendent in a white wedding dress and accompanying veil. The

30. Ruth Vanita, Love's Rite: Same-Sex Marriage in India and the West, Penguin India, 2005. Professor Ruth Vanita describes marriages, elopements, the legal attempts of parents to retrieve daughters who have eloped with a woman, and suicides of female couples whose life together has been blocked.
31. See Vanita (2005). Bina Fernandez, Humjinsi: A Resource Book on Lesbian, Gay and Bisexual Rights in India, India Centre for Human Rights and Law, 2002, lists joint suicides at pages 113-116. See also Darshana Sreedhar, Mapping the Queer Movement in Kerala, published in the magazine of the Kolkata based lesbian organization, Sappo for Equality, magazine title In Her Own Voice, June, 2011; Darshana Sreedhar, Sahayatrika in its Making: Mapping the Queer Movement in Kerala, paper prepared for the September 2011 National Queer Conference, Kolkata, organized by Sappho for Equality, copy in possession of the author. Darshana Sreedhar is an M.Phil student at the Centre for Studies in Social Sciences, Kolkata.

bridesmaid – a man – stole the show in a tangerine-coloured frock with matching parasol. Tommy Chen, 28 and gay, married a lesbian friend to try to claim Hong Kong housing benefits available only to heterosexual couples. Mr. Chen's partner plans to marry Yao Wai-wai's partner ... to claim the same benefits.[32]

Two married couples and two subsidized apartments. Why not? The event was a media splash, with coverage by the BBC and the South China Morning Post.

Near Tiananmen Square, on Valentine's Day, 2009, two lesbians in flowing white wedding dresses, and two gay men, in black tuxedos, went through wedding ceremonies. Pictures appeared in international media and in the English-language China Daily.

Organisers gave out roses and flyers to onlookers to promote social acceptance of same-sex relationships and support of same-sex marriage laws. For the past few years sociologist Li Yinhe has been submitting proposals at the People's Congress to enact same-sex marriage legislation.[33]

On February 14th, 2010, in Thailand, two lesbian couples attempted to register their relationships, one couple in Chiang Mai, the other in Pathum Thani. Both were "politely turned down."[34]

Taiwan, which hosts Asia's largest annual pride parade, held the biggest Asian wedding protest event in August, 2011.

About 80 lesbian couples tied the knot in Taiwan's biggest same-sex "wedding party", with organizers saying yesterday they hoped the island will become the first place in Asia to legalise gay marriage.[35]

Around 1,000 people had purchased tickets for the event, including visitors from China, Thailand and the US.

Even though gay marriage is not legal in Taiwan, the organisers do not expect a government crackdown. The cabinet in 2003 drafted a bill to legalise same-sex marriages and allow homosexual couples to adopt children, the

32. Hong Kong gays wed for welfare, BBC, March 25, 2002; Hong Kong gay man and lesbian marry to protest unequal treatment, March 30, 2002, www. fridae.com; Hate mail over sham marriage fails to deter gay activist couple, South China Morning Post, April 1, 2002, 3.
33. Activists hold mock wedding photo session on Beijing streets, fridae.com, February 16, 2009; China Daily, Year of Gay China, reprinted in fridae.com, December 29, 2009.
34. Paisarn Likhitpreechakul, Still not the same, The Nation, February 14, 2012, 1B.
35. AFP, Liberated lesbians say I do, Bangkok Post, August 22, 2011, 7.

first in Asia to promise to do so, but it has not yet been reviewed by parliament.[36]

A Bit of Progress in Asia

Three governments in Asia have given some support to recognizing same-sex marriages, Taiwan, Nepal and Vietnam.

Taiwan

As noted above, when Chen Shui-bian was mayor of Taipei, he sent a representative to the same-sex wedding ceremony of popular author Hsu Yoshen and his partner Gary Harriman in Taipei in November 1996. When Chen Shui-bian was president, in 2001, the Ministry of Justice drafted legislation recognizing marriage and adoption rights, which went to the cabinet for review.[37] In 2003 there seemed to be movement on the issue:

> *United Daily News, a local newspaper quoted the Presidential Office as saying: "The human rights of homosexuals have been gradually recognised by countries around the world. To protect their rights, people [of the same sex] should have the right to wed and have a family based on their free will," it added.*[38]

In a televised debate between candidates for the presidency in March, 2008, Ma Ying-Jeou, who won the subsequent election, noted that he had allocated funds for the gay pride events in Taipei when he had been mayor of the city, a policy that started in 1999. He boasted that "Taipei is the freest city to live in if you're gay." He stated that "sexual orientation is inborn and needs to be both respected and tolerated." He said "gay rights are part of human rights." On marriage, he planned to engage in public dialogue on the issue to generate understanding and consensus, saying he was "respectful but cautious" on same-sex marriage. The candidate of the Democratic Progressive Party,

36. AFP, Here come the brides, Bangkok Post, August 10, 2011, 7.
37. Taiwan may legalise same-sex unions, fridae.com, March 12, 2002; Taiwan considers gay "marriages", child adoption, fridae.com, June 27, 2001.
38. Taiwan moves to recognize gay marriages, fridae.com October 28, 2003; Taiwan's proposed same-sex marriage legislation delayed, fridae.com, December 10, 2003.

Frank Hsieh, said that problems, such as joint tax filings and adoption should be resolved "step by step" before marriage would be considered.[39]

An editorial in the English language China Post in Taipei in September, 2011, was titled "Taiwan could lead Asia with full recognition of gay rights."

... as [President] Ma once noted, "Gay rights are a part of human rights." The fight for equal rights for gays has been described as "the last major human rights struggle." How a nation treats its gay citizens is a good indicator of the general progressiveness of its society. It would likely cost President Ma a little political capital to directly call for legalizing gay marriage in Taiwan, but the overall benefit to the nation and the region could be worth it. Taiwan's people for the most part do not have strong religious objections to homosexuality and there is little organized opposition to gay rights here. All that's needed for this nation to become a bellwether for Asia is a nudge in the right direction from those in power.[40]

In Taiwan's campaigns for international recognition, it had become important to stress that Taiwan, unlike the mainland, had democracy and supported human rights. This had led Chen Shui-bian to support the ending of the death penalty, reforms of aboriginal policy and homosexual equality rights. All of these made Taiwan worthy of respect and recognition.

In August, 2012, the Deputy Director-General of the Centers for Disease Control in Taiwan publicly called for opening marriage. As in India, his argument for equal treatment was based on concerns with encouraging stable relationships for health purposes.[41] The theme for the 10th Anniversary LGBT Pride Parade in Taipei, by far the largest in Asia, in September, 2012, was "Revolutionary Marriage: Equal Marriage Rights and Diverse Partnership."[42]

Nepal

The Nepal Supreme Court in 2008 gave a judgment broadly upholding gay, lesbian and transgender rights, and instructing the government to proceed with the drafting of legislation to implement the decision. Opening marriage

39. Philip Hwang, Taiwan presidential elections candidates discuss same-sex marriage in televised debate, fridae.com, March 17, 2008.
40. Taiwan could lead Asia with full recognition of gay rights, China Post, Taipei, September 10, 2011.
41. Lung Rei-yun, Elizabeth Hsu, Health official calls for legalization of same-sex marriage, Focus Taiwan News Channel, August 20, 2012.
42. Ho Yi, Events mark gay pride birthday, Taipei Times, August 21, 2012, 3.

was to be one of the reforms. The process of drafting a new constitution has been on-again, off-again. Full implementation of the Supreme Court decision has not yet occurred, but there have been some administrative reforms. Sunil Pant, founder of Nepal's Blue Diamond Society, and a member of the legislature, is confident that Nepal will be the first Asian country to have modern legal same-sex marriage.

The developments in Nepal reflected the reformist possibilities created by the ending of the civil war. The commitment to draft a new constitution was part of that transition. The Blue Diamond Society had emerged over the previous decade as the largest and best organized LGBT organization in Asia. It gained financial support from Norway, and in the litigation was assisted by the International Commission of Jurists. The judicial breakthrough was possible because of an activist Chief Justice and the leadership of Sunil Pant and other activists.

Vietnam

In 2012, the government of Vietnam began the process of drafting a new law on marriage and family. Discussions and consultations were to result in draft legislation to go to the legislature in March, 2013. In July, 2012, the Minister of Justice said it was time to consider a legal framework for same-sex couples – giving very practical reasons for such a reform:

The Justice Ministry now says a legal framework is necessary because the courts do not know how to handle disputes between same-sex couples living together. The new law would provide rights such as owning property, inheriting and adopting children.

"I think, as far as human rights are concerned, it's time for us to look at the reality," Justice Minister Ha Hung Cuong said Tuesday [July 24th] in an online chat broadcast on national television and radio. "The number of homosexuals has mounted to hundreds of thousands. It's not a small figure. They live together without registering marriage. They may own property. We of course, have to handle these issues legally.[43]

In May the [Justice] Ministry sent out a consultative letter to concerned agencies to seek their opinions on same sex relationships. The letter de-

43. Margie Mason, AP, Unlikely Vietnam considers same-sex marriage, Jakarta Post, July 30, 2012, 2. Of course the numbers of homosexuals would not have increased. What has changed is their visibility and an evolving public recognition of the realities of sex and gender diversity.

scribed same-sex marriage as being inevitable according to human rights principles. However, it also said that "given the sensitivity of homosexuality and unforeseen consequences of same sex marriage on cultural and traditional family values, it is too early for Vietnam to legalise same sex marriage."

On 12 June 2012, the Institute for Studies of Society, Economy and Environment (iSEE) – a not-for-profit research organization that was involved in the launch of PFLAG Vietnam – was invited to a meeting with department of civil and economic law that is tasked to draft the marriage law revision. The representatives from the ministry of justice expressed their desire to have a dialogue with LGBT communities in Hanoi and Ho Chi Minh City, organize meetings between LGBT and same-sex relationship with experts from Vietnam and other countries, and educate the public on same-sex relationships.[44]

The Committee of Social Affairs of the National Assembly, as part of their consideration of possible revisions to the law on marriage and family, invited LGBT activists to make a presentation on same-sex marriage on October 8th, 2012.

Other Jurisdictions in Asia

Japan requires that a Japanese national who is entering into a foreign marriage obtain, in advance, a certificate from the Japanese government indicating basic information about both parties, including marital status, age, sex and nationality. In March, 2009, Japan began issuing such documents in cases where the foreign marriage was a legal same-sex marriage. The certificate is designed to facilitate the ability of the foreign spouse to live with the Japanese national back in Japan.[45]

In 2011, Judge Vimal Kumar in Gurgaon Sessions Court, close to Delhi, gave a same-sex couple the same protection from harassment and violence from family members that Indian courts have extended to male-female couples who were persecuted for inter-caste or inter-religious relationships. It was a significant step.[46]

44. Sylvia Tan, Will Vietnam become the first Asian nation to legalise same-sex marriage?, fridae.com, 1 August 2012, www. fridae.com, accessed August 6, 2012.
45. Japan OKs same-sex marriages abroad, Wockner International News No.780, April 6, 2009, copy in possession of author.
46. Gurgaon court recognizes lesbian marriage, Times of India, July 29, 2011.

In Hong Kong immigration officials have been quietly handing out special "relationship visas" for partners of gay professionals coming from overseas.[47] Singapore, it seems, does something similar for the same-sex partners of expatriates entering on a work permit.

The first openly gay lawmaker elected in Hong Kong, in September, 2012, said he would work for a non-discrimination ordinance and for same-sex marriage.[48] Japan has had a lesbian and a transgender elected to local or prefectural governments. The first openly gay man was elected to a ward in Tokyo in April, 2011, and promised to work for a partnership ordinance that would cover all unmarried couples, giving equal rights to marriage.[49]

Modern Legal Recognition of Same-Sex Relationships in the West

Accepting that the issue of legally recognizing same-sex relationships has emerged as a current issue in Asia, it may be useful to set out how such recognition has occurred over the last 30 years in Western legal systems.

There are three ways in which same-sex relationships have been given legal recognition:

a. *Ascription.* This refers to the legal recognition of actual relationships, often for specific purposes (like social benefits, inheritance, or immigration sponsorship). Couples do not have to register or go through a marriage ceremony. Recognition is given by courts, legislation or administrative practice. Those seeking rights have to assert and perhaps prove the existence of their relationship.[50]
b. *Registration.* This refers to laws which allow same-sex couples to register with a government agency. They are then entitled to some or all of the legal rights and obligations of marriage. Registration systems are separate from marriage, even in countries like the United Kingdom in which all of the rights and obligations of marriage are given to registered partners.

47. Kent Ewing, In Hong Kong, a quiet advance for gay rights, Asia Times, July 15, 2011.
48. Hong Kong's first openly gay lawmaker: Raymond Chan Chi-chuen, www.fridae.asia, September 12, 2012.
49. Japan Times, First openly gay candidate wins in Tokyo ward, April 26, 2011.
50. Such relationships are often called 'de facto' or 'common law' relationships. This kind of legal recognition often began with the recognition of unmarried heterosexual couples. The recognition was then extended to same-sex couples.

c. *Marriage*. In many countries same-sex couples can now marry, entering into the same legal relationship that the law provides for heterosexual couples.

Ascription

Two decisions of the United Nations Human Rights Committee have upheld equal pension rights for same-sex couples as for unmarried heterosexual couples (without any requirement of registration or marriage).[51] The Committee ruled that the denial of pension rights to the survivor in a same-sex relationship was discriminatory and violated the provisions of the *International Covenant on Civil and Political Rights* (which many countries in Asia have signed).

Survivor tenancy rights to rent controlled apartments have been upheld in cases involving same sex couples – in the Netherlands by legislation in 1979 – in New York by a judicial decision in 1989[52] – in Europe by decisions of the European Court of Human Rights in 2003 and 2010.[53]

Equal rights by ascription have been upheld in Colombia by a Constitutional Court ruling in January, 2009,[54] and in Brazil by Supreme Court order in 2011[55] Canada allowed the recognition of same-sex relationships for immigration sponsorship purposes (before marriage was introduced).

51. *Young v Australia*, 2003, CCPR/C/78/D/941/2000, *X v Colombia*, 2007, CCPR/C/89/D/1361 /2005. In *Joslin v New Zealand* the Committee rejected a claim to marriage on the basis of the specific gendered language in the *International Covenant on Civil and Political Rights*: CCPR/C/75/D/902/1999. See Office of the UN High Commissioner for Human rights, Born Free and Equal: Sexual Orientation and Gender Identity in International Human Rights Law, 2012, 53.
52. *Braschi v. Stahl*, 1989, 543 N.E. 2nd 49.
53. In the 2003 decision in *Karner v. Austria*, the European Court of Human Rights recognized a same sex relationship for the purposes of successor tenancy rights (repeated in 2010 in *Kozak v Poland*).
54. Colombia's Constitutional Court Rules for Equality, January 28, 2009 (press release, copy in possession of the author).
55. Reuters, Brazil's supreme court recognizes gay partnerships, May 5, 2011; AP, Court grants legal status to gay unions, Bangkok Post, May 7, 2011, 5.

Registration

Denmark enacted its *Registered Partnership Act* in 1989, which extended all the rights of marriage to same-sex couples who registered, with two exceptions. Same-sex couples did not gain adoption rights and they were not entitled to have a ceremony in the state Lutheran Church. One partner had to be a citizen or permanent resident (a common requirement for marriage in parts of Europe, so not a provision that discriminated against same-sex couples). Immigration sponsorship rights were part of the package.

The Danish legislation was copied in the Netherlands, Sweden, Norway, Finland and Iceland. Many other jurisdictions enacted similar laws for 'registered partnerships', or 'civil unions' or the 'social solidarity' pacts in France. Some came close to equal rights with heterosexual marriage, but many were clearly quite limited in the rights involved. The rights in the UK are identical for marriage or registered partnership.[56] A registration system in Washington State in the US was called the "everything but marriage" law, for it gave all state-level rights, but not the word "marriage." Registration systems were adopted in many states or provinces in Canada and the United States. New Zealand and some Australian states have such systems.

In the Nordic area the laws have been strengthened to include adoption rights and in some places ceremonies in the state church are possible.[57] As well the Nordic states agreed to mutually recognize registered partnerships (just as marriages in one state are usually automatically recognized as of legal effect in other countries).

The UN Human Rights Committee told Ireland to ensure that its proposed registration law did not provide lesser rights to same-sex couples, including in areas of taxation and welfare benefits.[58]

56. There are two differences in the UK: (a) non-consummation does not make the registration voidable, and (b) adultery alone is not a basis for ending the partnership. See Joshi at 441.
57. Legislation introduced in Denmark on March 14th, 2012, will allow weddings in the state Evangelical Lutheran Church. AFP, Denmark submits gay church wedding bill, Bangkok Post, March 16, 2012, 9.
58. Office of the UN High Commissioner for Human Rights, Born Free and Equal, Sexual Orientation and Gender Identity in International Human Rights Law, 2012, 53.

Marriage

The Netherlands opened marriage to same-sex partners in 2001. The Dutch lead has been followed in Argentina, Belgium, Canada, Denmark, Iceland, Norway, Portugal, South Africa, Spain and Sweden. Luxembourg and Finland are expected to make the change soon. Same-sex marriages can take place in the Federal District of Mexico City and those marriages are recognized throughout the country. Some judges in Brazil have converted same-sex civil unions into marriages, though that is currently under appeal.

The reforms solve problems for transgendered individuals and intersexuals, as well as homosexuals. Any two people can marry.

In May, 2011, the Gallup Poll reported that a majority of Americans (53 % to 45 %) believed that same-sex couples should have the same marriage rights as straight couples.[59] A poll released in April, 2012, had 47 % supporting marriage, and 43 % opposed.[60] As well reports say that extending marriage has majority support in Australia, and New Zealand.[61]

In July, 2011, New York State opened marriage, becoming the sixth state in the United States to do so (as well as the District of Columbia). In early 2012, Washington State became the seventh and Maryland the eighth. In 2008 the California Supreme Court opened marriage. A referendum reversed that ruling. In 2010 a challenge to the referendum, brought in federal court, opened marriage again. That decision was upheld in February, 2012, by the Ninth Circuit Court of Appeals, treating California as a special case because all substantive rights had already been extended with registration and because some legal same-sex marriages had already been allowed. Opponents of opening marriage are trying to appeal to the Supreme Court, but need leave to appeal, which may or may not be granted.[62] Some lower courts in the US have now ruled unconstitutional the Federal *Defense of Marriage Act*, which bars federal recognition of same-sex marriages.[63] That issue may go on appeal to the Supreme Court.

59. Connubial bliss in America, The Economist, July 30, 2011, 32.
60. AFP, Poll: Americans okay with guns, gay marriage, Bangkok Post, April 27, 2012. The poll was conducted by the Pew Research Center, a major polling organization.
61. AFP, Same-sex marriage proposal gets crushed in parliament, Bangkok Post, September 20, 2012, 5. Opening marriage was rejected in the Australian House of Representatives by 98 to 42, in a period of some political instability, though polls indicate majority support.
62. AP, Gay marriage ban backers seek Supreme Court review, July 31, 2012.
63. The ban on gays and lesbians openly serving in the US military has been ended by Congress, after strong urging from President Obama. In 2011 US embassies in vari-

Many couples have become marriage tourists. At least 2,700 Australians have entered into same-sex marriages overseas, according to census data released in June, 2012. Most have married in Canada, where there is no residency requirement (except in Quebec). We see a 'bounce-back' effect, when couples come back home and seek recognition of their foreign legal marriages, in the same way that foreign heterosexual marriages are routinely recognized as legally valid. A Hong Kong activist and his partner flew to Canada. Back home again, they asked Hong Kong to recognize their legal Canadian marriage. Israelis married in Canada won recognition of their marriages back home in Israel. New Yorkers won recognition of their Canadian marriages long before marriage was opened in their home state. UK law treats foreign marriages as civil unions (which gave the same rights as marriage, without the name).

In October, 2011, British Prime Minister David Cameron announced his support for opening marriage:

Conservatives believe in the ties that bind us; that society is stronger when we make vows to each other and support each other. So I don't support gay marriage despite being a Conservative. I support gay marriage because I'm a Conservative.[64]

On March 15th the British government announced a public consultation on legalizing same-sex marriage. The government proposed allowing same-sex couples to enter into a civil marriage or a registered civil union. Scotland 'jumped the gun' and announced on July 25th, 2012, that it would open marriage.

We have reached a tipping point. Major changes in policies and laws continue with some regularity. In May, 2012, Francois Hollande was elected President of France. In his campaign he pledged to open marriage, continuing the policy of his predecessor as Socialist party leader, Segolene Royal. He has a legislative majority, and will be able to follow through on the promise. President Obama in the United States expressed personal support for extending marriage on May 11th. His administration had already refused to support the restrictive national *Defense of Marriage Act*, taking the position in court that it is an unconstitutional denial of equal rights. Federal authorities announced on July 30th that the government would not deport the foreign same-sex partners of Americans, recognizing the relationships as establishing

ous parts of the world, for the first time, hosted receptions marking the International Day against Homophobia.

64. David Cameron, Conservative Party Autumn Conference, October 5, 2011.

"close family ties," a sharp reversal of policy.[65] The Democrat party's national convention in September, 2012, included the extension of marriage in its platform.[66] Marriage, however, is a matter for the individual states, so the next steps are largely up to the states and the courts.

With the Obama statement, the heads of governments of three of the five permanent members of the UN Security Council – UK, France, US – support extending marriage. The opposition Social Democratic Party in Germany supports opening marriage. In June, 2012, Denmark, which had pioneered 'registered partnerships' in 1989, moved on to full marriage. In August, 2012, marriage legislation passed first reading in the New Zealand Parliament, moving on to public consultations. In the same month, legislation was introduced in the Australian State of Tasmania. Tasmania had been the last jurisdiction in Australia to decriminalize, but reversed its image by pioneering registration, and now moving to support equal marriage. Marriage is, however, a matter for national law, and the Australian House of Representatives and Senate both rejected an extension of marriage in September, 2012. Earlier a review of national laws and regulations had eliminated all discrimination against same-sex couples, and opinion polls suggested majority public support for opening marriage.[67]

A Pattern for Change?

The Netherlands is an example of a country where recognition went through three stages – firstly ascription – secondly a registration system – finally marriage.

This kind of process, working through stages, is not surprising. For many people, lesbian and gay issues are new and unfamiliar because modern homophobia has kept lesbian and gay people "in the closet" for so long.

65. Julia Preston, Same-Sex Couples Granted Protection in Deportations, New York Times, September 28, 2012.
66. Adam Nagourney, Gay Democrats Celebrate a Newfound Visibility, New York Times, September 5, 2012.
67. AFP, Same-sex marriage proposal gets crushed in parliament, Bangkok Post, September 20, 2012, 5. In the House there was a free vote for members of the governing Labor Party, which divided on the issue. The main opposition coalition had no free vote and opposed. See also, Dan Harrison, Judith Ireland, Senate rejects gay marriage bill, Brisbane Times, September 20, 2012.

Dealing with specific issues, like survivors pensions or hospital visitation rights, introduces the public to the kind of issues that are involved. When such specific issues are resolved by ascription, it is easier to move onto a more general system of recognition of same-sex relationships through a registration system.

If a registration system is achieved, there is little reason to continue to deny the status of "marriage" to the couples involved. It completes a policy of equal respect.

We have had 33 years since ascription began in the Netherlands in 1979. We have had 23 years since registration began in Denmark in 1989. We have had 11 years since marriage began in the Netherlands in 2001. These issues are no longer "in the closet." They are in the newspapers, on television, on the internet, every day.

Little reason now to proceed slowly, through stages.

Changing Marriage (1)

Some think that opening marriage to any two people will change marriage (either for the worse or the better). Perhaps it will change marriage by

a. distancing it from a family model which values children,
b. weakening commitments to fidelity within marriage,
c. reinforcing marital privilege,
d. ending assumptions of inequality of partners within marriage, or
e. working against patriarchy.

All of these propositions are problematic.

- Gay and lesbian couples are raising children in great numbers now in the West. Studies confirm that they are good parents. As good, at least, as heterosexuals.
- If homosexual promiscuity is seen as a problem by society, then supporting equal marriage makes sense to try to establish more stable norms. The 'stereotype' of gay promiscuity, relative to heterosexual norms, has been rejected by the European Court of Human Rights. Homosexuality and promiscuity have no necessary correlation, though there is impact on such patterns from the discrimination and marginalization which make enduring homosexual relationships more difficult.

- Legal marriage is privileged. It is recognized by law. It involves a set of rights and obligations, and is supervised by family courts. Would extending marriage simply repeat this pattern of privileging marriage over other forms of cohabitation, creating 'good gays' (married), and 'bad' ones (unmarried)?[68] In parts of the West the rights and obligations of marriage have been extended to 'de facto' or 'common law' couples, that is, couples living in marriage-like relationships. Unmarried heterosexual cohabitants are increasingly common in the West and in Asia, and their recognition in law in the West has often preceded the recognition of same-sex couples. Because marriage rates have been dropping in most developed countries, and in many parts of Asia as well, patterns of ascription are increasingly a part of any modern system of family law, Increasingly the rights and obligations flowing from either marriage or ascription are available to any couple. De facto couples (as Vietnam recognizes, for example), present legal issues for the state in terms of property division, inheritance, spousal maintenance, child care, etc.. It was the high rate of cohabitation outside marriage in France that initially prompted its registration system, which is open to heterosexual and homosexual couples. Opening marriage does not end the use of ascription to resolve the issues that naturally arise.
- Marriages are less unequal now as education levels and job opportunities for women increase. More women are studying in universities than men. Two-income families are a modern norm in the West. All relationships will have some elements of inequality, but less than in the past.
- Patriarchy is being challenged, with or without marriage equality.

Some who support individual equality, and for that reason would oppose exclusions from marriage, nevertheless regard marriage as carrying too much baggage of sexual conformity and old sex/gender roles to be a worthy goal for anyone. No problem. They can choose not to marry. No system makes legal marriage compulsory. Equal rights can still be extended by ascription, in parallel with marriage, focused on issues of property, dependency and care of children.

Others oppose the focus on marriage as forsaking a larger agenda. It is only about 'us', they argue. These critics hearken back to the 'liberation' agenda

68. See Yuvraj Joshi, Respectable Queerness, 43 Columbia Human Rights Law Review, 415 (2012); Mariana Valverde, A New Entity in the History of Sexuality: The Respectable Same-Sex Couple, 32 Feminist Studies, 155 (2006); Douglas NeJaime, Marriage, Cruising, and life in Between, 38 Harvard Civil Rights and Civil Liberties Law Review, 511 (2003).

of the early gay rights movement, which challenged state regulation of relationships, and sought broad social change. It is certainly true that the developments on marriage have been occurring in what is otherwise a fairly conservative period in terms of social change. It is the privileged gays who will benefit from marriage, these critics argue. Instead of a self-focused campaign, they long for alliances with marginalized sectors in society. For better or for worse, that is not happening.[69]

Changing Marriage (2)

Meanwhile, marriage has been changing in fundamental ways.

- The long term shift from 'extended families' or 'multigenerational families' in favor of 'nuclear families', continues to take place in Asia.
- Marriage rates have dropped dramatically in many countries, including Japan, South Korea, Taiwan and Singapore.[70] Many women now choose careers over marriage and children. Cohabitation, without legal marriage, is common.
- In socially conservative South Korea and Japan many men, who cannot find wives locally, use agencies to arrange for marriages with women from China, the Philippines, or Vietnam. This is a major change in marriage patterns.[71]

69. Joshi argues in these terms. Peter Tatchell, the Australian/British activist, founder of Outrage and a regular blogger, often writes about the loss of the liberation agenda. His 'equal love' campaign argues for heterosexual access to registered partnerships as well as homosexual access to marriage. Urvashi Vaid both supports extending marriage and seeking alliances for broad social change.
70. "In the richer countries of East and South-East Asia, like Japan, Singapore, South Korea and Taiwan, a third or more of local women are not marrying; and those who do wed late, at 31 or 32." International Marriages – Herr and Madame, Senor and Mrs, The Economist, November 12, 2011, 63 at 64. See also, Asia's lonely hearts: Why Asian women are rejecting marriage and what that means, The Economist, August 20-26, 2011, 17-20. In China "extramarital relationships are increasingly accepted in society" according to Chinese researcher Pei Yuxin. See Sexuality Policy Watch Promoted an Inter-Regional Dialogue about Sexuality and Geopolitics, ILGA Asia e-newsletter, November 29, 2011, accessed at http:// ilga.org December 4, 2011.
71. Both the Republic of Korea and Japan have generally seen themselves as monocultural and racially uniform. They are not countries of immigration. Intermarriage across national boundaries has been a major departure from their closed demographic patterns. In South Korea, more than 35 percent of fishermen and farmers who mar-

- Divorce is flourishing. In much of the West it now ends 50 % of marriages. US Roman Catholic Bishops in 2009 said that the social sanctions and legal barriers to divorce "have all but disappeared."[72] In 2010 China had more divorces than marriages.[73]
- The availability to women of reliable contraception (with the advent of 'the pill' in the 1960s) has made both marriage and procreation more optional than in the past.
- Birth rates have dropped in all parts of the world. The richest countries all face population decline (countered in some by immigration).[74]
- The raising of children has no necessary linkage to marriage in the contemporary West. Many couples, married or unmarried, are childless by choice. Single parent families are common. Individuals can adopt children. Increasingly, so can same-sex couples. Alternative insemination, surrogacy and various reproductive technologies have created new possibilities for individuals and couples, without regard to sexual orientation, marriage or other factors.
- In much of the West the rights and obligations of marriage have been extended to unmarried heterosexual couples, often designated as 'de facto' or 'common law' couples. This shift made it politically easier to extend rights and obligations to same-sex couples by ascription.

Why, then, would gays and lesbians give such priority to equal access to marriage? The answer is two fold:

ried in the year up to May 2009 took foreign brides, mainly from China and Vietnam: Lawrence Bartlett, AFP, Imported brides popular as money mixes Asian marriages, Bangkok Post, August 12, 2010, 2010, 3. Sex-selective abortion is not a factor in Japan or South Korea.

72. Marriage: Love and Life in the Divine Plan, A Pastoral Letter of the United States Conference of Catholic Bishops, November, 2009, line 69.
73. AFP, Mass wedding but massive divorce rate, Bangkok Post, October 8, 2011, 5. 1.96 million divorces. 1.2 million marriages.
74. Globally, the average fertility rate has roughly halved in the past half century from five in the mid-1950s to 2.5: A new science of population, The Economist, May 19, 2012, 83, citing John May, World Population Policies, Springer, 2012. In 2011 the fertility rate in the United States dropped below the 'replacement rate' of 2.1, to 1.9, below both France and the United Kingdom: see Virility symbols, The Economist, August 11, 2012, 32. Founding father Lee Kuan Yew, in a national day address in August, 2012, lamented that the day could come when Singapore would "fold up" because of declining births: Jan Lund, DPA, Singapore's singles urged to procreate, Bangkok Post, September 1, 2012, 4.

Access to marriage can solve a number of specific problems in one blow – think of inheritance, hospital visitation, immigration and benefits.

There is another problem. Minorities are more complicated than majorities. Majorities emerge from long periods of economic, social and cultural integration and assimilation. Sexual minorities have a lot in common with cultural minorities in their relations to majority populations. They are difficult for majority people to understand. Not only are they different, but they are internally diverse. Majorities are also internally diverse, but they function on a day to day basis by emphasizing common values, common patterns of living and programs of assimilation.

Everywhere majorities don't really want to pay a lot of attention to minorities. They are busy with many other things. Running a modern state is no easy task. Strategically, a minority needs to get the attention of the majority with simple, easily understood demands. Reductionism is a necessary strategy.

Talking to the Larger Society

The claim to marriage is a simple, easily understood demand. It tells heterosexuals that they are not the only people who deserve a normal, unstigmatized life. It captures the goal of equality with great clarity. It resolves many legal issues for same-sex couples (and for transgender and intersex people). And it does this both comprehensively and with a simple, clearly stated reform.

Marriage is now a credible demand. Marriage is open in major jurisdictions – Argentina, Canada, South Africa, New York State – not just small liberal northern European countries like Sweden and the Netherlands. The idea can no longer be dismissed as impossible by Asian politicians. It is a real issue. It will happen in Asia.

What country will lead the way? Maybe Nepal. Maybe Taiwan. Maybe Vietnam.

Gender Relations and Third Country Nationals – Some Thoughts from a Greek Perspective

Eirini Tsifopoulou, Effrosyni Bakirtzi

1. Introduction

Once known as a country of large-scale emigration, during the last few decades Greece has been transformed into a country of destination for thousands of foreigners. In recent years, due to its geographical position at the crossroads of three continents, the country has also become a host state for thousands of immigrants and refugees. Further, due to the right to free movement of European citizens, the mobility of EU citizens is a reality and often EU or Greek citizens move, work and found their families with other European citizens or third country nationals in other EU member states.[1]

Various *life events* govern the legal status of these people (e.g. marriages, civil partnership acts, births, adoptions, changes of name, nationality etc.). These events are recorded in civil status records by the relevant state authorities, usually where the events have taken place. However, while EU or third country nationals are often called upon to provide the necessary proof of these events, for instance either in their host state or in their home state, the public records do not necessarily have the same legal effects in other states. Supplementary formalities are frequently required. This is because each state

1. European citizens, living and creating families in a different location and jurisdiction at which their civil status registrations have been made, are often confronted with many obstacles and practical difficulties when wishing to exercise their rights in the context of a European area of justice in civil matters; see for instance COM(2010) 747 final, *Green Paper on Less Bureaucracy for citizens: promoting the free movement of public documents and recognition of the effects of civil status records*; COM(2010) 603 final, *EU Citizenship Report 2010: Dismantling the obstacles to EU citizens' rights*, p 5.

has its own rules about life events, within a domestic, legal and social framework that varies from state to state.

The adoption of a modern legal framework facilitates the exercise of civil rights deriving from life events,[2] enhances legal certainty and contributes to the better social integration of foreign nationals in a society. Specific examples of bureaucratic legal requirements for the registration of those events in public records show this link and significantly contribute to the analysis of the issues at stake. This is one of the challenges the Greek legal system has been called upon to address in recent years. At the same time, this has been one of the less explored legal areas. The reality shows that a more harmonised system is necessary when 'life events' are taking place and when states are called upon to recognize the effects of registration of life events on civil status records.[3]

The aim of this article is to identify challenges related to life events and changes to the civil status of third-country nationals in Greek territory. It describes contemporary legal developments that facilitate family structures based on selected cases which reflect the social and political reality, especially with regard to issues of gender relations and their implications.

2. Main legal status issues

2.1. General legal context

In the past, the legal status of the foreign population did not cause significant problems to the Greek legal system. Usually, problems with regard to changes in life events came up in marriages between Greek and foreign nationals,

2. See for instance the CJEU judgments in cases of *Konstantinidis* and *Dafeki*, both Greek nationals and permanent residents in other EU member states (Germany). The CJEU judgments established the principle of free movement of civil status records (Case C-168/91, *Konstantinidis*, E.C.R., 1993, I-1191; Case C-336/94, *Dafeki*, E.C.R., 1997, I-6761). The Court noted that member states have to respect foreign certificates 'unless their accuracy is seriously undermined by concrete evidence related to the individual case in question.'
3. See COM(2010), 171 final, *Action Plan Implementing the Stockholm Programme*. The action plan provides a roadmap for the implementation of EU political priorities set out in the Stockholm Programme for the area of justice, freedom and security and includes legislative proposals, among others, relating to civil status documents.

and concerned the registration of civil marriages and the recognition of their effects in the Greek legal order.[4]

With the massive immigration into Greek territory, national authorities prioritised legislation related to the residence and work permits of individuals, while little attention was paid to gender and family relations[5] and the adoption of a proper legal framework for their relevant civil status certificates. However, the reality shows that most foreign nationals live in various family structures[6] and their life-changing events create a series of legal issues that must be carefully regulated, because usually they involve more than one legal system and raise conflict-of-law issues. Furthermore, these events must be properly registered in public civil status records and their effects must be mutually recognised.

The recognition of the effects of civil status records has a significant effect both on a person's status and on their gender relations, and is strongly connected with various legal rights, including family, social, civil and political rights.[7] In Greece, the proper registration of life events allows third country nationals to exercise certain rights related to their legal residence rights, family reunification rights, social security rights, citizenship rights, etc.[8] Despite the complexity of the issues, the relevant legal framework has been rather fragmented and based on several sources, such as national laws, EU legisla-

4. Civil marriage was established in Greece in 1982 (Act 1250/1982). Before that, there have been great problems with regard to gender relations in civil marriages outside Greece and with regard to parent-child relations and the rights of children who were considered as born out of wedlock.
5. This reaction of policy-makers is not unusual worldwide, see for instance H. Motomura, 'We asked for Workers, but Families Came: Time, Law, and the Family in Immigration and Citizenship', vol. 13, Virginia Journal of Social Policy and the Law, 2.
6. See relevant data, among others, in M. Baldwin-Edwards, 'Immigrants in Greece: Characteristics and Issues of regional distribution', MMO Working Paper No 10 (2008).
7. See COM(2010) 747 final, *Green Paper on Less Bureaucracy for citizens: promoting the free movement of public documents and recognition of the effects of civil status records.*
8. See, for instance, the right to acquisition of Greek citizenship due to birth in Greece and by naturalisation, in Greek Citizenship Code, arts. 1A and 5 respectively. See also Act 3536/2007 (art. 18 par. 4) where, among other requirements, a birth certificate properly registered in the Greek civil status records gives the child and the foreign parent the right to residence permit (in an effort to regulate illegal immigration flows), and Act 3731/2008, where a similar birth certificate gives the right to second-generation immigrants to a permanent residence permit.

tion and a number of multilateral or international conventions.[9] It is characteristic that the relevant Greek law on registration of life events in civil status records[10] does not provide for any specific rules facilitating the life events of foreigners in Greece while at the same time it provides for Greek nationals who live abroad.[11]

Furthermore, each state determines which law is applicable in a cross-border situation based on the connecting factor set out in its private international law. The nationality or the habitual residence of the interested parties is frequently used as a criterion and is a connecting factor that regulates changes in life events and resolves conflict-of-law issues. The applicable law, thus determined, varies considerably from one state to another. This fragmented legal framework creates further bureaucratic formalities and barriers to exercise certain rights or to register life events (such as legal impediments on the right to marry). Relevant efforts, especially by the Greek Ombudsman and the State Legal Council, have proven to be valuable and have, to a great extent, been adopted by the administration.

The following sections of this article give explicit examples and illustrate the various approaches adopted in legislation and legal practice.

2.2. Marriage

Marriage as a legal institution is a form of partnership between two persons that is created by a formal act of registration and has a number of legal effects. Furthermore, it has profound effects on the legal status of the individuals who become husband and wife. Marriage, as well as family life, is especially protected by the Greek Constitution[12] and is expressly enshrined in var-

9. See, for instance, Bern Convention on the recording of surnames and forenames in civil status registers, 1973 (Act 1655/1986); Hague Convention on Protection of Children and Co-operation in respect of Inter-country Adoption, 1993 (Act 3765/2009); see also the International Commission on Civil Status (CIEC) which contributes to the harmonisation and unification of civil status and family law by drawing up international conventions such as the Convention introducing an international family record book (1973) etc.
10. Act 344/1977.
11. Due to large emigration flows, legislation has been designed to facilitate registration of life events of Greek nationals and their families abroad, providing for organisational structures that better serve their needs; see Act 344/1976 on civil status records and rules for the Athens Special Registry, with the responsibility to keep records of civil status events of Greek citizens abroad (art. 43).
12. Greek Constitution art. 21 par. 1.

ious international and European conventions.[13] Two types of marriage exist in Greece; the civil and the religious marriage. The religious marriage is recognised by the state as equivalent to the civil one. Same-sex marriages have not been recognized so far.

Legal impediments and formal requirements to marriage in Greek territory are specifically defined in the Greek Civil Code. The formalities have been a field of conflict between EU citizens or third country nationals who wish to exercise the right to marry and the administrative authorities responsible for issuing the relevant marriage licence.[14] There are many cases involving situations where the two partners had the legal capacity to marry but could not comply with the relevant formal requirements. The certificate of 'no impediment' is a good example, among others, of a requirement for the issue of a marriage licence. This certificate does not exist in many jurisdictions, and foreign nationals or EU citizens who are not able to produce such a document are discouraged from exercising the right to marry.[15] After a series of complaints and recommendations before the Greek Ombudsman, public authorities have now replaced the above certificate with a submission of a personal declaration of the same content when applying for a marriage licence.

Moreover, the presence of both parties is also required[16] and aims to ensure that the parties are free to marry and give consent to do so. A proxy marriage is not recognised in the Greek legal order and, irrespectively of whether it is or not a common practice in the country of origin of the parties, the couple cannot exercise the right to family reunification.[17]

Another formality with regard to refugees and asylum seekers who want to exercise the right to marry is the requirement for legal residence in Greece. A valid passport and formal documentation, such as a visa or residence permit, are necessary for the public authorities that issue the marriage licence,[18] per-

13. See for instance ECHR art. 8 and art. 12.
14. According to Civil Code art. 1368.
15. Similar problems have been addressed in other EU member states; see *Green Paper on Less Bureaucracy for citizens* (n 7).
16. Civil Code art. 1350.
17. Greek Ombudsman, Report No 150153/19984/2012, in a case concerning a 'telephone marriage' and a subsequent application of one of the parties for a visa in the Greek Embassy in Islamabad for family reunification purposes.
18. Based on Act 3386/2005 art. 84 par. 1 on 'Obligations of Public Agencies and Officers.'

haps in an effort to prevent marriages of convenience.[19] Since the above categories of third country nationals were unable to produce such documents, the only solution was to refer the matter to the judicial authorities.[20]

This requirement made the exercise of the right to marry impossible for the above categories of people and has been challenged many times by the Greek Ombudsman.[21] The challenge was based on many grounds and on the balance between domestic family law and the protection of the fundamental right to family life and the protection of family, especially with regard to the political refugees and asylum seekers who, by definition, probably lack such official documentation from their countries of origin.[22]

However, the right to marry cannot be subjected to conditions that impair its substance and deprive certain categories of persons from exercising it. Thus, recently the relevant rules were amended with regard to foreign nationals who have the right to international protection as political refugees or enjoy the status of supplementary protection and the problem has been resolved with specific provisions for the replacement of the above documents and formalities.[23] Now, it suffices to present, for instance, the act of recognition of the person's status as a political refugee or the status of supplementary protection.

Beyond that, the Greek Ombudsman has argued, in the same cases, that a legal residence in Greece is a requirement for a marriage licence that is not provided for by the Greek Civil Code, and is also irrelevant to the right to marry as a civil right[24] and to the nature of the institution of marriage. However it is still mandatory, both in civil and religious marriages, based on immigration laws.[25] The previous illegal residence of a third country national in Greece has also been an impediment often invoked by the governmental authorities in the exercise of family reunification rights.[26] Such an obstacle has

19. See Study on marriages of convenience within ICCS member states, International Commision on Civil Status, available at: http://www.ciec1.org/Etudes/Fraude/MariagesSimules-ENG-sept2010.pdf (accessed on 16.11.2012).
20. According to Civil Code art. 1368, see Greek Ombudsman, Report No 3875.04.2.2/25.7.2007 'Political refugees' right to marriage.'
21. Greek Ombudsman, Report No 3875.04.2.2/25.7.2007 'Political refugees' right to marriage.'
22. See the Geneva Convention on the protection of refugees, 1951, art. 25 par. 1 (Act 3989/1959).
23. See Act 3536/2007 art. 18 par. 10, in combination with Act 3386/2005 art. 84 par. 1.
24. See Civil Code art. 4 on the civil rights of foreigners.
25. Act 3386/2005 art. 84 par. 1 on 'Obligations of Public Agencies and Officers.'
26. Directive 2003/86/EC implemented by Presidential Decree 131/2006 and167/2008.

been challenged on several bases, including the absence of reasons of public interest and national security against the person in question, the right to the protection of family life, the best interests of children to live with both parents etc., with a positive response from public authorities.[27]

Finally, an extra burden for third country nationals is the obligation to declare their marriage to the immigration authorities,[28] as well as any other change in their personal status, within a deadline and with monetary fines in the case of a delay. However, these authorities are irrelevant to the marriage establishment and, further, the requirement is an additional burden to third country nationals beyond the mandatory registration to the public registrars.

2.3. Registered partnership

A new development in the marriage institution took place in 2008, with the adoption of registered partnership in Greece.[29] The civil registered partnership is a legal institution that is more or less proportionate to marriage, with several legal effects on the status of partners, which affects the civil status of the persons involved. It is signed before a notary and must be registered in the public civil status records, as also happens with marriage.

The partnership law requires the common agreement of parties, the presence of both parties before a notary, the legal capacity to marry and satisfaction of minimum age, the different sex of the parties and, further, registration in public civil status records.[30] The adoption of civil partnership follows similar developments in other EU member states. It has been a necessary development in cases where legal or administrative impediments to a marriage in Greece exist in international couples. Further, it facilitates such family structures, especially when the couple has children, as the partnership law provides similar rules to marriage and prioritises the best interests of the child.[31]

In practice, the registered partnership law leaves many aspects of gender relations unregulated, compared to similar partnership acts of other EU member states, and has not been very popular so far. First of all, it excludes the

27. Greek Ombudsman, Report No 148757/24172/2012, in a case of an Albanian national or Report No 132406/27905/2011 in a case of Ukrainian national, with positive response on behalf of the public authorities.
28. Act 3386/2005 art. 73 par. 2.
29. Act 3719/2008.
30. Ibid arts. 1 and 2.
31. The registered partnership act includes provisions on the surname of children, parenthood etc., Act 3719/2008 arts 8-10.

exercise of important rights for couples, such as social security rights.[32] Further, and with regard to EU or third country nationals, it creates legal uncertainty on fundamental international private law issues. The legal characterisation of the partnership act as a marriage, or as a contract, is of particular importance from the perspective of Greek international private law, as it defines the applicable rules that may be different in each case.[33] It also raises issues with regard to the formal requirements and validity of the partnership law (the minimum age of parties, for instance) and the legal consequences in the civil and personal status of the foreign partner.[34]

A good example with regard to third-country nationals is whether the partnership gives rights for immigration purposes. The provisions on registered partnership law create legal uncertainty with regard to the exercise of family reunification rights, the personal status of the immigrant partner and the rights deriving from this status. A simple question would be whether such a registered partnership allows the unmarried partner to exercise the right to family reunification, by proportional application of family reunification rights of married spouses. The same insecure situation exists with the dissolution of the civil partnership with regard to the partner who is a foreign national. The question is similar, whether a right to acquire an autonomous residence permit after the dissolution of the partnership exists, in an analogous application of the right of divorced/separated spouses.[35]

Taking into account the purpose of such a registered union in regulating modern family structures, and the purpose of the right to family reunification in facilitating family reunion and the integration of foreign nationals to the society, it is rather unfortunate that no explicit provision has been adopted in the relevant laws.[36] It remains to be seen, at the implementation level, wheth-

32. Opinion of the Greek State Legal Service No 258/2010.
33. See Civil Code art. 13 par 1 (b), or art. 11.
34. See analysis of various conflicts of law issues in Z. Papasiopi – Pasia, 'The applicable law in civil registered partnership (Law 3719/2008 art. 13) and the effects on the personal status of foreign partners' in Nomiki Viviliothiki, EfAD 11/2010, p. 1147-1155 (in Greek).
35. Act 3386/2005 as amended, arts 60 par 1 on family members of third country nationals and 62 par 1 on family members of EU citizens.
36. Both in Act 3719/2008 on registered partnership and in Act 3386/2005 (arts. 55-64) as amended by Act 3448/2006, 3536/2007, 3613/2007, 3731/2008, 3772/2009 and 3801/2009 on 'Codification of Legislation on the Entry, Residence and Social Integration of Third-Country Nationals on Greek Territory' available in English in http://www.synigoros.gr/?i=foreigner.el. metanastis-nomoi.55204 (assessed 16.11.2012).

er the interpretation of relevant provisions on the 'family members'[37] does not restrict application of reunion rights to such unions.[38] Finally, no other forms of cohabitation or de facto unions are recognised in the Greek legal order for the purpose of exercising family reunification rights.

On the other hand, despite the relevant discussions, registered partnerships have only been made available to different-sex couples. The relations of same-sex couples living in Greece, who cannot choose to get married either, and the practical question of whether a partnership contracted abroad is recognised or not in the domestic legal order,[39] especially when both partners are not Greek nationals, have been left unregulated.

A relevant case on same-sex couples was referred to the State Legal Service. It involved a question about the right to registered partnership of either two British nationals or a British and a Greek national, at the British Consulate in Athens.[40] The Service invoked the *ordre public* and public morality exceptions[41] and refused to recognise the registration of such partnerships in the Greek public records. While the answer for Greek nationals follows the domestic law, the negative answer with regard to European or third-country citizens, according to the minority opinion, is unlikely to be valid based on the above argument. In any case, the registered partnership would be a first step towards the regulation of such relations in the future.

Recently, a committee for the reform of partnership law was established[42] and has already submitted a proposal on the direction to provide the right to registered partnership with no distinction between opposite-sex or same-sex couples.[43]

37. See Presidential Decree 131/2006 art. 4.
38. Several EU member states allow reunification of an unmarried partner either under the registered partnership or an evidence-based stable long term relationship, see COM(2008) 610 final, Report from the Commission to the European Parliament and the Council on the Application of Directive 2003/86/EC on the right to Family Reunification.
39. The problem is common in many EU member states http://europa.eu/ youreurope/citizens /family/couple/registered-partners/index_en.htm (assessed 16.11.2012).
40. See Opinion of the Greek State Legal Service No 432/2006.
41. See Civil Code art. 33.
42. ON 29/7/2010.
43. Act 3719/2008 art. 1.

2.4. Gender relations and name changes

2.4.1. Introduction

Changes in gender relations often raise legal issues concerning changes of name. Common issues that usually occur concern the surnames of foreigners who are wives of Greek citizens. Marriages between Greek and foreign nationals, as well as childbirth, often create issues with regard to the registration of the surname of the wife or child.

The name/surname is the basic identity element in the Greek legal system and is, thus, connected to the fundamental civil and social rights of the individual. Within the Greek legal framework of civil status certificates, name is defined as the first name (or forename or given name), surname (or last name or family name), maiden name, father's name and mother's name; these name elements are all important for identifying the person within his/her family, professional and social relationships. Moreover, the name/surname is closely related to the personal life of each individual and provides him/her with rights according to the principle that *"all persons shall have the right to develop freely their personality and to participate in the social, economic and political life of the country."*[44]

The right to bear and change a certain name is subject to administrative and legislative restrictions which aim at safeguarding the so-called *certification of identity* as well as the safety of transactions in general; therefore, this right may be subject to certain public law restrictions. However these restrictions have to be compatible with the right to respect for private life,[45] including the right to establish and develop relationships with other human beings, in professional or business contexts as well as other contexts.[46] Such restrictions can be justified on the grounds of public interest.[47] In any case, the State has broad discretionary power while exercising its own regulatory competence. For example, the State can require the use of a surname for someone

44. As it is stated in the Greek Constitution art. 5 par 1.
45. See European Convention of Human Rights art. 8. Although article 8 ECHR does not expressly refer to names, the Court has held that name issues fall within the scope of the right to private life.
46. See case Burghartz v. Switzerland, Application No. 16213/90, ECHR Judgment of 22 February 1994.
47. See case Stjerna v. Finland, Application No. 18131/91, ECHR Judgment of 25 November 1994 regarding the change of surname and Guillot v. France, Application No. 22500/93, ECHR Judgment of 24 October 1993, and Johansson v. Finland, Application No. 10163/02, ECHR Judgment of 6 September 1997, regarding the name parents want to give to their child.

who wanted to bear no surname[48] or the state can order the phonetic and grammatical adjustment of a surname of foreign origin.[49]

The Court of Justice of the EU has also dealt with cases concerning national laws/regulations and administrative practices of EU member states regarding nationality and civil status issues which relate to the exercising of the fundamental freedoms guaranteed by the Treaty on the Functioning of the European Union (article 21), in particular those involving the freedom to move and reside freely within the territory of the member states.[50] All these decisions[51] aim at safeguarding and protecting the freedom of movement and establishment within the territory of the EU member states.

Referring to the European legal framework regarding the right to bear and change a certain name is important because it is part of the Greek legal order.

48. See case The former King of Greece and others v. Greece, Application No. 25701/94, ECHR Judgment of 23 November 2000.
49. See case Mentzen alias Mencena v. Latvia, Application No. 71074/01, ECHR Judgment of 7 December 2004.
50. See Cases C-274/96 Bickel and Franz [1998] ECR I-7637, paras 15 and 16, Grzelczyk [2001] ECR I-6193, paragraph 33, and D'Hoop, [2002] ECR I-6191, paragraph 29.
51. One of the most important CJEU decisions – Garcia Avello (Case C-148/02 Garcia Avello [2003] ECR I-11635) – concerned the application filed by a Spanish national and his Belgian wife to change their children's surname; the main issue was the registry of their children possessing a dual nationality (Spanish and Belgian) at the Belgian civil status records with a double surname (the father's surname followed by the mother's surname according to Spanish name law).

    The CJEU continued with two other decisions – Stadt Niebüll (Case C-96/04, Standesamt Stadt Niebüll [2006] ECR I-03561) and Grunkin and Paul (Case C-353/06, Grunkin and Paul [2008] I-07639) – coping with the issue of recognition of a child's surname in one Member State, as determined and registered in another Member State in which the child was born and has been resident since birth. Another interesting decision is the relatively recent one Runevié-Vardyn and Wardyn (Case C-391/09, Runevié-Vardyn and Wardyn [2011] ECR I-0000) where it was examined whether national rules requiring that the surnames and forenames of natural persons must be entered on certificates of civil status in a form which complies with the rules governing the spelling of the official national language, are compatible with EU law and more specifically with articles of 18 and 21 TFEU.

2.4.2. Name law cases in Greece

In Greece, derogations from the principle of stability and immutability of name/surname[52] can be permitted under certain circumstances. With regard to gender relations, there has been an amendment of the provisions of the Greek Civil Code, which regulates the surname that spouses have after marriage.[53] More specifically, each spouse has the right to, or can make an agreement to, add the other spouse's surname to his/her surname; this statement is made before the civil status registrar and has validity until it is withdrawn. The aforementioned provision can be applied to foreigners should the applicable law on their surnames be Greek.

Matters regarding the surname of foreigners that are wives of Greek citizens can often cause identity problems before the Greek administration. The key issue here is whether the wife's surname is modified with marriage. The Greek State Legal Service has published different opinions upon this matter.

One of the cases regarded a foreign woman who was the wife of a Greek citizen and whose surname had been changed to that of her husband. Her passport, which had been issued by foreign authorities, mentioned her husband's surname as her surname, but all her other Greek legal papers (for example her residence permit) remained unmodified. Upon her request to modify her surname in the Greek legal documents, the State Legal Service expressed two diverse opinions: the first – and prevailing one – explained that the Greek surname on her passport could not have any legal effect with regard to the applicable law regulating the spousal personal relationships. In other words, the Greek applicable law regulating the surnames of spouses after marriage did not provide for such a change in the wife's surname and, therefore, the Greek legal documents could not be modified by virtue of the surname in her passport. The other opinion – which had not been followed in this case – argues that her surname should have been modified in her Greek legal documents according to the modification of her passport which had been issued by foreign authorities. This is because the latter change of surname in the passport should have a legal impact on matters regarding her identity in the Greek legal order. This second opinion seems more plausible as the principle of stability and immutability of surname is hereby protected.[54]

52. This principle is on the core of most national systems; however, different rules on the attribution of the name exist in most countries. Many legal orders provide for derogations from that principle allowing the amendment of one's name/surname.
53. In 2008 by Act 3719/2008 art. 28.
54. See Opinion of the Greek State Legal Service No 24/2004 (3rd Department).

The challenge here in the field of recognition of foreign documents in the Greek legal order lies in the fact that, in each and every case, the public administration has to check with the applicable foreign law or the real circumstances with regard to the identity elements of the foreigner and then decide whether such modifications can be applied in the Greek legal documents of foreigners. In order to clarify these issues, the public administration may request further information from the foreign authority or the submission of a declaration on honor containing the identity elements of the individual that are at issue.[55]

The reverse case scenario concerns Greek female citizens who were married to foreigners before 1982[56] and, therefore, had acquired their husband's surname; these women can use their maiden name again under the principle of the constitutional equality principle and articles 8 and 14 of the ECHR.[57]

Therefore, the common problems that the Greek administration and courts are facing are the various conflicts within the texts of legal documents, which certify the civil status of third country nationals and their family members in Greece (i.e. discrepancies of names/surnames/father's or mother's names). In particular, when two or more legal orders are involved or there is a transnational element in a certain situation, then private international law rules, together with private international law treaties, are called upon to guarantee that the name issues will be regulated consistently. At European level, an important step towards less bureaucracy for citizens of the EU is the European Commission's Green Paper[58] for promoting free movement of public documents and recognition of the effects of civil status records.

2.5. Legal status of children and gender relations

An increasing number of children are being born from relationships outside of marriage/civil partnerships. Several legal problems occur in this situation, originating from the child support obligation. The child shall be registered immediately after birth and has the right from birth to a name, nationality, and to know and be cared for by his or her parents.[59] Among other issues, the most complicated ones concern the establishment and registration of paterni-

55. See Opinion of the Greek State Legal Service No 3/2003 (Individual Case).
56. See Act 1329/1983 art. 54 par. 3.
57. See Opinion of the Greek State Legal Service No 337/2005 and case Burghartz v. Switzerland, Application No. 16213/90, ECHR Judgment of 22 February 1994, par. 27.
58. *Green Paper on Less Bureaucracy for citizens* (n 7).
59. UN Convention on the Rights of the Child, 1989, arts. 7 and 8.

ty, as in many countries there is no automatic presumption of parentage of children born out of wedlock, as well as of the nationality of the child.

A similar situation with legal impediments to marriage occurs when one of the parents is not legally resident in Greece. The recognition of a child born out of wedlock by his/her father takes place before a notary with the consent of the mother.[60] Until recently, the recognition could not take place because of the lack of legal residence documents, usually of the mother as a third country national. This happened because the notary was obliged to ask for the mother's legal documentation before her consent, a formality required by law with severe penalties in the case of the non-compliance of the notary. Even in cases where the mother was a Greek national or EU citizen and the father had no legal residence, the latter could not recognize the child for the same reason, irrespective of the consent of the mother. The only solution was to refer the case to the judicial authorities and issue a court order establishing the paternity, with additional costs in terms of time, money and legal certainty.

The situation has recently moved in the right direction for various reasons, including the prevailing interests of children. Thus, now there is an exception of the requirement for a legal residence permit in case of recognition of a child before the notary and for the registration in civil status records when one of the two parties is Greek, EU citizen or legally residing in Greece.[61]

The proper recognition of a child out of wedlock not only gives the child the right to know and be cared by his/her parents, but also the right to acquire Greek citizenship.[62] In the case of an American woman born in the United States out of wedlock, she applied to become a Greek citizen because of her father's Greek origin and, among other documents, she had to submit a birth certificate. However, this certificate was solely a birth registration by the mother alone; it included the name and surname of the father, but not a formal recognition on behalf of the father. In this case, the Greek authorities held that such a birth certificate, with no supplementary documents showing the express recognition of the child born out of wedlock, could not be accept-

60. Civil Code art. 1475.
61. Law 3386/2005 as amended, art. 85 on Obligations of notaries public-Penalties, '*The above provisions shall not include the preparation of powers of attorney to lawyers in order to represent third-country nationals before courts, and the preparation of notarial deeds relating to the recognition of a child born out of wedlock, when one parent is Greek or other EU Member State national or third-country national legally residing in Greece.*'
62. UN Convention on the Rights of the Child, 1989, art. 7; Greek Citizenship Code, art. 1, 2, and 10 on 'Naturalization of Foreign Nationals of Greek Origin who live abroad', which requires submission of a birth certificate.

ed as a proof of origin from a Greek father.[63] This decision is in line with the control of mandatory requirements on recognition of a child according to Greek family law, which had not been fulfilled in this case. However, it also reveals the different approach of legal systems in the civil status issues of their citizens and finally deprives a person from the right to acquire the citizenship of his/her father.

Furthermore, a child has the right to a name from birth. An additional problem that the Greek administration often has to deal with is the recording of the name of a foreigner father or mother on the birth certificate, naming or baptism act. More specifically, the issue of the mother's surname and maiden name is regulated by article 14 of the Greek Civil Code and, consequently, when the couple has different nationalities, the applicable law regulating their surnames is that of the last common residence of their marriage.

However, there have been a number of cases before the State Legal Service and the Greek Ombudsman where surnames have been recorded for foreign women married to Greek citizens in their civil status registrations, while different surnames were recorded in the birth certificates of their children.[64] These discrepancies result from the practice of the Greek administrative authorities of giving a surname to foreigners – mothers of Greek citizens that is different from the one defined by the law of their own nations. Such problems have been solved by modifying the mother's surname in the birth certificates of the children or requesting the submission of an identity certificate issued by the foreign authorities.

Finally, under article 5 par. 1 of the Greek Constitution which provides for the free development of one's personality, the Greek case law has recognized that a person can correct his/her name/surname by court order if the name/surname has undesirable consequences for the individual which can be

63. Court of First Instance Rode 15/2003; See a similar case in Greek Ombudsman Report No 14564/2004 'Nationality of foreigner, who invokes recognition as a child out of wedlock from a Greek father' and concerned an American citizen born in California, USA, who could not provide the proof needed of her origin from her Greek father but has just birth certificate out of wedlock with the name of the Greek father. On the contrary, see Supreme Court 1255/2006, where in a case from Massachusetts, USA, a criminal order including a preliminary decision on the recognition of the child was considered by the Greek legal system as enough evidence of recognition of the child by the father.
64. See Opinion of the Greek State Legal Service No 509/2006 (3rd Department) and Conclusion of the Greek Ombudsman 2445.07.2.2/18.5.2007.

justified,[65] for example when the name/surname sounds wrong in some way. There was a particularly interesting case brought before the Greek courts in which a child was born in Albania and given the name Helious. He was later adopted by Greek parents, baptized Christian orthodox and given the name Stylianos; consequently, the relative baptism act was issued. After the Greek nationality of the said person was established by the authorities according to the provisions of Greek law, the relevant Municipality issued his birth certificate under the name Helious. As this name could have caused undesirable consequences to the individual because it is not Christian and fine-sounding, the court ordered its correction in the birth certificates of the Greek and the Albanian Registrar.[66] The reasoning of the court order argued that the applicant had legal interest in justifying such a correction and the Greek courts had jurisdiction to decide upon the said application.

3. Concluding remarks

Life events, such as a marriage/partnership act, birth, adoption etc., and their registration are fundamental to a person's identity and civil status, and necessary for the effective exercise of various social, economic and political rights.[67]

This short overview of selected life events and their related problems show that these issues demand increasing attention from Greek legislator, administration and every person implementing the relevant laws. Therefore, it would be plausible to modernize and codify the legal provisions with the aim to eliminate high bureaucracy and complexity of legislation and increase predictability for citizens. Some positive steps have already been taken by Greek legislator related, but not restricted, to the elimination of legal impediments to marriage, the adoption of registered partnership law and the facilitation of family reunification rights. These steps are consistent with the European and international standards of the protection of private and family life and the right to marry.

However, unnecessary restrictions not justified by the nature of the rights involved still exist. These require an understanding of the different legal or-

65. See decisions of the Athens Appeal Court 2064/2005 and the One member Court of First Instance of Rethymno 175/2006.
66. See decision of the Athens Appeal Court 1661/2005.
67. See also the recent Opinion of the Committee of the Regions on *'Less bureaucracy for citizens'* (2012/C 54/05).

ders involved in various life events and enhanced cooperation with the foreign citizens and their countries of origin. In many cases the legislator transfers the responsibility to resolve complicated legal issues to the notaries, civil registrars, and finally to the judicial authorities in case the law provides no solution, with additional cost to citizens.

The strengthening of the capacity of public administration to interact with third country nationals certainly contributes to the effective implementation of the new positive legislation changes. Above all, a comprehensive legal framework would *bring legal certainty and clarity* through a coherent set of rules and would be a more effective reaction to the reality. At the EU level, the proposal for a European certificate to be used for any administrative formalities in all EU member states would potentially avoid further procedures involving civil registrars[68] and facilitate the increasing mobility of EU citizens.

In conclusion, the legislator has become progressively more aware of the significance of the interests of all parties involved in life events. The domestic legislator's efforts in the direction of identifying and removing obstacles to exercising rights, particularly in cross-border situations, is an important step towards promoting the inclusion of third country nationals in society. At the EU level interesting developments will take place in this direction.

68. *Green Paper on Less Bureaucracy for citizens* (n 7), p 10.

Biographical Notes

Eylem Ümit Atılgan graduated from Ankara University Faculty of Law. She completed her MA in Philosophy of Law with her thesis *The State Theory of Aristoteles*, and her PhD in Sociology of Law. She has been awarded with the Turkish Social Science Association Young Scholars' prize in the Social Sciences for her thesis *Habitus of Juvenile Delinquency in Urban Areas.*
In addition to her books *Space and Possibility: Habitus and Penal Liability* (2006), *"Justice can be bypassed sometimes ..." Judges and Prosecutors in the Democratization Process*, (2009 co-authored with Mithat Sancar), she has a lot of articles published in various journals. She was a visiting scholar at Humboldt University, Berlin in 2011-2012, and works at Ankara University Faculty of Law as an associate professor.

Effrosyni Bakirtzi graduated as a lawyer from the Law School of the Faculty of Law of the Aristotle University of Thessaloniki in Greece and then completed a Master's degree in International and European Law at the same university. She practiced law in Greece and worked as scientific researcher at the K.U. Leuven (Catholic University of Leuven) in Belgium. Her main research interests are international, European and comparative social security law, EU internal market issues, international economic law, international private law and migration law. She is the co-author of a book on *"Civil status certificates with a foreign element from a Greek judicial and administrative practice perspective."*

Åsa Gunnarson is professor in tax law and scientific leader at Forum for Studies on Law and Society, Umeå University. Her fields of interest are feminist legal theory, gender perspectives on taxation and budgeting, social citizenship and cross-disciplinary gender studies. She has been a member of the steering committee for the Centre of Gender Excellence Program Challenging Gender at Umeå University. At present she is leading an international network based project about Feminist Studies on Taxation and Budgeting. The network has presented this new field of gender studies *in Challenging Gender Inequality in Tax Policy Making: Comparative Perspectives*, edited by Kim

Brooks, Åsa Gunnarsson, Lisa Philipps and Maria Wersig. Oxford: Hart Publishing. In the field of feminist legal theory she published the book Genusrättsvetenskap in 2009 together with Eva-Maria Svensson.

Ingrid Lund-Andersen is Professor, Dr. jur. at the University of Copenhagen, Faculty of Law. From 1978 to 2010 she worked at the University of Aarhus, School of Law. She is the author of *Familieøkonomien* (The Family Economy), 2011, and the co-author of *Retsstillingen for Ugifte Samlevende* ('The Legal Situation of Cohabitants'), 1988, *Familieret* ('Family Law'), 5th ed., 2003 and *Familieret* ('Family Law'), 2th ed., 2012. Her research fields are Family Law, the Rights of the Child and the Legal Position of Cohabitants and Same-Sex Partnerships, and she has published numerous articles on these subjects in national and international journals. She is a national expert at the Commission on European Family Law (CEFL).

Kenneth McK. Norrie, Law School, University of Strathclyde has taught law for thirty years and has been Professor of Law since 1995. He was Head of Strathclyde Law School in Glasgow, Scotland between 2001 and 2007. He has also held visiting positions in Regensburg (Germany), Vienna (Austria), Sydney (Australia), Cape Town (South Africa) and Wellington (New Zealand). He has published widely in family law, private international law, and defamation and privacy. He has been a parliamentary adviser on legislation dealing with cohabitants' rights, adoption and child protection. His major research interests within family law include child protection law, and the legal recognition and regulation of same-sex families.

Theis Munthe-Brun is a graduate student at the Department of English, Germanic and Romance Studies at the University of Copenhagen, Denmark. He is currently researching and writing his master thesis on the independence of India and British civic identity.

Greta Olson is Professor for English and American literature and cultural studies at the University of Giessen and a general editor of the *European Journal of English Studies* (EJES). The author of *Reading Eating Disorders* (2003) and '*Criminal Animals' and the Rise of Positivist Criminology* (De Gruyter 2014), she has edited *Current Trends in Narratology* (2011) and *9/11 – Ten Years After* (2011). She has also co-edited *Obama and the Paradigm Shift—Measuring Change* (2012) with Birte Christ), *In the Grip of the Law* (2004) with Monika Fludernik as well as a special issue of EJES on law, literature, and language with Martin Kayman. Her research interests are interdisciplinary and include trans-Atlantic politics, Law and Literature/Culture, punitivity, narratology, animal studies, and feminist and gender studies.

Mira M. Ramhøj is currently a PhD student at the Center for Studies of Legal Cultures at the Faculty of Law, University of Copenhagen. She holds a law degree from the Faculty of law at the University of Copenhagen. Her field is family law. Her PhD topic is concerned with the legal process of change in Morocco, primarily women's status according to the Moroccan Family Law.

Hanne Petersen is Dr. jur. and professor of legal cultures at the Center for Studies of Legal Culture, University of Copenhagen. She was Jean Monnet Scholar at the European University Institute in Florence 1993-94, professor of jurisprudence and sociology of law at University of Greenland, Ilisimatusarfik 1995-99, professor of Greenlandic sociology of law at University of Copenhagen 2001-2006 and adjunct professor of law at University of Tromsø 2007-2010. From 2011-2013 she was Hedda Andersson guest professor at Lund University as part of the Gender Equality priority of Lund university. She has participated in a number of international research projects amongst others EU-projects on issues of gender, religion and legal transition.

Douglas Sanders, Professor Emeritus, Faculty of Law, University of British Columbia (1977-2003); Visiting Professor, Masters Program in Business Law, Faculty of Law, Chulalongkorn University, Bangkok (1998-2008); member of the governing board for the Doctoral Program in Human Rights, Mahidol University, Bangkok (2005-present). Professor Sanders represented the International Lesbian and Gay Association at the United Nations in the year and a half it had consultative status in 1993-4 (that status has since been restored). He has written widely on issues relating to indigenous and tribal peoples, as well as on human rights and specifically sexuality rights. His entry 'Sex and Gender Diversity' was published in Forsythe, Encyclopedia of Human Rights, OUP, 2009. And see 'Out at the UN' in Weissbrodt, Rumsey, *Vulnerable and Marginalized Groups and Human Rights,* Elgar, 2011. He lives in Bangkok, Thailand.

Ánde Somby is a Sámi person and a yoiker. He graduated from the Faculty of Law at University of Oslo in 1987. He has worked in the Ministry of Municipal Affairs in Norway, been an assistant judge and been practicing as an attorney of law. He got his PhD in Law in 1999. His thesis was "*Rhetoric of Law.*" Currently he is an associate professor at the Faculty of Law at the University of Tromsø in Norway.

Eirini Tsifopoulou is a PhD Fellow at the University of Copenhagen, Faculty of Law. She graduated from the Aristotle University of Thessaloniki, Faculty of Law, and has a Master's degree in International and European Law from the same University. She also has a Master's degree in International Dispute Settlement from the Graduate Institute of International and Development Studies and the University of Geneva. She has worked as a lawyer in Greece and is the co-author of a book on *'Civil status certificates with a foreign element from a Greek judicial and administrative practice perspective.'*

José María Lorenzo Villaverde is PhD student at the Faculty of Law of the University of Copenhagen. He completed his studies in Law and in Journalism in the University of Santiago de Compostela (Spain). His PhD project is a comparative family law study regarding the legal recognition of same-sex couples in Spain and Denmark. His main areas of interest are family law, sexual orientation law and private international law in family matters.

Miriam Koktvedgaard Zeitzen is Assistant Professor at Department of Cross-Cultural and Regional Studies at University of Copenhagen, Denmark. She received her Ph.D. in Social Anthropology from University of Cambridge, England. Her dissertation research focused on elite Malay polygamy in urban Malaysia, and Muslim polygamy in Southeast Asia remains a central research interest. She is currently doing research on fundamentalist Mormon negotiation of the right to practice polygamy in Canada and the United States of America, focusing on gender, religion and legal culture perspectives.